Sunset

Northern California
—TRAVEL GUIDE—

North Coast

Shasta-Cascade

Wine Country

Sierra Nevada

San Francisco

Bay Area

Central Valley

Monterey Peninsula

By the Editors of Sunset Books
and Sunset Magazine

Sunset Publishing Corporation
Menlo Park, California

Research and Text
Barbara J. Braasch

Book Editor
Phyllis Elving

Coordinating Editor
Suzanne Normand Mathison

Design
Cynthia Hanson
Kathy Avanzino Barone

Maps
Eureka Cartography

Our thanks...

to the many people and organizations who assisted in the preparation of this travel guide. Special appreciation goes to city and county visitor bureaus, chambers of commerce, and other visitor service agencies throughout Northern California.

We would also like to thank Joan Beth Erickson and Pamela Evans for their editorial contributions to this manuscript and Lois Lovejoy for her illustration of the California poppy.

Photographers

R. Valentine Atkinson: 2, 114; **Larry Brazil:** 34; **Carr Clifton:** 47, 78, 106; **Betty Crowell:** 127; **Mark Gibson:** 18, 26, 31, 39, 42, 55, 70, 119; **Jeff Gnass Photography:** 86, 91; **Dave G. Houser:** 58; **Rolland A. Meyers:** 10, 67; **Chuck Place Photography:** 111; **Mickey Pfleger/Photo 20-20:** 122; **Galen Rowell:** 50; **David Ryan/Photo 20-20:** 23; **Larry Ulrich Photography:** 15, 63, 75, 83, 94, 98, 103.

Cover: Warm sunset glow enriches the vibrant hue of San Francisco's Golden Gate Bridge. View is looking north from the city's Baker Beach toward the Marin Headlands. Cover design by Susan Bryant. Photography by Jeff Gnass Photography.

Editor, Sunset Books
Elizabeth L. Hogan

First Printing May 1991

Prairie Creek Redwoods State Park, carpeted and canopied in greenery, contains some of the last remaining old-growth redwoods along the northern coast.

Contents

Discovering Northern California

"Kaleidoscopic"—that's the word to describe Northern California. From waterfall-laced mountains to grape-filled valleys, giant redwood forests to sandy coastal stretches, and slumbering ghost towns to one of the world's most cosmopolitan cities, this region really does offer something for everyone, any time of the year.

This is an area devoted to outdoor recreation, and your choices are almost unlimited. You can hike, camp, fish, boat, cycle, beachcomb, run river rapids, and climb mountains. Swimmers and windsurfers take to the lakes and rivers in summer, and winter finds skiers heading for slopes at dozens of high-country resorts. Tennis players and golfers pursue their games year-round, thanks to the mild climate.

San Francisco—famous for its bay, bridges, hills, waterfront, and fine food—draws a majority of Northern California's tourists with its big-city attractions. Together with the surrounding Bay Area cities (as far south as San Jose), it's the region's largest cultural, business, and industrial center.

Scenic riches

The best of Northern California's diversions were created by nature—Yosemite Valley and Lake Tahoe in the mighty Sierra Nevada range, Mount Shasta, the Big Sur coast, Redwood National Park, and more. These scenic splendors, and the wealth of outdoor recreation such areas make possible, lure visitors and residents alike. But if you're looking for solitude, you can head for the mountain wilderness north of Redding.

Northern California boasts the state's most dramatic coastline and the majority of its mountains, forests, natural lakes, and rivers. The region encompasses the continent's highest waterfall (Yosemite Falls) and the world's tallest trees.

That's not to say you won't find man-made attractions. Popular destinations beyond San Francisco include Sonoma, with its Spanish landmarks; the Napa Valley wine district; Monterey's historic buildings and waterfront; Carmel's quaint shops; and Mendocino, with its dramatic coastal setting and artsy atmosphere.

Sacramento, the main city in the agriculturally important Central Valley, is often overlooked by tourists. Its river setting, historic waterfront, and world-famous railroad museum, however, make it well worth visiting. East of the valley in the foothills of the Sierra are remnants from the days when gold created California.

The northern half of the state also has its share of theme parks (Marine World/Africa USA and Great America, for example), zoos, museums, galleries, shopping centers, and an array of wineries to tour. And it offers such unique diversions as the Skunk train that chugs through the redwoods up north, the island prison of Alcatraz offshore from San Francisco, a Russian fort on the Sonoma coast, and the Santa Cruz Boardwalk, one of the coast's few fun zones remaining from another age.

A golden frontier

Mountain men, Russian fur traders, Spanish explorers, and Franciscan monks—all had a hand in creating Northern California. But it took the shouts of "Gold!" in 1848 to turn the world's attention to San Francisco and the Sierra foothills.

Sir Francis Drake had set anchor along the coast in 1579, claiming the region for England. Yet it was Spanish explorers and accompanying Franciscan monks who began settlement, nearly two centuries later. They built forts in San Francisco and Monterey and extended a chain of missions as far north as Sonoma.

Monterey became Alta California territorial capital for both Spain and Mexico (after its declared independence in 1822). Still, the Spanish-Mexican reign had less of an influence in Northern California than it did in the south. The U. S. flag had already been raised at Monterey and San Francisco two years before Mexico finally surrendered its territory to the United States in 1848.

And then gold was discovered. The fabled wealth of the Mother Lode helped achieve statehood for California by 1850. It catapulted San Francisco into prominence as the financial center for those who made their fortunes in the mines. And gold fever called global attention to the area,

Rodeo competitions, Dixieland jazz, ethnic and historic celebrations, art fairs, and festivities celebrating everything from jumping frogs and racing crabs to wine, pumpkins, and garlic—lively events throughout the year showcase Northern California's diversity. Below are 15 of the region's most colorful celebrations. For a calendar of events throughout the state, contact the California Office of Tourism (address on page 4).

AT&T Pebble Beach National Pro-Am, late January–early February at Pebble Beach. Legendary golf tournament shows off the Monterey Peninsula's renowned golf courses. Sightseers have a field day as celebrities and high-profile sports figures team with top golfers for several rounds. Contact: (408) 372-4711 outside California or (800) 541-9091 within the state.

Chinese New Year, February in San Francisco. North America's largest Chinese community salutes the lunar new year with the Golden Dragon parade, Miss Chinatown USA pageant, martial arts demonstrations, and cultural events. Contact: (415) 391-2000.

World Championship Crab Races, mid-February (Saturday of Presidents' Day weekend) in Crescent City. Dungeness crabs claw their way down a short race course; the winner is returned ceremoniously to the sea. The celebration climaxes with a huge crab feed. Contact: (707) 464-3174.

Mendocino Whale Festival, mid-March in Mendocino. Bring your binoculars to scan the sea for migrating whales, then join in wine tasting, boutique and gallery browsing, and other activities. Contact: (707) 964-3153.

Cherry Blossom Festival, mid- to late-April in San Francisco. This street party in Japantown celebrates spring with entertainment by kimono-clad performers, martial arts experts, and masters in origami (paper folding), ikebana (flower arranging), and bonsai (tree pruning). You can take in a tako drum concert, attend a Japanese film festival, and sample teriyaki, yakitori, sushi, and other treats in the food bazaar. Contact: (415) 922-6776.

Jumping Frog Jubilee, third weekend in May in Angels Camp. Mark Twain publicized the first frog jump in this gold country community; now hundreds of colorfully named frogs jump in various divisions. Contact: (209) 736-2561.

Dixieland Jazz Jubilee, Memorial Day weekend in Sacramento. Jazz takes over California's capital city for a 4-day jam session with lively performances by more than 100 bands from around the world. Contact: (916) 372-5277.

Carmel Bach Festival, last three weeks in July in Carmel. Outstanding baroque music draws classical music enthusiasts to this coastal town each summer for performances of instrumental and choral works, young people's concerts, recitals, and lectures. Book 3 months ahead for weekends. Contact: (408) 624-1521.

California Rodeo, mid-July in Salinas. Top cowboys compete during one of North America's biggest rodeos. Other events include horse races, horse show, chili cookoff, barbecue, and square dancing. Contact: (408) 757-2951.

Gilroy Garlic Festival, last full weekend in July in Gilroy. Garlic-lovers by the thousands feast on garlic-seasoned recipes from appetizers to desserts in Gourmet Alley. Though food is its main attraction, the festival also features lively entertainment, cooking demonstrations by celebrity chefs, and an arts and crafts show. Contact: (408) 842-1625.

California State Fair, mid-August through Labor Day in Sacramento. The state's largest agricultural fair (held at the Cal Expo grounds) includes a carnival, exhibits, and top-name entertainment. Contact: (916) 924-2000 or (916) 924-2032.

Monterey Jazz Festival, third weekend in September in Monterey. Venerable 3-day event draws many top jazz performers. Contact: (408) 373-3366.

Valley of the Moon Vintage Festival, late September in Sonoma. This oldest of California's wine festivals celebrates the harvest with the "blessing of the grapes," an old-fashioned grape stomp, and re-enactments of events from Sonoma history. Wine tasting and food sampling take place in and around Sonoma's historic town square. Contact: (707) 996-2109.

Half Moon Bay Art & Pumpkin Festival, mid-October in Half Moon Bay. You can pick out your Halloween pumpkin, then enjoy a giant street fair featuring regional artists and craftspeople, food booths, and varied entertainment. Contact: (415) 726-9652.

Gold Country Christmas, Thanksgiving weekend to mid-December in various towns: *Placerville*, Festival of Trees, (916) 621-5885; *Columbia*, Christmas Lamplight Tour and Miners' Christmas Celebration, (209) 532-4301; *Auburn*, Old Town Auburn Village Christmas, (916) 885-5616; *Coloma*, Christmas in Coloma, (916) 622-3470.

bringing an influx of people from around the world who were looking for something more permanent than gold. Many of these immigrants played important parts in Northern California's development.

Over the years, San Francisco's unique blend of races, cultures, and lifestyles has transformed it from a sleepy pueblo into a Pacific Basin gateway. Central Valley agriculture, too, owes much to the early farmers who came here from other parts of the world.

About this book

Based on the state's regional differences, we've chosen a boundary line for Northern California that extends from the coast at San Simeon (site of Hearst Castle) east across the Coast Range into the Central Valley as far south as Fresno.

Then this imaginary border turns northward along the Sierra Nevada range just south of Yosemite National Park.

The area below this boundary is described in Sunset's companion *Southern California Travel Guide*.

This book begins with one of the world's most visited cities, San Francisco, starting point for most Northern California visits. Subsequent chapters cover the surrounding Bay Area, the Monterey Peninsula, Napa and Sonoma wine valleys, the northern coast, the mountainous reaches north of Redding, the Sierra Nevada region, and the Central Valley.

The map on page 7 shows how we've divided the state, chapter by chapter. Regional maps within each chapter, and detailed downtown maps of San Francisco, Monterey, and Sacramento, are included as further aids in planning driving or walking tours.

A special guide at the back of the book breaks down Northern California by activity. Look here for specifics on camping in national and state parks, plus directories of golf courses, ski resorts, boat cruises, whale-watching excursions, river runs, underground explorations, and train trips.

Some destinations may be covered in special features or in the activity guide as well as in the chapter describing that region; use the index at the back of the book to make sure you locate each entry.

A note on prices and hours: we've made every effort to be up to date. Admission fees and hours are constantly changing, however, so check locally to be sure.

When to visit

Thanks to its equable climate, Northern California is a year-round destination, though there are "best" seasons for various areas.

Coastal temperatures are mild the year around, with extremes a rarity. Spring and autumn are especially good times to tour the coast—you'll find clearer and warmer weather than in summer, when fog frequently blankets the region, especially in the morning and evening. Winter brings the year's

Global Dining

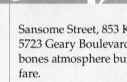

No matter what cuisine you choose, you'll probably find it among San Francisco's 3,300 restaurants. Along with trendy California cuisine eateries and more traditional European and American favorites, this city abounds in restaurants spotlighting Pacific Rim and other lesser-known fares.

The ethnic dining spots listed here are but a small sampling of what's available. The tab at such places is usually low to moderate; we've noted any exceptions. Unless mentioned, you won't need reservations weekdays, though you may have to wait for an empty table in small establishments. Most are open for both lunch and dinner.

Afghanistani. *The Helmand*, 430 Broadway, (415) 362-0641. Locally acclaimed exotic fare, closed Sunday; you might call ahead.

Brazilian. *Bahia*, 41 Franklin Street, (415) 626-3306. Open weekdays for spicy seafood, music; reservations advisable for both lunch and dinner.

Cambodian. *Angkor Wat*, 4217 Geary Boulevard, (415) 221-7887. Longtime favorite, closed Monday.

Chinese. Of hundreds of possibilities, try *China Moon Cafe*, 639 Post Street, (415) 775-4789, for Chinese-California blend; popular with theater crowd, expensive. *Hunan Restaurant* at three locations (924

Sansome Street, 853 Kearny Street, 5723 Geary Boulevard) has bare-bones atmosphere but fine spicy fare.

Ethiopian. *Rasselas*, 2801 California Street, (415) 567-5010. Spicy food, good jazz bar.

Greek. *Stoyanof's*, 1240 9th Avenue, (415) 664-3664. Turkish and eastern Mediterranean specialties, closed Monday.

Indian. *North India Restaurant*, 3131 Webster Street, (415) 931-1556. Well-prepared curries and tandoori.

Japanese. *Tachibana*, 301 Mission Street, (415) 957-0757. Traditional favorites and American versions of Asian appetizers; popular for lunch, closed weekends.

Korean. *Korea House*, 1640 Post Street, (415) 563-1388. Well presented fiery food.

Spanish. *Alejandro's*, 1840 Clement Street, (415) 668-1184. Good tapas bar, not open for lunch.

Thai. *Khan Toke Thai House*, 5937 Geary Boulevard, (415) 668-6654. Pleasantly prepared seafood, poultry, and meats; Sunday dancing.

Vietnamese. *Golden Turtle*, 2211 Van Ness Avenue, (415) 441-4419. Long list of delicacies, closed Monday.

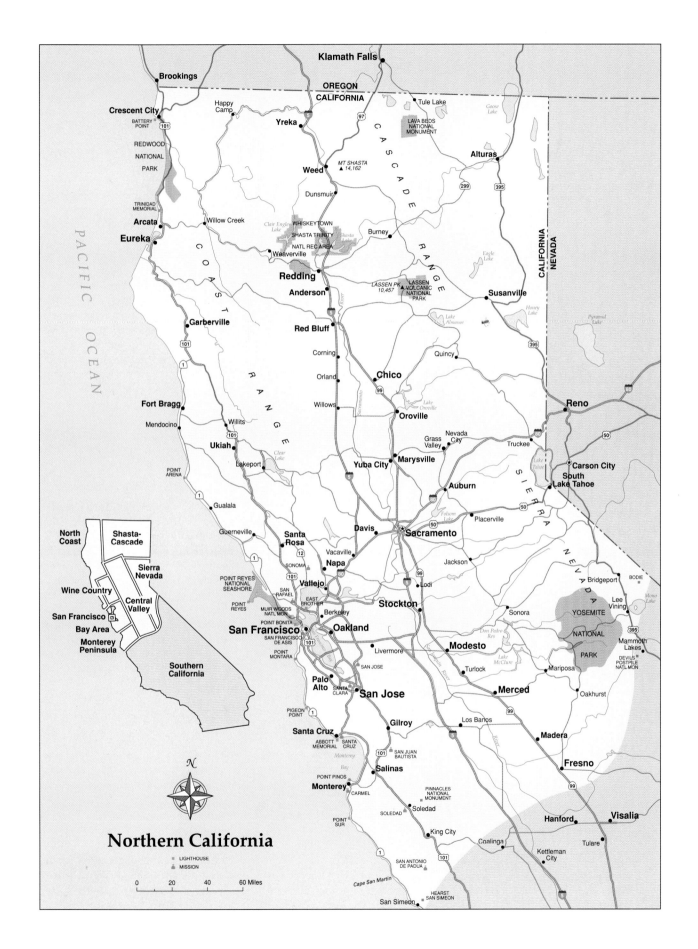

Northern California

- ▲ LIGHTHOUSE
- ▲ MISSION

0   20   40   60 Miles

supply of rain, decreasing as you head south. Crescent City and Eureka in the north receive twice as much precipitation as do Santa Cruz and Monterey on down the coast.

As you move inland, the seasons become more pronounced. Summers get hotter (with relatively little humidity), winters colder (with occasional snow). Spring and autumn are the best times to visit Sacramento and the Central Valley, and also the gold-rush ghost towns nestled in the Sierra foothills. These destinations sizzle in mid-summer, and the valley is subject to low-lying fogs in winter.

The Sierra Nevada has the most dramatic seasonal changes. Summer days are warm, ideal for outdoor activity, the nights cool. Autumn brings a crispness to the air and creates dramatic splashes of red and gold foliage, and winter's usually heavy snowfalls make the mountains a mecca for skiers. Some Sierra highways do close for the winter at the first snowfall, and others require chains over high mountain passes.

The mountains to the north are best visited from spring to early autumn. Many small-town attractions and accommodations in this part of the state are closed in winter.

How to get around

San Francisco and the Greater Bay Area serve as Northern California's main gateway—with three international airports (San Francisco, San Jose, Oakland), two railway terminals (Oakland and San Jose), Greyhound bus terminals, port cities, and a network of teeming freeways.

Sacramento, at the intersection of major east-west and north-south routes, is served by many major airlines, Amtrak, and Greyhound.

Freeways. Northern California's major north-south corridor is Interstate 5, a fast albeit not too scenic route which streaks north through the Central Valley en route to the Oregon border. Other principal north-south highways include U.S. 101, State 99, and State 1, the latter a slow but dramatic route up the coast.

The main east-west artery, Interstate 80, crosses the Sierra into California west of Reno, Nevada. U.S. 50 enters the state from the east at Lake Tahoe, then joins Interstate 80 at Sacramento.

The only freeway congestion you're likely to find in Northern California lies around the Greater Bay Area and, to a lesser degree, the Sacramento metropolitan area. While freeways into San Francisco damaged by the 1989 earthquake are being repaired, traffic on other routes is heavier than usual. To save time, avoid normal commute hours.

Public transportation. Ways to get around specific areas within Northern California are discussed in each chapter. Besides San Francisco's picturesque cable cars and ferries, the Bay Area is served by the modern Bay Area Rapid Transit System (BART) plus municipal bus lines and trains. In other large cities, buses reach most attractions; the capital city shuttles visitors to and from its Old Sacramento attractions.

Tours. Don't overlook sightseeing tours as a means of getting around. They give good background information and spotlight the high points of an area. For details, check with your travel agent, hotel desk, or area visitor center.

Where to stay

Northern California accommodations range from sophisticated city hotels and elegant coastside resorts to guest ranches, small bed-and-breakfast inns, motels, and RV parks. In heavily traveled areas, advance reservations are almost always advisable in summer and on weekends year-round.

This guide takes a look at some San Francisco "boutique" hotels, North Coast bed-and-breakfast inns, and a variety of guest ranches. Other notable accommodations are mentioned throughout the book. For more comprehensive suggestions in any given area, write or call the contacts listed on the first page of each chapter.

Many of Northern California's national and state parklands offer camping facilities; for some choices see pages 120–122. For a listing of national forest campgrounds, contact the Office of Information, U.S. Forest Service, 630 Sansome Street, Room 529A, San Francisco, CA 94111; (415) 705-2874.

The U.S. Bureau of Land Management (2800 Cottage Way, Sacramento, CA 95825) can also provide camping information.

Information sources

Advance planning will help you make the most of your Northern California trip. For up-to-the-minute information on transportation, accommodations, dining options, and special events, contact the local visitor and convention bureaus and chambers of commerce listed in each chapter.

For general information about the state, contact the California Office of Tourism (address on page 4). Another good source of information is the Redwood Empire Association (also listed on page 4); this organization publishes a booklet (small fee) about coastal and Wine Country counties from San Francisco north to the Oregon border.

Every May the Department of Fish & Game (1416 9th Street, Sacramento, CA 95814) publishes a free pamphlet outlining current hunting and freshwater and saltwater fishing regulations for the coming year.

Handicapped travelers. In the last few years California has made great progress in assisting disabled travelers. Special license plates and permits, available from the state's Department of Motor Vehicles, allow the physically impaired to park in convenient slots close to entryways. California also honors permits and plates issued by other states. For additional information, contact the Department of Motor Vehicles, P.O. Box 942869, Sacramento, CA 94269-0001; (916) 732-7243.

Many attractions provide free or rental wheelchairs. And most new and recently refurbished hotels have a few rooms equipped especially for the handicapped. For referrals, contact the California Travel Industry Association, 2500 Wilshire Boulevard, Suite 603, Los Angeles, CA 90057; (213) 384-3178.

Senior citizens. Older travelers will receive hotel and transportation discounts, special dining rates, and reduced entrance fees at many places. The age of eligibility varies widely, so ask about special fares in advance.

Cuisine in California

Northern California has been influencing what America eats and drinks for more than a century. From food staples to regional recipes, the area has a rich history of culinary innovation.

The state's fertile farmlands, vast pasturelands, and hundreds of miles of coastal waters have created a bountiful harvest of fresh ingredients to inspire Northern California chefs. And because of the region's diverse ethnic makeup, varied international tastes have become basic fare here.

The following is a sampling of historic Northern California culinary specialties, including some that date back to gold-rush days.

Coffee. From the earliest days of the gold rush, the smell of roasting coffee has infused the air in San Francisco. By 1890, the city boasted 27 coffee and spice mills, 24 importers, and more than 100 coffee houses.

Three of the country's java giants started here: Folger's, MJB, and Hills Bros. You can sample the dark-roasted blends introduced more than 50 years ago at such places as Caffe Malvina, Caffe Trieste, and Cafe Italia in North Beach.

Stan Delaplane, the late San Francisco newspaper columnist, is credited with introducing Irish coffee in the 1950s. He showed Buena Vista Cafe bartenders how to mix this coffee, whiskey, and cream concoction. The stomach-warming drink can still be sipped at the BV (2765 Hyde Street).

Sourdough bread. Whether the "starter" for this distinctive bread came from the French and Basque settlers who arrived in 1840, the Alaska prospectors—called "sourdoughs"— who rushed here in 1849, or some unknown quality in San Francisco's atmosphere is still debated. But the Boudin brand of sourdough, made by San Francisco's first bakery, is still a favorite.

Chocolate. Domingo Ghirardelli arrived in San Francisco in 1849 via Italy and South America and quickly set up shop as a purveyor of spices, liqueurs, and chocolate. Less than 20 years later, he produced his famous ground chocolate. Take a look at the original equipment at the Chocolate Manufactory in Ghirardelli Square, his old factory.

Another Bay Area chocolate company, Guittard, has been around since 1868. Most of its production is used for cooking and to coat candies.

Jack cheese. This mild, semisoft cheese is another Northern California native. Two of the best-known brands, Sonoma and Vella, are made in the city of Sonoma. You can tour the plants on a visit to the city.

Dungeness crab. Some 140 years ago, Italian fishermen searching the waters around San Francisco for salmon, mackerel, herring, and smelt discovered a crustacean called Dungeness crab. During crab season (November to mid-June), you can sample it at Fisherman's Wharf as a walk-away cocktail in a paper cup.

Fortune cookies. No one is sure who made the first fortune cooky, but some credit Makoto Hagiwara, the developer of the Japanese Tea Garden in San Francisco's Golden Gate Park, with its creation in 1909. You can taste an up-to-date version at the teahouse or watch cookies being made in Chinatown's Golden Gate Fortune Cookies Company (56 Ross Alley).

Green Goddess Salad. One of the most popular items on the Garden Court menu at San Francisco's Sheraton Palace Hotel, this salad was created in the 1920s at the request of actor George Arliss, who was performing in a production called *Green Goddess.* The original dressing recipe calls for anchovy fillets, green onion, minced parsley, tarragon, mayonnaise, tarragon vinegar, and chives.

Joe's Special. This dish was born at New Joe's restaurant in San Francisco in 1932. When the chef informed a late-night customer that there was nothing left to eat but spinach, onions, mushrooms, ground beef, and eggs, he was told to "mix 'em together." It's still a favorite entrée.

Hangtown Fry. Restaurants from San Francisco to the Sierra serve the gold-rush favorite first prepared in Placerville, then called Hangtown. The dish of scrambled eggs, oysters, and bacon was reportedly a condemned prisoner's last request.

Steam beer. San Francisco's Anchor Brewing Co., founded in 1896, was the only steam beer survivor of Prohibition. Though devotees of this Potrero Hill brew admire its classic flavor, no one is certain what "steam beer" means.

Bottled water. From the Martinez area comes Alhambra Water, a company that benefited by being able to supply potable water after the 1906 earthquake. You can watch the operations of two Napa Valley bottled water plants, Calistoga and Crystal Geyser, both in Calistoga.

Wine. Long-lived wineries attest to the region's close ties between wine and food. Tours and tastings take place at such Napa Valley survivors as Beaulieu, Beringer, Inglenook, and Charles Krug; Buena Vista and Simi in Sonoma Valley; and Mirassou, Wente, and Concannon in the Greater Bay Area.

San Francisco

Polls consistently rank San Francisco in the top 10 of the world's favorite cities. The beautiful setting certainly has a lot to do with its allure. Pacific Ocean and San Francisco Bay waters enclose the city on three sides. And San Francisco's naturally air-conditioned climate, carefully preserved Victorian architecture, 19th-century cable cars, and cosmopolitan attitude all contribute to its popularity.

Then, too, this is a *manageable* city for visitors. Its compact size concentrates its considerable charms within a small area, making them easily accessible even without a car.

This is a city built on hills. Someone once said that if you get tired of climbing them, you can always lean against them. But it's from these peaks that you get the well-touted views—fog rolling in over the Golden Gate Bridge, cargo ships heading into the harbor, and sailboats tacking past islands in the channel.

Connecting links

Whether you drive across San Francisco's bay-spanning bridges or merely glimpse them from one of many observation spots, you'll notice their importance to the city.

Most glamorous of the bridges is the Golden Gate, one of the longest single-span suspension bridges ever built (6,450 feet). It's a bridge you can walk and bike across, enjoying a gull's-eye look 220 feet down. The turnout at its

View from the top of Twin Peaks stretches east across the city and the Bay Bridge all the way to Oakland in the East Bay.

north end offers exceptional city views. Motorists pay tolls only when entering San Francisco from the north.

The San Francisco–Oakland Bay Bridge is the city's main connection to the east. A hardworking double-decker, part suspension span and part cantilevered, it tunnels through Yerba Buena Island on its 8¼-mile route across the bay. Tolls are collected westbound only.

Tales of a city

San Francisco became a city quite out of proportion to its actual size from the first cry of "Gold!" in 1848. With a population of less than 725,000 in an area of less than 47 square miles, it's still a big city without being big.

It has qualities common to all of the world's great cities: rich historical background, great diversity of activity, cultural depth, and pervasive charm. And its problems are those of a large city, often magnified because they occur in such a compact area: traffic congestion, environmental concerns, and an ever-growing number of homeless.

Costanoan Indians had lived in the Bay Area for thousands of years before the Spaniards, in 1776, established a military post at what is now the Presidio and founded Mission San Francisco de Asis. But the pueblo drowsed until the mid-1800s, when the gold rush and the subsequent silver bonanza made it a magnet for those who hoped to get rich—and sometimes did. The city was changed forever.

By the start of the 20th century the city, which had already been rebuilt seven times after devastating fires, boasted a population of 342,000. Then came the 1906 earthquake and fire, which destroyed 28,000 buildings and killed 500 people. San Franciscans rebuilt once more, showing off their new

look at the Panama-Pacific International Exposition in 1915.

Those early tourists wouldn't recognize today's city: ultramodern skyscrapers jostle venerable Victorians, old factories have become shopping areas, and part of the once-raucous Barbary Coast provides sedate quarters for antique dealers, attorneys, and architects.

Another serious earthquake occurred in 1989, and though San Francisco suffered less damage than other parts of the Bay Area, some freeways are still being repaired and realigned.

A cultural mosaic

Its early settlers, a unique blend of races and cultures, set the pattern for San Francisco's tolerant attitude. Over the years the city has been enriched by the colorful traditions of Chinese, Japa-

Contacts

These agencies offer information on attractions and accommodations. See additional contacts throughout this chapter.

San Francisco Convention & Visitors Bureau
201 3rd St., Suite 900
San Francisco, CA 94103-3185
(415) 974-6900

Visitor Information Center
Hallidie Plaza, Lower Level
Powell and Market Streets
(P.O. Box 6977)
San Francisco, CA 94101-6977
(415) 391-2000

nese, Southeast Asian, Italian, Hispanic, and other ethnic groups. Some 50 foreign language publications are currently sold around town.

A more recent addition to the city's cultural heritage is its gay community, now estimated to comprise about 15 percent of the total population.

Planning a trip

Part of the pleasure of visiting San Francisco is the ease with which a visitor can move from attraction to attraction. A car is not a necessity—you can get around on foot or aboard public transportation.

The city is noted as being eternally springlike, which means that it's seldom hot (and often foggy and cold in summer, when tourists least expect it). September and October are usually the warmest months, January the coldest (average 55°).

The San Francisco Visitor Information Center at Hallidie Plaza (address on page 11) can provide additional travel details. For an around-the-clock rundown of events, call (415) 391-2001.

Accommodations. A sampling of city hotels is shown on page 16; contact the visitors bureau (page 11) for a complete guide. You can call hotels directly or book through a travel agency or reservation service such as San Francisco Reservations, (800) 333-8996, and San Francisco Lodging, (800) 356-7567.

Getting there. Major north-south highways into San Francisco are U.S. 101 and State 1. Interstate 280 also reaches the city from San Jose. Interstate 80 is the most direct east-west corridor.

Some 35 domestic and foreign carriers serve San Francisco International Airport, 14 miles south of the city via U.S. 101. Oakland and San Jose have alternative international airports. An information board in the baggage claim areas of each of the three SFO terminals lists ground transportation, including door-to-door shuttles and limousines. Most major car rental agencies have desks here. A free shuttle connects airport terminals.

SFO Airporter shuttles ($7 one-way, $11 round-trip) run every 20 minutes

from 5 A.M. to midnight between the airport and Union Square area hotels. Cab fare into the city is about $25.

Amtrak train and Greyhound bus passengers arrive at the Transbay Terminal, 1st and Mission streets. (Train passengers are transported across the bay by bus from Oakland.)

From the Transbay Terminal, regional bus lines also connect the city with destinations around the Bay Area. AC Transit buses, (415) 839-2882, serve the East Bay; Golden Gate Transit, (415) 332-6600, reaches the North Bay; and SamTrans, (415) 761-7000, heads south to the airport and peninsula cities. CalTrain commuter train service extends south to San Jose; for information, call (415) 557-8661.

Getting around by car. It's wise to avoid driving in the heart of the city. Streets are crowded, parking limited and expensive.

After the 1989 earthquake put the Embarcadero Freeway out of business, the city posted color-coded directional signs to help visitors find their way to Fisherman's Wharf, Chinatown, and North Beach. Drivers from the East Bay should leave Interstate 80 at the Embarcadero exit; from the South Bay, exit U.S. 101 at Civic Center. Then follow the green boot of Italy, the red Chinese lantern, or the orange crab to your destination.

San Francisco Municipal Railway. The city operates one of the country's most convenient and efficient fleet of buses, light-rail vehicles, and cable cars. Route information is published in the Yellow Pages, or you can call 673-MUNI for specific help. A comprehensive route map is sold at stores throughout the city.

You'll need exact change—currently about $1 ($2 on cable cars), reduced rates for seniors and disabled. Free transfers can be used on any Muni vehicle. Passports valid for one day ($6) or three days ($10) are sold at the visitor information center (address on page 11) and STBS outlets (see page 14).

Cable cars. Riding San Francisco's "municipal roller coaster" is not only fun, but an excellent means of transportation on congested streets.

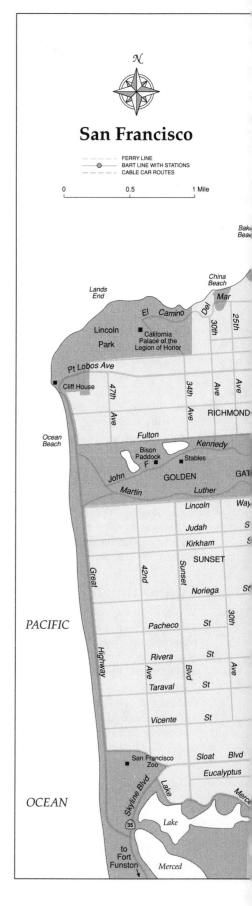

to
Marin
County

San   Francisco   Bay

Ferry to Angel Island,
Tiburon, Vallejo
Ferry to Alcatraz Island
Ferry to Sausalito
Ferry to Tiburon
Ferry to Vallejo

Golden
Gate
Bridge

Fort Point

Golden   Gate
National   Rec   Area

Marina Green

Crissy Field

Doyle   Dr

Lincoln   Blvd

Lincoln   Blvd

PRESIDIO

Presidio Army
Museum &
Pershing Square

Palace of
Fine Arts/
Exploratorium

Marina   Blvd

Fort
Mason

Pier 45   Fisherman's
Wharf
Hyde St
Pier
Aquatic
Park

Anchorage

Cannery

Beach   Bay   St

Ghirardelli
Square

Pier
43½   Pier
41   Pier 39

Pier 35

Columbus   Ave

Grant

Powell   St

Montgomery

Coit
Tower

TELEGRAPH
HILL

The Embarcadero

Pier 7

BART Transbay Tube
to Oakland

Ferry to
East Bay

Drumm

Main   St

Bay
Bridge

MARINA

Lombard   St

Union   St

Broadway

Washington

RUSSIAN
HILL

Taylor   St

NOB HILL

NORTH
BEACH

CHINA
TOWN

Portsmouth
Square

FINANCIAL
DISTRICT

Battery

Transbay
Bus Terminal

Julius Kahn
Playground

Ave

PACIFIC
HEIGHTS

Divisadero

Steiner   St

Webster

Fillmore   St

Laguna

Gough   St

Polk   St

Leavenworth   St

St

Ave

Union
Square

Howard

Folsom

Harrison

1st St

West   Pacific

Washington   St

Sacramento   St

California   St

Sutter   St

Van Ness Ave

Larkin   St

Geary   St

O'Farrell

2nd   St

Mtn Lake
Park

St

St

7th   Ave

Geary   Blvd

Stanyan   St

Masonic   Ave

Turk   St

Fulton   St

Fell   St

Japan
Center

St Mary's
Cathedral

JAPANTOWN

CIVIC
CENTER

City Hall

Opera
House

Market   St

Mission   St

SOUTH OF
MARKET

Moscone
Center

4th   St

5th   St

6th   St

3rd   St

Bryant

Brannan

6th   St

California   St

Clement   St

Balboa   Ave

St

Arguello   Blvd

Park   Presidio Blvd

Univ of
San Francisco

Alamo
Square

Freeway
Closed

7th   St

8th   St

9th   St

10th   St

11th   St

80

PARK

De Young/
Asian Art
Museum

Conservatory
of Flowers
McLaren
Lodge

Calif Academy
of Sciences

Playground

Oak   St

Duboce   Ave

St

St

St

Japanese
Tea Garden

Strybing
Arboretum

Stow
Lake

JF
Dr

Haight   St

Frederick   St

HAIGHT

Ashbury St

Clayton   St

Buena
Vista
Park

15th   St

J. Randall
Museum

Mission
Dolores   17th   St

16th   St

St

St

St

St

Folsom

Harrison

Bryant

Potrero   Ave

De Haro   St

Arkansas   St

Pennsylvania

101

280

3rd

7th   Ave

10th   Ave

Univ of Calif
SF

Castro   St

Douglass   St

19th   St

20th

22nd

24th   St

27th

CASTRO

Mission
Dolores
Park

MISSION

Mission   St

South Van Ness Ave

Valencia

Guerrero   St

Dolores   St

20th

23rd

St

St

POTRERO

Twin   Ave

Clarendon   Ave

TWIN
PEAKS

Market   St

Twin   Peaks   Blvd

NOE VALLEY

30th   St

Army   St

Evans   Ave

Jerrold   Ave

Closed   For   Repairs

Cargo   Way

19th   Ave

14th   Ave

Dewey Blvd

O'Shaughnessy   Blvd

Portola   Dr

MT
DAVIDSON

Yerba Buena   Ave

Sigmund
Stern
Grove   Dr

Courtland   Ave

Industrial   St

Oakdale   Ave

Quint   St

Mendell   St

Freeway

BAYVIEW

Monterey   Blvd

Bosworth St

San Jose   St   Ave

280

101

Junipero Serra Blvd

Ocean   Ave

City College
of SF

San Jose   Ave

Alemany   Blvd

Mission   St

Silver Ave

University   Ave

McLaren
Park

3rd   St

Keith   St

Thomas Ave

HUNTERS
POINT

San Francisco
State Univ

Holloway   Ave

to Daly City,
San José

to SF Intl Airport,
San José

The two lines that leave from the turntable at Powell and Market streets (Hallidie Plaza) reach the waterfront. Cars marked "Bay and Taylor" clang through the edge of Chinatown and along a section of North Beach en route to Fisherman's Wharf. "Hyde and Beach" cars bypass most of Chinatown and North Beach but provide grand bay views and hang-on-tight rides to Aquatic Park.

The California Street line runs from the foot of Market Street, through the financial district and Chinatown, up steep Nob Hill, and west to Van Ness Avenue.

It's best to buy tickets ($2) before boarding; be prepared for long lines. Look for self-service ticket machines at terminals and major stops. All-day passes are also available there.

Bay Area Rapid Transit. This modern, direct, and comfortable subway system links San Francisco with Daly City to the south and with the East Bay (the latter via a tube under the bay). BART trains run to midnight daily (weekdays from 4 A.M., Saturday from 6 A.M., Sunday from 8 A.M.). Discounted senior and children's tickets are also available; call (415) 464-7133. Downtown San Francisco has four stations (see map on page 19). Phone (415) 788-BART for other details.

Ferries. Several ferry companies provide daily transport as well as sightseeing. Golden Gate Ferries serve Sausalito and Larkspur in Marin County from the Ferry Building at the foot of Market Street; call (415) 332-6600 for fares and schedules. The Red & White Fleet, (415) 546-BOAT, makes daily runs to Sausalito, Tiburon, and Vallejo (shuttle to Marine World). Oakland/Alameda service is operated by the Blue & Gold Fleet; for information, call (415) 522-3300.

Tours. Gray Line offers several popular guided sightseeing tours, including a 3-hour look at the city and a trip to Chinatown at night. Other companies offer limousine and minivan tours; check with your hotel desk, the visitors bureau (page 11), or the Yellow Pages.

You can join the knowledgeable City Guides, (415) 558-3981, for a free walking tour. The Foundation for San Francisco's Architectural Heritage, (415) 441-3004, is another good choice (small fee). For other specialized walks, check with the visitors bureau.

Harbor tours operate from piers at Fisherman's Wharf (see page 124).

Dining. The city's 3,300 restaurants offer every kind of dining, from haute cuisine to family-style meals. Service comes at cloud level at posh aeries on Nob Hill and downtown. For a list of restaurants offering fare from Afghanistani to Vietnamese, stop by the visitor center (page 11); also see page 6.

For inexpensive choices, try "walkaway" seafood cocktails at Fisherman's Wharf, dim sum in Chinatown, sushi in Japantown, tacos in the Mission District, and pasta in North Beach.

Entertainment. San Francisco has always had a zest for performing arts. At least 15 legitimate theaters flourished here in 1850 amid the saloons of the Barbary Coast, and ebullient audiences threw gold nuggets at the feet of the performers. The pace has not slackened.

City entertainment includes everything from trendy nightclubs South of Market to quiet piano bars and lively discos in downtown and Nob Hill hotels. The Civic Center is home to renowned opera, symphony, and ballet companies. For plays and musical shows, theaters are concentrated downtown on Geary, Mason, and Market streets and on the waterfront at Fort Mason. Check the visitors bureau or the weekend entertainment sections of the local newspapers for current events.

Club Fugazi (678 Green Street in North Beach) is the venue for the city's longest-running musical revue, the zany *Beach Blanket Babylon*, presented cabaret-style Wednesday through Sunday nights plus Sunday matinees. For reservations, call (415) 421-4222.

Stop by San Francisco Ticket Box Office Service outlets (STBS) on the Stockton Street side of Union Square or at One Embarcadero Center (street level) for half-price day-of-performance tickets or full-price tickets for future events. The Union Square office is open noon to 7:30 P.M. Tuesday through Saturday; Embarcadero is open 10 A.M. to 6 P.M. daily except Sunday. For recorded information, call (415) 433-STBS.

Spectator sports. San Francisco hosts professional baseball (Giants) and football (49ers); both teams currently share the stadium at Candlestick Park, 8 miles south of the city off U.S. 101. Across the bay, the Oakland A's baseball team and the Golden State Warriors basketball team perform in the Oakland Coliseum. San Jose has pro hockey (Sharks).

The Cow Palace sports arena on Geneva Avenue in Daly City is the site of the Grand National livestock exposition, horse show, and rodeo every October.

A Bay Model

For a graphic illustration of the immensity of the West's largest estuary, cross the Golden Gate Bridge to visit Sausalito's impressive hydraulic model of San Francisco Bay and Delta region. Though only a thousandth of the bay's actual size, the scale model takes up 1½ acres in a warehouselike stucture.

A tape tour describes tidal movement, flow and current of water, and other forces affecting the sea.

Anecdotes about Humphrey the humpback whale and the area's humming toadfishes enliven the tour.

Operated by the U.S. Army Corps of Engineers, the visitor center is open 9 A.M. to 4 P.M. Tuesday through Saturday. Admission and tape tour are free. From U.S. 101, take the Marin City/Sausalito exit east and head south on Bridgeway; turn left on Marinship Way, and follow the signs.

Called the city's municipal roller coasters, cable cars provide thrills and views. This line terminates downhill at the Hyde Street Pier, where you can climb aboard several vintage ships at San Francisco's Maritime National Historical Park.

At one time the names of San Francisco's grand hotels could roll right off your tongue: Clift, Fairmont, Mark Hopkins, Palace, St. Francis, and Sir Francis Drake. These are still top-notch contenders (the Sheraton Palace reopened in 1991 after an 18-month renovation), but they've been joined by other well-known names.

In addition to the oldtimers, the downtown roster of major hotels now includes Grand Hyatt, Hilton, Holiday Inn, Huntington, Hyatt Regency, Mandarin, Marriott, Meridien, Nikko, Pan Pacific, Parc Fifty Five, Park Hyatt, Ritz-Carlton, and Stanford Court.

Motels (mostly along Van Ness Avenue and Lombard Street) and bed-and-breakfast inns are scattered throughout the city. Twenty chain hotels, from Best Western to Westin, are located south of the city at the airport.

"Boutique" hotels are another popular lodging option. These small hotels (under 150 rooms), often recently renovated and conveniently located, usually offer such complimentary services as breakfast, tea, or limo transfers. Our sampling focuses on what's available around Union Square.

Rates begin around $100 at some, climb well upward at others. For a complete list of San Francisco hotels, contact the visitors bureau (address on page 11).

Campton Place Hotel, 340 Stockton Street; (415) 781-5555. Small, elegant, top-of-the-line hotel with traditional European ambience; 126 rooms and a restaurant rated one of the city's finest. Complimentary limo.

Cartwright Hotel, 524 Sutter Street; (415) 421-2865. Built in 1915 and renovated in 1990, with 114 antique-furnished rooms; coffee shop for breakfast only. Complimentary afternoon tea.

Hotel Diva, 440 Geary Street; (415) 885-0200. Ultramodern hostelry in a transformed 1912 building; 107 rooms with down comforters, safes, minirefrigerators, and VCRs (video library in lobby). Complimentary continental breakfast and morning limo.

Donatello, 501 Post Street; (415) 441-7100. Intimate, grande-luxe hotel; 95 rooms furnished with many 18th- and 19th-century antiques; top-rated Ristorante Donatello.

Inn at Union Square, 440 Post Street; (415) 397-3510. Charming English country atmosphere with European-style service; 30 antique-decorated rooms, some with garden views. Complimentary breakfast, afternoon tea with goodies, and evening wine and hors d'oeuvres on each floor.

Hotel Juliana, 590 Bush Street; (415) 392-2540. Rotating art collection from local galleries hangs in the 107 guest rooms. Complimentary limo to Financial District, evening wine, coffee and tea all day.

Kensington Park Hotel, 450 Post Street; (415) 788-6400. Intimate lobby, 84 Queen Anne–styled rooms, just off Union Square. Complimentary continental breakfast, afternoon high tea and sherry.

Monticello Inn, 127 Ellis Street; (415) 392-8800. Ninety-one rooms in renovated 1906 building; popular Corona Bar & Grill. Complimentary breakfast, evening wine, and limo service.

Orchard Hotel, 562 Sutter Street; (415) 433-4434. Renovated 1907 building with 96 rooms; large lobby offering cocktails beneath crystal chandeliers; Sutter Garden Restaurant. Complimentary coffee, limo.

Petite Auberge, 863 Bush Street; (415) 928-6000. Twenty-six country French–furnished rooms, 18 with fireplaces. Complimentary breakfast buffet, afternoon tea, wine and hors d'oeuvres, morning paper, home-baked cookies, and terry robes.

Prescott Hotel, 545 Post Street; (415) 563-0303. Opened in 1989 with 109 traditional-styled rooms; Postrio Restaurant featuring Wolfgang Puck's cuisine.

Regis Hotel, 490 Geary Street; (415) 928-7900. Luxury hotel with Louis XVI styling, French and English antiques in its 86 rooms; Regina's restaurant. Complimentary morning limo.

Hotel Union Square, 114 Powell Street; (415) 397-3000. The 131 rooms have honor bars, hair dryers, comforters, and remote-control TV; Mermaid Seafood Bar & Bar is off the lobby. Complimentary continental breakfast and limo.

Vintage Court Hotel, 650 Bush Street; (415) 392-4666. European-style decor with 106 rooms; outstanding French cuisine in Masa's—rated by some as the city's best restaurant. Complimentary morning coffee and tea, limo, afternoon wine.

White Swan Inn, 845 Bush Street; (415) 775-1755. London-style inn with 26 antique-decorated rooms featuring sitting areas and fireplaces, wet bars and refrigerators. Complimentary breakfast; afternoon tea, wine, and sherry; home-baked cookies; newspaper; shoeshine.

York Hotel, 940 Sutter Street; (415) 885-6800. Ninety-six room hotel with high-ceilinged, Victorian-style lobby; Plush Room cabaret and bar; wet bars, coffeemakers, and vanities in guest rooms; and 24-hour executive gym. Complimentary continental breakfast, limo.

Unlocking the City

One way to grasp the city on your own is to follow the 49-Mile Drive past important scenic and historic points. Later you can return to explore areas that interest you most.

Marked by blue, white, and orange seagull signs, the drive takes you along some congested downtown streets. For that reason, it's best enjoyed on Sunday. Pick up a free map at the visitor center (address on page 11), and start anywhere along the route.

City hills

For a good overview, climb the city's hills. The following are the most accessible and interesting.

Nob Hill. This posh crest is easily reached by any of the city's three cable car lines. Disembark at California and Powell for a spectacular look down California to the bay. The lofty plateau has long been synonomous with the city's elite. Before the 1906 earthquake, it was the site of grand mansions; the imposing brownstone at California and Mason (now the Pacific Union Club) is the single complete survivor.

Several of the city's most luxurious hotels (Fairmont, Mark Hopkins Inter-Continental, Huntington, Stanford Court, and Ritz-Carlton) rise atop or around the hill. Other cachets include the California Masonic Memorial Temple at California and Taylor, a spacious auditorium for performing arts, and Gothic-style Grace Cathedral across the street, begun in 1910 and consecrated in 1964. The east entry doors at the Episcopalian church are gilded bronze replicas of the Ghiberti doors at the Florence Baptistry.

Telegraph Hill. At the northeast corner of the city, Telegraph was named for the semaphores once used to signal ships. Coit Tower at its summit was built as a memorial to volunteer firemen from funds left by Lillie Hitchcock Coit, a great fire buff. Even the 210-foot tower's shape roughly resembles a hose nozzle. Inside, 25 murals of "Life in California, 1934" were painted by WPA artists. An elevator to an observation platform operates daily (small charge). To get there, take Lombard Street from the west.

Russian Hill. West of Telegraph, bounded roughly by Polk, Taylor, Broadway, and Bay streets, Russian Hill is an area of small green parks and quaint cottages squeezed amidst apartment buildings. Filbert between Hyde and Leavenworth is one of the city's steepest streets; brick-paved Lombard between Hyde and Leavenworth is its most crooked.

Twin Peaks. Situated in the center of the city, the Twin Peaks are noted for some of the best views of the Bay Area. Now a 65-acre park, the crests are particularly popular lookouts at night. To get there, take upper Market Street west to Twin Peaks Boulevard.

City streets

Knowing these famous and not-so-famous streets will help you get around.

Market Street. The city's best-known thoroughfare slices diagonally across town from Twin Peaks to the Ferry Building. Heart of the gay community lies around Market and Castro; the strip south of Union Square is a continuation of the downtown shopping center.

Across from the Ferry Building at the foot of Market lies Justin Herman Plaza; its monumental Vaillancourt Fountain is a walk-through arrangement of 101 concrete boxes.

High-rises accent the street's lower end. The 20-story building at Market and Bush rises above a pleasant park (popular at lunch). At 555 Market you can stroll through gardens outside the 43-story building or see a free Chevron petroleum exhibit inside (9 A.M. to 4 P.M. weekdays).

At Market and New Montgomery streets stands the refurbished Sheraton Palace Hotel, built by silver king William Ralston in 1875. Its glass-roofed Garden Court—a historical landmark—is a popular dining spot.

Geary Street. The city's oldest street, Geary extends west from Market all the way to Sutro Heights Park near the ocean. En route it passes some of the city's smartest shops, Union Square, the theater district, stunning St. Mary's Cathedral on Gough Street, and Japantown (page 24).

Mission Street. Paralleling Market Street to the south, Mission cuts through the South of Market (SoMa) district, home to trendy restaurants, clubs, and galleries—see page 21. Upscale hotels edge close to the Moscone Convention Center, a block south of Mission between 3rd and 4th streets. Mission Street takes an abrupt turn south after it crosses Van Ness Avenue, heading into the heart of the Hispanic Mission District (see page 24).

California Street. Taking off from Market at Justin Herman Plaza, California extends all the way west to Lincoln Park, site of the California Palace of the Legion of Honor museum. En route, it climbs from the canyons of the financial district through colorful Chinatown to the heights of Nob Hill.

Union Street. Passing North Beach and upper Grant Avenue, Union becomes a shopping and dining compound after crossing Van Ness. In pre–gold rush days, the district became known as Cow Hollow, the city's dairyland.

The Octagon House at Gough Street, built in 1861, is open for tours (donations) from noon to 3 P.M. the second and fourth Thursday and second Sunday of every month except January. Another vintage charmer a few blocks south, the Haas-Lilienthal House at Franklin and Jackson, welcomes visitors from noon to 4 P.M. Wednesday, 11 A.M. to 4:30 P.M. Sunday; there's a nominal admission.

Polk Street. The 10-block length of Polk between Union and Pine streets—one of the city's main gay areas—sandwiches antique stores, galleries, and restaurants between odds-and-ends emporiums.

At the heart of downtown shopping, Union Square serves as an outdoor setting for colorful city festivals; underneath is a large parking garage. On its west side stands the elegant Westin St. Francis Hotel, a 1906 earthquake survivor.

Downtown

Unlike many big cities, San Francisco still has its government, financial, and major retail centers centrally located downtown. Stretching roughly from Van Ness Avenue to the waterfront, this downtown area encompasses the Civic Center, Union Square, the Financial District, Embarcadero Center, historic Jackson Square, and the revitalized South of Market district.

Chinatown and North Beach, two colorful sections in the heart of the city, are discussed on pages 22 and 24. For shopping highlights, see page 20.

Civic Center

A monumental group of federal, state, and city structures, Civic Center extends east from Franklin Street to the United Nations Plaza (scene of lively produce markets on Wednesday and Sunday) at Market and 7th streets. The buildings that make up the performing arts center lie along Van Ness Avenue, and around them spreads a fresh crop of restaurants, inns, galleries, bookstores, and antique shops.

Public buildings. Ornate City Hall, a model of French Renaissance grandeur crowned by a lofty dome higher than the nation's capitol, presides over Civic Center Plaza. Underneath, Brooks Hall adds exhibit space to the Civic Auditorium complex. The History Room at the Main Public Library (east of the plaza) holds maps, photographs, and exhibits salvaged from the 1906 earthquake; call (415) 558-3949 for hours.

Performing Arts Center. West of City Hall along Van Ness Avenue is one of the country's largest performing arts centers. The War Memorial Opera House (home to fine opera and ballet companies) is bracketed by the gleaming modern Louise M. Davies Symphony Hall on the south and the War Memorial Veterans Building on the north. Center tours are offered every half-hour Monday (except holidays) from 10 A.M. to 2:30 P.M.; you can also tour Davies on Wednesday and Saturday afternoons (moderate admission). Phone (415) 552-8338 for details.

The Veterans Building (Van Ness and McAllister) was the site of the signing of the United Nations Charter in 1945. It houses the intimate Herbst Theatre and the Museum of Modern Art, acclaimed for its abstract expressionist works. The museum is open 10 A.M. to 5 P.M. Tuesday through Friday (to 9 P.M. Thursday), 11 A.M. to 5 P.M. weekends. Admission is $4 adults, $2 seniors and

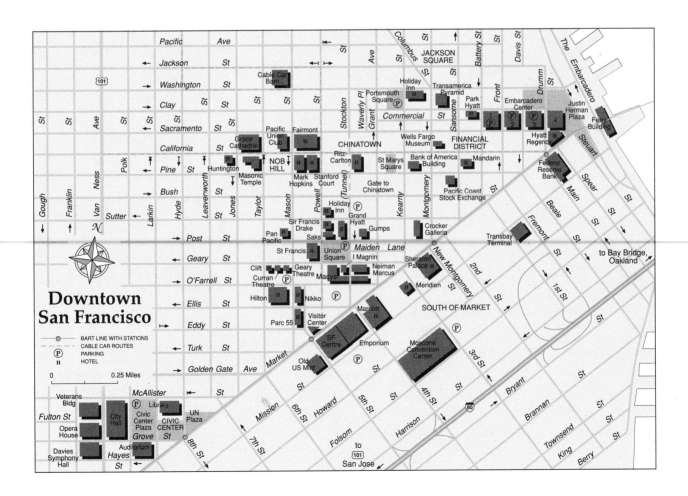

San Francisco is a world market-place with everything from tourist trifles to antique treasures for sale. Most shops are open 7 days a week, with extended evening hours on certain weekdays.

The d.a.s. Bus (Dining and Shopping) offers loop service to Pier 39, Fisherman's Wharf, Union Square, North Beach, Union Street, Chinatown, South of Market, and Civic Center. For fares and schedules, call (415) 775-SHOW.

Don't overlook museum and gallery stores. Check out the San Francisco Zoo (Sloat Boulevard at Skyline), San Francisco Opera Shop (199 Grove Street), Museum of Modern Art (401 Van Ness Avenue), and Craft & Folk Art Museum at Fort Mason (Building A) for T-shirts, books, posters, and many one-of-a-kind items.

To buy souvenirs and support a cause at the same time, shop at the Greenpeace Store (890 North Point) for handcrafted and recycled items or the UNICEF Store (3419 Sacramento Street) for international gifts.

Downtown, Union Square's wealth of stores, convenient parking, good restaurants, and nearby attractions make it hard to bypass. Only a few blocks away lie other unique malls, and farther afield you'll find discount outlets, crafts galleries, and trendy boutiques.

Union Square. This is San Francisco's answer to Rodeo Drive in Beverly Hills. Elegant department stores and richly appointed specialty shops cater to an upscale crowd, but their decor makes them fun to browse. When you tire, a variety of restaurants and hotel dining rooms offer a change of pace.

Serious shoppers concentrate on the blocks bounded by Geary, Powell, Post, and Stockton streets. Besides the large stores like Neiman

Marcus, Saks Fifth Avenue, I. Magnin, and Macy's, take a look at Gump's (250 Post Street), famous for its Orientalia, and FAO Schwarz (48 Stockton), a playland for children. Sutter Street has art galleries and exclusive clothing stores.

San Francisco Shopping Centre. Spiral escalators reach 9 floors of shops and restaurants in this vertical mall at Market and Powell streets. Nordstrom department store occupies the top 5 stories; more than 90 boutiques and 9 restaurants fill the rest of the space.

The large Emporium department store just up Market Street, connected by walk-throughs to the Centre, is one of the city's oldest retailers.

Crocker Galleria. This three-level center on the block bounded by Post, Kearny, Sutter, and Montgomery streets encompasses more than 50 boutiques, restaurants, and services under a spectacular glass dome. Modeled after Milan's vast Galleria Vittorio Emmanuelle, it's the place to look at the wares of American and European designers. Two rooftop gardens offer picnic possibilities.

Embarcadero Center. On the site of San Francisco's other-era produce market, this high-rise complex of offices, stores, restaurants, and hotels near the waterfront north of Market Street resembles a city of the future. You can park in the garage and spend the day wandering around. Information boards at the base of the escalators will help orient you.

South of Market. You don't really need a map to shop the discount and factory outlets South of Market—just follow the crowds. Discount shopping in the city is so popular that several guidebooks have been published on the subject, and special bus tours are available; check with the visitor center (page 11).

Stores usually open around 10 A.M. and close about 5 P.M.; most are closed Sunday. Go early; merchandise can become a mad tangle by mid-day.

Six-Sixty Center (660 3rd Street) has 20 outlets offering savings on brand-name shoes, clothing, and accessories. Happy Times, across the street, discounts jewelry, watches, and sunglasses.

Yerba Buena Square (Howard and 5th streets, open daily) offers outlets for toys, coats, dance and exercise wear, and more.

Among San Francisco designer outlets worth visiting are Esprit (Illinois and 16th streets, open daily, sportswear); Eileen West (39 Bluxome Street, women's clothing); and Gunne Sax (35 Stanford Alley between 2nd and 3rd streets, open daily, period-look prom dresses and other women's clothing).

Waterfront. While most of the stores at Fisherman's Wharf and Pier 39 sell souvenir-type merchandise, street vendors often display good handicrafts. But your best bet for crafts and unique gifts will be the Anchorage, Cannery, or Ghirardelli Square malls (see pages 27–28 for information).

Union Street. Trendy upscale shops west of Van Ness Avenue in the 1500 to 2200 blocks mingle happily with bakeries, cafes, and lively bars. Victorians have been transformed into shopping malls, and passages between buildings lead to small courtyards and antique-filled backyard barns.

Sacramento Street. A browsable 5-block area south of the Presidio between Lyon and Spruce streets is reminiscent of early Union Street. Interspersed with vintage homes are galleries, boutiques, and coffee houses.

students, free 12 and under (free for all the first Tuesday of the month). The museum will move to South of Market in 1993 (see below right).

Around Union Square

The 20-odd blocks around Union Square are a magnet for shoppers, diners, and theatergoers. You can park in the cavernous garage beneath the square to stroll around this walkable area. (Two other convenient garages are Mason-O'Farrell and Sutter-Stockton.)

The square. The landscaped square (bounded by Geary, Powell, Post, and Stockton streets) got its name from a series of 1860 pro-Union demonstrations. Its 97-foot monument to victory in the Spanish-American war and the Westin St. Francis hotel across Powell Street are 1906 earthquake survivors.

Today, its benches are lined with a motley assortment of street artists, panhandlers, and people feeding the pigeons. But it's also the site of fashion shows, rallies, concerts, and colorful events like the annual Cable Car Bell Ringing Contest in June.

Around the square. Framing the square and fanning out around it are such noted stores as Neiman Marcus, I. Magnin, Saks Fifth Avenue, Macy's, Gump's, and FAO Schwarz (see page 20 for more shopping details). West on Geary lie the Curran and Geary theaters and the venerable Clift Hotel (its Redwood Room bar is a favorite pre-theater stop).

Sutter Street, a block north of Union Square, showcases an array of haute couture, art, and antique stores in the 300 to 500 blocks. Two blocks east is the glass-canopied Crocker Galleria shopping center.

The fountain in the plaza of the Grand Hyatt north of the square on Stockton near Sutter gives a whimsical picture of city history. It was created by sculptor Ruth Asawa, who also designed fountains at Ghirardelli Square and Japantown's Buchanan Mall.

On the east side of Union Square across Stockton lies Maiden Lane, a pedestrianway that began life as the Barbary Coast's most lurid red light district. Architecturally, the lane's chief claim to fame is the yellow brick gallery at 140, designed by Frank Lloyd Wright in 1948 as a prototype for New York City's Guggenheim Museum.

Financial district

North of Market Street, impressive office buildings shade the narrow slot that is Montgomery Street, San Francisco's business center. Heart of the district is the Pacific Coast Stock Exchange (Pine and Sansome streets), where business begins around 6 A.M. to coincide with New York trading. At lunchtime, well-clad crowds hurry through the doors of such dining temples as Doro's, Ernie's, Jack's, Sam's Grill, Tadich Grill, and Tommy Toy's.

It's hard to realize that this dapper domain of bankers and brokers was a muddy morass deemed "impassable, not even jackassable" in gold-rush days when A. P. Giannini founded his Bank of America at the corner of Montgomery and California.

Two high-rises offer bird's-eye views: the Bank of America's 52nd-floor Carnelian Room restaurant and bar (see page 30) and the 27th floor of the 853-foot-high Transamerica Pyramid at 600 Montgomery Street.

Three banks have free museums open during banking hours. The Wells Fargo History Museum, 420 Montgomery Street, brims with memorabilia from the 1800s to 1915. The Bank of California's one-of-a-kind gold collection, 400 California Street, includes privately minted coins and Western currency. The Bank of Canton's Pacific Heritage Museum, Commercial and Montgomery streets, looks at contributions made to the state by Pacific Rim immigrants.

Embarcadero Center

Laced on three levels by landscaped plazas and malls, this 10½-acre complex near the waterfront combines offices, shops, restaurants, and hotels in five soaring towers. Its showplace is the Hyatt Regency at the foot of California. Another hotel, the Park Hyatt, faces Battery Street.

In the neighboring Federal Reserve Bank (101 Market Street), a surprisingly interesting World of Economics display describes banking with cartoons, electronic devices, and computer games. Stop by at noon for a 20-minute movie. You can see the free exhibits weekdays from 9 A.M. to 4:30 P.M.

Jackson Square

Built on the wharves and ships of those hungry for gold, this historic district is roughly bounded by Washington, Columbus, Pacific, and Sansome streets. It's now a quiet enclave of tiny alleys and tree-lined streets, a far cry from its rowdy Barbary Coast beginnings.

Converted into a showplace for designers in the 1950s, it became home to attorneys, architects, and ad agencies when the decorators fled south to design complexes around Potrero Hill. Some of the elegant buildings house antique shops and restaurants.

Landmarks of interest on Jackson Street include the original iron-shuttered A. P. Hotaling Co. liquor distillery (451), the factory used by Domingo Ghirardelli for his chocolate works (415–31), and an early 1850s survivor supported by ship masts (472), used as the French Consulate from 1865 to 1876.

South of Market

Explore the industrial neighborhood south from Market Street to find some of the city's trendiest nightclubs, eateries, discount shops, gay clubs, and avant garde galleries, museums, and theaters. This is a funky community with warehouse-size buildings, later-day apartments, wino bars, and train tracks. Parking is tight weekdays.

SoMa's gentrification started with the 1981 opening of Moscone Convention Center (Howard between 3rd and 4th streets), now the focal point for upscale hotels such as the Meridien and Marriott, discount outlets (see page 20), and restaurants. Part of the Yerba Buena Center construction across the street is the new Museum of Modern Art, scheduled to move here in 1993.

Most art galleries are sprinkled along Folsom Street, and several popular restaurants and clubs cluster around 11th and Folsom.

Neighborhoods

Most of San Francisco's immigrants settled in tightly knit communities—a happy circumstance for anyone who has ever prowled Chinatown's back alleys, enjoyed a *caffelatte* in North Beach, joined a spring festival in Japantown, or eaten nachos in the Mission District.

San Francisco's districts are often called cities within a city, and they grow and change just as the city itself does. For example, the funky Haight-Ashbury residential district at the east end of Golden Gate Park, home to flower children in the 1960s, is as likely to attract young professionals these days. And the predominantly gay Castro area south of Market has become increasingly gentrified, its Victorians spruced up and its streets lined with boutiques and pubs.

Chinatown

Benevolent dragons and stone lions guard the green-tiled gateway to Chinatown at Grant Avenue and Bush Street. The center for the largest Asian community in North America, Chinatown covers an area of about 24 square blocks between Kearny, Mason, Bush, and Broadway.

The 8-block stretch of Grant Avenue attracts most tourists. But more local flavor is found along the cross streets and side alleys paralleling Grant. You'll find typical Chinese markets and food stores along the northern reaches of Stockton Street and around Broadway. Plan to explore the avenue on foot, as the streets are narrow and very heavily congested.

A neighborhood stroll. Busy, crowded Grant Avenue bulges with shops, restaurants (venerable favorites with Westerners include Empress of China, Kan's, and Imperial Palace), bars, bakeries, teahouses, theaters, and Asian markets. Fine wares from China, Taiwan, and Hong Kong mingle with curios made in Korea, Japan, and the U.S. One local axiom: the best stock is never found in the front of the shop.

Old St. Mary's Church, a landmark since 1854, stands at Grant and California. This Gothic structure was built largely by Chinese laborers with granite from China and brick brought around Cape Horn from New England.

Diagonally across the street is St. Mary's Square, a quiet little park with sculptor Beniamino Bufano's imposing marble and stainless steel statue of Sun Yat-sen, founder of the Chinese Republic and onetime Chinatown resident. Underneath the park lies a parking garage (entrances on Kearny, Pine, and California).

The Bank of Canton branch at 743 Washington (east of Grant) is another landmark. From 1909 to 1949 the building held the Chinese Telephone Exchange; operators memorized as many as 2,400 names and numbers of Chinatown subscribers.

Waverly Place, a 2-block stretch paralleling Grant Avenue west between Washington and Sacramento streets, reveals some of Chinatown's colorful old buildings and few remaining temples. Of special interest is the Tien Hou Temple (top floor of 125 Waverly), which dates back to gold-rush days. Tourists might take note: the main shrine is dedicated to the protectress of travelers.

Down the street on Waverly is the Chinese Culture and Art Center, where instructors teach calligraphy, *tai chi chuan,* Chinese violin, and butterfly harp during weekend classes.

Continue west to Stockton Street; the lively food stalls and markets in the 1000–1200 blocks sell everything from squawking chickens and ducks to crocks of pickled vegetables and packages of rare herbs and fragrant teas. Buyers gather not only to shop, but also to socialize.

Portsmouth Square. Just east of Grant Avenue, between Washington and Clay, is the place where Captain John B. Montgomery raised the American flag in 1846 to proclaim the Mexican village a possession of the United States. Named for Montgomery's ship, the

square today is a landscaped park atop a parking garage.

Portsmouth Square may not have a Chinese name, but it is the area's village plaza. In the early morning, students practice *tai chi chuan* exercises; by afternoon elders gather for chess and conversation while youngsters romp in the nearby playground.

Museums. Two museums help unlock the history and culture of this famous section of town. The Chinese Culture Center (750 Kearny Street), on the third floor of the Holiday Inn on Portsmouth Square, offers a collection of contemporary and historical art. The free gallery is open Tuesday through Saturday from 10 A.M. to 4 P.M.

The free Chinese Historical Society Museum, 650 Commercial Street, is a small downstairs gallery with a treasurehouse of Chinese-American artifacts, among them unusual tools from early herb shops and a small, flat-bottomed boat dating back to the bay's first shrimping industry. You can visit Wednesday through Sunday from noon to 4 P.M.

Walking tours. Guided tours can uncover Chinatown's hidden heart. Docents from the Chinese Culture Center lead a 1- to 2-hour Chinese Heritage Walk with stops at an herb shop, fortune cooky factory, Buddhist temple, and other architectural and historical gems ($9 adults, $2 children under 18). A culinary tour also is offered ($18 adults, $9 children under 12). For details and reservations, call (415) 986-1822.

Several other walking tours of the area are conducted by knowledgeable locals; for a complete list of options, check with the visitors bureau (address on page 11).

North Beach

Not really a beach at all, this district between Chinatown and Fisherman's Wharf acquired its name in the 1850s when a finger of bay extended inland

Stone lions guard the ornate gateway to Chinatown at Grant Avenue and Bush Street. Most tourist shops and restaurants lie along Grant, but side-street prowls reveal temples, museums, and workshops.

to the sunny shore cradled between Telegraph and Russian hills. The bohemian era of the 1950s and a later influx of Chinese newcomers erased some of the original Italian imprint, but North Beach is still a distinctive neighborhood.

An enticing mosaic of cappuccino houses, cafes, bakeries, and Italian specialty stores is found on and around aptly named Columbus Avenue north of Broadway's titillating nightspots. Remnants of the 1950s Beat Generation live on in the City Lights Bookstore at 216 Columbus (onetime gathering spot for Beat poets) and neighboring Vesuvio cafe and bar.

Beach Blanket Babylon packs Club Fugazi at 678 Green in an area of moderately priced, family-run Italian restaurants. And photos and relics of old days are on display in the North Beach Museum, located above Eureka Federal Savings at 1435 Stockton Street. The free museum is open during regular bank hours.

Heart of this Little Italy is Washington Square (Columbus Avenue and Union Street), actually a pentagon adorned with a statue of Benjamin Franklin. Just as early immigrants gathered here to socialize with neighbors, oldtimers today sit on benches conversing with friends in Italian.

The annual blessing of the local fishing fleet in October begins with a procession from the twin-spired Church of Saints Peter and Paul, across Filbert Street from the square. Spiritual home of city Italians, the church now also offers masses in English and Cantonese.

The upper floors of the building at the southwest corner of Union and Stockton serve as a retirement home for elderly Italians, while the ground floor is occupied by Fior d'Italia, the city's oldest Italian restaurant.

Japantown

More than 12,000 people of Japanese descent live in San Francisco. Though the first Japanese arrived in the 1860s, it wasn't until after the 1906 earthquake that many chose to rebuild homes in this area west of downtown, bounded by Post, Geary, Laguna, and Fillmore streets.

For visitors the focal point is the Japan Center at Post and Buchanan, a 5-acre, pagoda-crowned complex of hotels, shops, theaters, restaurants, and sushi bars. Street signs are in both Japanese and English.

Colorful ceremonies take place in the central plaza, including the week-long Spring Cherry Blossom Festival in April.

A little over a mile from Union Square, Japantown is easy to reach on public transportation; take a bus west along Geary and get off at Buchanan or Laguna. Motorists can park in the center's underground garage.

Mission District

The Latino section of the city is unfamiliar to many tourists, but in this colorful area south of Market Street you'll find vibrant outdoor murals, lively street markets, galleries of traditional and contemporary art, and some outstanding food.

You can also see the city's oldest building. The Mission District's heart is Mission San Francisco de Asis (called Mission Dolores), founded in 1776 by Father Junipero Serra. The 1791 mission church at 16th and Dolores streets survived the 1906 earthquake to claim senior status among San Francisco structures. Note the Indian art on the ceilings and the ornate altar. A small museum displays artifacts, and the cemetery is a final resting place for San Francisco pioneers. The mission is open from 9 A.M. to 4 P.M. daily (small admission fee).

District streets are crowded and parking is at a minimum, so it's easiest to take BART from downtown. From the station at 24th and Mission, wander east on 24th Street for 10 blocks to York Street, with a small detour into Balmy Alley, to see more than 30 murals. The Precita Eyes Mural Center conducts tours the first and third Saturday of the month; for information and reservations, call (415) 285-2287.

The free Galeria de la Raza, 2851 24th Street (open Tuesday through Saturday, noon to 6 P.M.), is a setting for traditional and contemporary art. The adjacent shop sells folk art.

For south-of-the-border taste treats, the 5-block stretch of 24th between Harrison and Hampshire streets has bakeries, candy stores, markets, and inexpensive eateries like tiny Roosevelt Tamale Parlor at 2817 24th Street.

Clement Street

In the Richmond District, some 3½ miles west of downtown, Clement Street (north of Geary Boulevard) is multicultural. In this section of town, bagel shops and Asian food markets jostle Russian bakeries and Greek delis.

With an estimated third of the city's Chinese population living nearby, it's not surprising that eateries lean heavily toward dim sum and roast duck. But a stroll along the friendly street (best from 1st to 12th or 19th to 26th avenues) also reveals a peppering of Irish bars and French bistros plus lots of Indonesian and Vietnamese restaurants. And Bill's Place (2315 Clement) is regarded as one of the best in the city for a hamburger.

Alamo Square

The classic view of a prim line of Victorian houses backdropped by downtown skyscrapers is taken from Hayes and Steiner streets in the Alamo Square Historic District. This picture-pretty setting also embraces the Imperial Russian consulate of czarist days (1198 Fulton Street) and a 1904 chateau (1000 Fulton) that was once home to the city's Roman Catholic archbishops, and then an inn.

Pacific Heights

Some of the city's finest homes lie around Fillmore Street north of California. Interspersed among the mansions are consulates, private schools, and posh condominiums. House browsing is best along Broadway between Webster and Lyon streets. Where Broderick crosses Broadway, the sidewalk is so steep it's a stairway. Climb up to the top; the views down to the bay are superb.

Small collections of treasures and historical tidbits form surprising additions to San Francisco's rich museum scene. Everyone in the family should find something of interest in this eclectic sampling. Many are free, others charge only nominal fees, and all close on major holidays.

African-American Historical and Cultural Society, Building C, Fort Mason; (415) 441-0640. This museum, art gallery, and history center devoted to African-Americans and black Californians is open noon to 5 P.M. Wednesday through Sunday. Admission: Donations.

Cable Car Museum, Powerhouse, and Car Barn, 1201 Mason Street; (415) 474-1887. Tours of the cable car control center are offered daily from 10 A.M. to 6 P.M. It's a treasure house of photos, scale models, and original cars designed by Andrew S. Hallidie in 1873. A 16-minute film shows continously. Admission: Free.

Cartoon Art Museum, 665 3rd Street, 5th Floor; (415) 546-9481. Exhibits highlight the history of cartoon art with illustrations and animation (Wednesday through Friday from 11 A.M. to 5 P.M., Saturday from 10 A.M. to 5 P.M.). Admission: $3 adults, $2 seniors and students, $1 children 12 and under. On the same floor is the free Explore Print! museum, with motorized models to explain printing processes (8:30 A.M. to 5 P.M. weekdays).

Craft and Folk Art Museum, Building A, Fort Mason; (415) 775-0990. Witty exhibits showcase contemporary crafts, American folk art, and traditional ethnic art from around the world (daily except Monday from 11 A.M. to 5 P.M., from 10 A.M. on Saturday). Admission: $1; free Saturday morning.

Fire Department Pioneer Memorial Museum, 655 Presidio Avenue; (415) 861-8000. Horse-drawn engines and other equipment that fought fires after the 1906 earthquake are featured in this tribute to early volunteer fire units, open 1 to 4 P.M. Thursday through Sunday. Admission: Free.

Friends of Photography, Ansel Adams Center, 250 4th Street; (415) 495-7000. Five galleries of creative photography showcase works by Ansel Adams and other photographers (11 A.M. to 6 P.M. Tuesday through Sunday). Admission: $3 adults, $2 seniors and students 12 to 17.

Jewish Community Museum, 121 Steuart Street; (415) 543-8880. A lively collection of art and artifacts explores Jewish culture past and present. You can visit Tuesday through Friday from 10 A.M. to 4 P.M. Admission: Free.

Levi Strauss, 250 Valencia Street; (415) 565-9153. To see the small museum chronicling the history of this San Francisco jeans giant, make a reservation for a 45-minute factory tour, offered at 10:30 A.M. Wednesday. Admission: Free.

Mexican Museum, Building D, Fort Mason; (415) 441-0404. Fine art collections focus on pre-Hispanic, colonial, folk, Mexican, and Mexican-American works. The museum is open Wednesday through Sunday from noon to 5 P.M. Admission: $2 adults, $1 seniors and children above 10.

Musée Mécanique, Cliff House, 1090 Point Lobos Avenue; (415) 386-1170. Rescued from former fun zones, 140 ancient amusement devices accept your quarters for games and music. A few modern video games beep at the back of this arcade, open from 11 A.M. to 7 P.M. weekdays, from 10 A.M. weekends. Admission: Free, but you pay to play.

Museo Italo American, Building C, Fort Mason; (415) 673-2200. This collection of Italian-American and Italian art, culture, and history focuses on contemporary artists. It's open Wednesday through Sunday, noon to 5 P.M. Admission: Free.

Museum of Ophthalmology, 655 Bush Street, Suite 300; (415) 561-8500. This engaging but serious shrine to mankind's attempts to improve vision displays 6,000 artifacts from as far afield as Sri Lanka and China. Hours are 8:30 A.M. to 5 P.M. weekdays. Admission: Free.

Old Mint, 5th and Mission streets, (415) 744-6830. Opened in 1874, this building contains restored rooms, western art, pioneer gold coins, and a pyramid of gold bars valued at $5 million. The mint is open Tuesday through Saturday from 9 A.M. to 1 P.M. with tours offered Saturday at 10 and 11:30 A.M. Admission: Free.

Society of California Pioneers, 456 McAllister Street; (415) 861-5278. A Children's Gallery featuring the state's history, gold-rush artifacts, and costumes is open weekdays from 10 A.M. to 4 P.M. (closed in August). Admission: Free.

Telephone Pioneers Communications Museum, 140 New Montgomery Street, Suite 111; (415) 542-0182. This display of telephone communication from the days of antique switchboards to the technology of the future is open weekdays from 10 A.M. to 2 P.M. Admission: Free.

Treasure Island Museum, Building l, Treasure Island; (415) 395-5067. Halfway across the Bay Bridge, this museum chronicles the history of military service in the Pacific, the 1939 World's Fair, and the China Clipper. It is open daily from 10 A.M. to 3:30 P.M. Admission: Free.

A chocoholic haven, the Chocolate Manufactory at Ghirardelli Square sells gigantic sundaes and splits; some of Domingo Ghirardelli's original candy-making equipment is still operating on the premises..

Along the Waterfront

San Francisco's waterfront is its chief drawing card. Attractions around Fisherman's Wharf and Pier 39 draw the most visitors, but you can also take a sightseeing tour around the bay, boat across to the former island prison of Alcatraz or to Angel Island (see page 37), board a flotilla of venerable ships, visit some noted museums, and explore a Spanish fort. Many of the sites are part of the Golden Gate National Recreation Area (page 29).

Piers are numbered from the Ferry Building at the foot of Market Street; even-numbered piers lie to the south, odd-numbered piers to the north. From the 1896 Ferry Building (site of the World Trade Center) along the Embarcadero southeast to the base of the Bay Bridge, a waterfront promenade provides a place to stroll.

Northwest at the foot of Broadway, 840-foot-long Pier 7 has been fitted with ornate lamps and a brass railing and opened to strollers and fishers (no license required). Pier 35 is the major dock for passenger liners.

Getting around. Parking lots around Fisherman's Wharf and garages across from Pier 39 and under Ghirardelli Square provide space for all but the busiest weekends. Traffic to the wharf is always congested, but it's particularly bad since the elevated Embarcadero Freeway was closed by earthquake damage in 1989 (and then demolished). Avoid driving by catching a cable car from downtown (even though lines can be long and waits exasperating), or taking a taxi.

You can also ride through the area by horse-drawn carriage (Carriage Charter at Pier 41), pedicab, or motorized cable car (Cable Car Charters at Piers 39 and 41), or see it from along the water's edge in a 17-foot inflatable boat (Bay Adventure, Pier 41).

Boat tours. The most striking views of San Francisco come from the water. Sightseeing boats leave from Piers 41 and 43½ near Fisherman's Wharf and from Pier 39's west marina. The *City of San Francisco*, a re-created bay steamer, offers dinner cruises from Pier 33 at the foot of Bay Street. For all cruise details, see page 124.

Fisherman's Wharf

Visitors far outnumber fishermen in the wharf district which stretches east from the Hyde Street Pier to Pier 39. Most of the activity is centered in the 22-square-block district around the pier at Jones and Jefferson streets, where you'll find what is left of San Francisco's fishing fleet.

This world-famous destination is a combination of tourist-oriented shops and galleries, offbeat museums, sidewalk stalls, and seafood restaurants. Along the dock, a vast open-air fish market offers oceans of steaming crabs, piles of prawns, and heaps of San Francisco sourdough bread.

The 312-foot submarine *U.S.S. Pampanito* tied up at Pier 45 saw action in the Pacific during World War II. It's now open for touring daily (from 9 A.M. to 9 P.M. in summer, closing at 6 P.M. weekdays the rest of the year). Admission is $4 adults, $2 students 12 to 17, and $1 ages 5 to 11, seniors, and military.

Dining. To many who come to the city, a visit calls for a meal at Fisherman's Wharf. The view is the big reason. Bayside tables let you see bobbing fishing boats and cavorting sea lions below you, while the towers of the bridges loom in the distance.

Specialties at seafood restaurants such as Scoma's (Pier 47) include fresh crab (season runs from November to July), cracked and served cold with lemon and mayonnaise; crab Louis, the classic wharf salad, served with sourdough bread; and cioppino, the heroic shellfish stew you dip into with your fingers.

Shopping. Waterfront district stores sell souvenirs ranging from seashell jewelry and T-shirts to bronze turnbuckles and model ships. The biggest retailer, Cost Plus Imports at 2252 Taylor Street, is a rambling bazaar of housewares, antiques, foods, jewelry, and home garden supplies.

At the west end of the district sprawl warehouses converted into stores and restaurants. Most famous is Ghirardelli Square (page 28); others include the Cannery and the Anchorage.

The Cannery (bounded by Beach, Leavenworth, and Jefferson streets) was constructed in 1894 by the Del Monte Company. Today, the restored brick building holds three levels of lively shops and restaurants and a comedy club. Jugglers, mimes, magicians, and musicians perform in the flower-filled courtyard.

The Anchorage occupies the block bounded by Jones, Leavenworth, Beach, and Jefferson. Its contemporary design is bedecked with nautical flags and banners, and a two-story anchor sculpture rises in the central plaza. When shopping palls, you can have a snack and watch street performers.

Pier 39

Once an abandoned cargo shipping pier, Pier 39 was transformed into a waterfront marketplace in the late 1970s. Just east of Fisherman's Wharf, the long pier (length of three football fields) embraces two levels of restaurants, tourist-oriented specialty shops, and entertainment areas.

One of its nicest features is the 5-acre waterfront park that stretches along the southwestern edge of Pier 39 as far as Pier 35. In the marinas flanking the pier, fishing boats and pleasure craft bob and sea lions bark. The Blue & Gold Fleet runs sightseeing excursions from here (see page 124).

There's no lack of free entertainment on the pier's stages, and children enjoy the double-deck Venetian carousel and the amusement arcade. The San Francisco Experience, a multimedia presentation of the city's colorful history, is offered daily every half hour from 10 A.M. to 10 P.M. ($6 adults, $5 seniors and military, $3 children ages 6 to 16).

A pedestrian bridge over Beach Street leads from a large parking garage to the pier's second level.

Alcatraz Island

Noted chiefly as a prison, Alcatraz was also the site of the first lighthouse and permanently fortified military outpost on the West Coast. Old Fort Alcatraz started housing military criminals in 1861, but it wasn't until after Prohibition in the 1930s that the island acquired the name "the rock" and its reputation as a secure site for America's most hardened criminals. Its roster of inmates included Al Capone and "Birdman" Robert Stroud.

The federal prison was abandoned in 1963, occupied in a protest movement by Native Americans from 1969 to 1971, and opened to the public in 1973 as a part of the Golden Gate National Recreation Area. Tours include a self-guiding trail, a slide show, and an audio tour of the cellblock featuring the voices of former guards.

Ferries depart Pier 41 daily every 30 minutes from 9:45 A.M. to 2:45 P.M. ($7.50 adults and children ages 12 to 18, $4 children ages 5 to 11). Get a ticket at least a day in advance during the busy summer season, from the ticket booth at Pier 41 or through Ticketron.

Visitors can stay on the island as long as they wish; the last boat back leaves at 4:35 P.M. Dress warmly, and wear comfortable shoes. For tour information, call (415) 546-BOAT or (800) 229-2784 within California.

Aquatic Park

Once part of the Golden Gate National Recreation Area (facing page), the bayside park east of Fort Mason is now the San Francisco Maritime National Historical Park. In addition to an acclaimed maritime museum and a flotilla of historic ships at Hyde Street Pier, the park contains a curving pier popular with anglers, bocce ball courts, grassy lawns alive with vendors, and one of the city's few sandy beaches.

Best way to reach the park is on the Powell and Hyde Street cable car; the turntable lies just east of the ship-shaped museum at Beach and Polk.

Investigate San Francisco's seagoing past at the *streamline moderne* Maritime Museum, which houses an extensive collection of meticulously crafted ship models, figureheads, nautical relics, photographs, and paintings. The free museum is open daily from 10 A.M. to 5 P.M.

Queen of the fleet at the Hyde Street Pier is the *Balclutha*, a regal three-masted sailing ship. Refurbished and restored, she looks like what she was: a Scottish-built square-rigger that plied the seas between the 1880s and the 1920s and logged 17 Cape Horn doublings.

Other ships include the schooner *C.A. Thayer*, river tug *Eppleton Hall*, ferryboat *Eureka*, scow schooner *Alma*, and steam tug *Hercules*. Admission to the pier is a modest $3 (free for seniors and children under 12). It's open from 10 A.M. to 6 P.M. daily.

Ghirardelli Square

Just south and west of the Hyde Street Pier, this shopping and dining complex covers the square block bounded by Beach, Larkin, North Point, and Polk streets. Though it was first a woolen works (Civil War uniforms were made here), Ghirardelli Square is better known for its years as a chocolate factory.

In 1964, the red-brick compound was renovated to contain an enticing miscellany of shops, galleries, restaurants, and a theater, all situated around an inviting plaza with an innovative fountain. Part of the square's charm lies in the outdoor cafes and the variety of food outlets available here. You can still see some of the machines used to make the rich chocolate at the Ghirardelli Chocolate Manufactory, noted for its ice cream concoctions.

Marina district

This lovely residential area with its Mediterranean flavor made headlines when it suffered extensive damage in the 1989 earthquake. But the damage has been repaired, and this stretch of waterfront still offers the best bayside viewing in San Francisco.

Fort Mason. Once Army land, Fort Mason is now the headquarters and visitor center for the Golden Gate National Recreation Area (facing page). Its old wharves and warehouses burst with museums (page 25), craft studios, theaters, bookstores, a vast maritime library (open to the public), workshops, and classrooms.

Greens, a top-rated vegetarian restaurant, serves up great views with lunch and dinner. Lawns and gardens offer picnic sites, and piers afford prime views along with fishing (California fishing license required).

Star of the show at the fort's Pier 3 is the *S.S. Jeremiah O'Brien*, an unaltered World War II Liberty Ship. A taped self-guided tour lets you clamber about the great welded-steel decks on your own. The ship is open 9 A.M. to 3 P.M. daily except holidays (small admission charge). The third weekend of each month (except May and December), the steam engine is fired up. An annual bay cruise on the third weekend of May includes a buffet luncheon; for information, call (415) 441-3101.

Fort Mason's main entrance is at Franklin and Bay streets. Best entrance for visitor attractions is Marina Boulevard at Buchanan Street.

Get maps and additional details from the information center in Building A, open 8:30 A.M. to 5 P.M. weekdays. For further information, call (415) 441-5705. To find out about guided walks, call (415) 441-5706.

Golden Gate Promenade. The 3½-mile shoreline walk between Aquatic Park and Fort Point leads to the Marina Green, a favorite place for flying kites, sunbathing, and jogging. Crissy Field, beyond, is a quiet stretch of shoreline that skirts the water's edge for about a mile; it's a favorite windsurfing spot. The orange-roofed building at the water's edge is the St. Francis Yacht Club.

At the end of the breakwater, a 20-pipe organ engineered by the Exploratorium (facing page) creates music through wave action.

To reach the end of the promenade, head west past a U.S. Coast Guard station to Long Avenue, which leads to Fort Point (page 30) and the Golden Gate Bridge. The hardy can climb the hill to the Golden Gate Bridge toll plaza and catch an inbound Golden Gate Transit bus back to the downtown area.

Palace of Fine Arts. The Greco-Romanesque rotunda at Marina Boulevard and Baker Street was built as a showcase for fine art exhibits for the 1915 Panama-Pacific International Exposition. The original building on the natural lagoon was plaster, but it was recast in concrete in 1967 to keep it from deteriorating. The palace now houses the Exploratorium museum and a 1,000-seat theater.

Exploratorium. This internationally acclaimed museum of science, art, and human perception delights both children and adults. There are some 700 exhibits to be manipulated, tinkered with, or activated by a push of a button. A visit to the Tactile Gallery, a pitch-black sensory chamber, requires reservations; call (415) 561-0362.

The museum, in the Palace of Fine Arts, is open Wednesday through Sunday from 10 A.M. to 5 P.M. (until 9:30 P.M. Wednesday) in summer. Hours the rest of the year are 1 to 9:30 P.M. Wednesday, 1 to 5 P.M. Thursday and Friday, and 10 A.M. to 5 P.M. weekends. Admission (valid for 6 months) is $6 adults, $3 seniors, $2 ages 6 to 17 (free the first Wednesday of the month and every Wednesday after 6 P.M.).

The Presidio

Location led to the Presidio's original founding by Spanish explorer Juan Bautista de Anza in 1776, and proximity to San Francisco kept it going. The U.S. Army needed the fort to protect the Pacific gateway. But in recent years, global action has passed it by.

An Urban National Park

Within a short distance of San Francisco's skyscrapers lies the country's largest urban national park. The Golden Gate National Recreation Area (GGNRA) sprawls over 74,000 acres, all the way from San Mateo County in the south to Tomales Bay in Marin County, offering diverse historic and scenic attractions.

On the north side of the Golden Gate, the park includes Marin's dramatic headlands, Muir Woods and Mount Tamalpais (see page 37), and Muir and Stinson beaches (page 68). South of the Golden Gate, the park extends out in the bay to Angel Island (page 37), wraps around San Francisco's northern and western waterfronts, and extends south into San Mateo County.

San Francisco's MUNI system provides transportation to most park attractions. For route information, call (415) 673-MUNI. For more information on GGNRA parklands, visit the headquarters in Fort Mason (open weekdays, 7:30 A.M. to 5 P.M.) or call (415) 556-0560. A detailed guidebook to all area attractions, published by the Golden Gate National Park Association, is available at many park locations and area bookstores.

The following is a brief rundown on waterfront attractions in the San Francisco part of the GGNRA. For detailed information, turn to the page reference given for each site.

Fort Mason. On the waterfront north of Fisherman's Wharf, this former Army post served as the embarkation point for Pacific-bound soldiers and supplies during World War II. Today, the recycled military warehouses brim with museums, theaters, galleries, classrooms, and a vegetarian restaurant. The last unaltered operational Liberty Ship, the *S.S. Jeremiah O'Brien,* is tied up at Fort Mason's Pier 3. (See page 28.)

Alcatraz Island. Guided tours tracing this 22-acre island's history from fort to federal prison leave from Pier 41 at Fisherman's Wharf. (See page 28.)

Golden Gate Promenade. This scenic bayshore walk with its magnificent waterfront views stretches 3½ miles from Hyde Street Pier to Fort Point and the Golden Gate Bridge. (See page 28.)

Fort Point. This brick and granite coastal fortification underneath the Golden Gate Bridge is open daily for tours. (See page 30.)

Presidio. The 1,440-acre military post at the city's northern tip (see above) will become part of the GGNRA after its scheduled closure in 1995. Rangers lead free weekend tours of the facility.

Baker Beach. On the northwest shore of the Presidio, Baker Beach is a good place to hike and fish (swimming is unsafe). Behind the beach is Battery Chamberlin, with a 95,000-pound cannon. Rangers lead tours on weekends; call (415) 556-8371 for details.

Cliff House. This San Francisco landmark, now a restaurant and museum, offers sweeping views of the Pacific Ocean and Marin coast. (See page 33.)

Ocean Beach. The 4-mile stretch of windswept sandy beach south of Cliff House is a dramatic place to hike, though unsafe for swimming.

Fort Funston. At the city's southwest corner (off Skyline Boulevard opposite Lake Merced), this fort was a military reservation from 1898 to 1972. Now its seaward bluffs are a popular launching spot for hang gliders. A loop trail offers grand views.

...Waterfront

This 215-year-old, 1,440-acre Army base overlooking the Golden Gate is scheduled for closure in 1995. Thanks to its rich history and grand scenery, the Presidio will become a national park administered by the Golden Gate National Recreation Area.

Until then, it's still a working Army post, through which you can walk, bicycle, and drive—a city within a city with more than 1,100 housing units, hospital, supermarket, churches, bowling alley, theaters, and 18-hole golf course.

On the wilder ocean and bay sides, the wind sculpts trees and hikers' hairdos. To the south, joggers and dog-walkers invade its woods and creeklands. The eastern part is the main post and hospital.

You can go anywhere in the Presidio unless it is marked otherwise. Pick up a free map showing points of interest at the Presidio Army Museum (see right), or join a ranger-led weekend tour; call (415) 556-0865 for reservations. Parking is easy, except on the lot near the Golden Gate Bridge toll plaza (try the free unpaved lot off Lincoln between the road to Fort Point and the bridge turnoff).

Presidio Army Museum. This free museum (open 10 A.M. to 4 P.M. Tuesday through Sunday) stands near the corner of Lincoln Boulevard and Funston Avenue on the east side of the Presidio.

Built in 1864, the building was the original post hospital. Displays on two floors document the fort's history from the Spanish period through the Vietnam era, with detours into Black military history and military propaganda. Models and dioramas of the 1906 earthquake and the 1915 Panama-Pacific Exposition are particularly interesting.

The two small shacks behind the museum, built as temporary housing after the 1906 earthquake, now contain exhibits.

Pershing Square. On the grassy square around which the museum lies, an old cannon is still fired daily when the flag is raised and lowered. The square was named for John J. Pershing, General of the Armies of World War I, whose home once stood here. In 1915, while Pershing was chasing Pancho Villa in Mexico, his house burned down. His wife and daughters perished; only a son escaped.

Fort Point National Historic Site. The most popular Presidio attraction is Fort Point, huddled directly under the south end of the Golden Gate Bridge. Completed in 1861, it was once the West Coast's principal defense bastion; its 126 cannons guarded the entrance to the bay from 1861 until the fort was abandoned in 1886—though it never saw actual battle.

The fort is open from 10 A.M. to 5 P.M. daily. Guides in period uniforms lead free tours that visit the restored powder magazine and cannon display; you're on your own in the bookstore.

Room to roam. Off West Pacific Avenue along the Presidio's southern boundary lie two places to pause: Mountain Lake Park (fitness course, playground, tennis courts) and, over the hill to the east, Julius Kahn Playground (picnic tables, tennis courts, baseball diamond, gated play area).

Sky-high Retreats

Restaurants and lounges scattered across the city welcome those looking for high—literally—society. These lofty vantage points range in age from the Top of the Mark, a 1939 landmark, to the View Lounge, Marriott's new vista site. You can go sky-high even if you only want to look.

Carnelian Room, 52nd Floor, Bank of America Building, 555 California Street; (415) 433-7500. Opens 3 P.M. weekdays, 4 P.M. Saturday, 10 A.M. Sunday; cocktails, dinner, Sunday brunch.

Cityscape, 46th Floor, San Francisco Hilton, O'Farrell Street between Taylor and Mason; (415) 776-0215. Cocktails daily from 5 P.M., dinner, Sunday brunch, nightly entertainment.

Club 36, 36th Floor, Grand Hyatt, 345 Stockton Street; (415) 398-1234. Cocktails daily from 2 P.M., live entertainment from 4 P.M.

Crown Room, 24th Floor, Fairmont Hotel, 950 Mason Street; (415) 772-5131. Buffet lunch and dinner Monday through Saturday, Sunday brunch, cocktails daily from 11 A.M.

Equinox, 18th Floor, Hyatt Regency, 5 Embarcadero Center (foot of California Street); (415) 788-1234. Revolving restaurant, daily lunch and dinner, cocktails from 11 A.M.

Oz, 32nd Floor, Westin St. Francis, 335 Powell Street; (415) 397-7000. Cocktails from 4:30 P.M., music for dancing (cover charge) nightly from 9:30 P.M.

S. Holmes, Esq., 30th Floor, Holiday Inn-Union Square, 480 Sutter Street; (415) 398-8900. Cocktails daily from 4 P.M. (from 8 P.M. Saturday), live entertainment Tuesday through Friday from 5 P.M.

Starlite Roof, 21st Floor, Sir Francis Drake Hotel, 450 Powell Street; (415) 392-7755. Cocktails daily from 4:30 P.M., dancing until 1 A.M.

Top of the Mark, 19th Floor, Mark Hopkins Inter-Continental, California and Mason; (415) 392-3434. Cocktails daily from 4 P.M., Sunday buffet brunch.

Victor's, 32nd Floor, Westin St. Francis, 335 Powell Street; (415) 956-7777. Cocktails daily from 5 P.M., dinner, Sunday champagne brunch.

View Lounge, 39th Floor, San Francisco Marriott Hotel, 727 Market Street; (415) 896-1600. Cocktails daily from noon, piano music.

Swans and ducks share the lagoon fronting the Palace of Fine Arts in the Marina District. The neo-classic structure (home to the Exploratorium museum) is the sole survivor of the 1915 Panama-Pacific International Exposition complex.

The West Side

San Francisco owes a great debt of gratitude to William Hammond Hall and John McLaren, two pioneer park designers whose vision and perseverance turned 1,017 acres of rolling sand dunes into one of the world's best-loved parks. Golden Gate Park stretches all the way across the western half of the city.

The city's western edge, defined by the Pacific Ocean, was part of an 1854 coastal fortification plan that established a natural greenbelt south as far as Fort Funston. The region is now part of the Golden Gate National Recreation Area (see page 29).

Golden Gate Park

San Francisco's premier park is a place for people to walk, play, and picnic in grassy meadows. Hiking and riding trails and bicycle paths wind through the urban oasis close to three museums, gardens, lakes, waterfalls, sports fields, polo grounds, tennis and horseshoe courts, lawn bowling greens, fly-casting pools, and an archery range.

A children's playground at the eastern end of the park has a handsomely restored 1912 carousel. Toward the western end of the park, a small herd of bison grazes in a paddock not far from a 9-hole golf course. Trail rides are available from the nearby stables; call (415) 666-7201 for reservations.

Two main drives—John F. Kennedy and Martin Luther King, Jr.—run the 3-mile length of the park. Some roads in the east end close to auto traffic on Sunday.

Stop by McLaren Lodge at the east end (Stanyan and Fell streets) weekdays for maps and brochures. Friends of Recreation and Parks offers free walking tours on weekends from May through October; call (415) 221-1311.

Three of the city's finest museums flank the Music Concourse (free outdoor concerts Sunday at 1 P.M.) in the eastern half of the park. Museum admission is free on the first Wednesday of the month.

A trio of distinctive gardens offers abundant floral displays. Note also the rhododendron dell near McLaren Lodge and the rose gardens near Stow Lake (center of park).

California Academy of Sciences. The West's oldest scientific museum (founded in 1853) includes a natural history center, an aquarium, and a planetarium. Crowd-pleasing exhibits include a simulated earthquake ride, California wildlife dioramas, "Life through Time" evolutionary evidence, and a gem and mineral display.

Among the most popular aquarium residents are penguins (feedings at 11:30 A.M. and 4 P.M. daily), dolphins and seals (fed every 2 hours beginning at 10:30 A.M.), turtles, octopi, and alligators.

The Fish Roundabout lets you stand in the center of a tank while a dazzling array of sharks, tuna, and other fish flash past around you. A re-created tidepool introduces children to starfish and hermit crabs.

Daily shows at the Morrison Planetarium revolve around a specially built star projector. One-hour performances (modest admission) take place at 2 P.M. weekdays, on the hour from 1 to 4 P.M. weekends and holidays. Laserium shows are offered some evenings; call (415) 750-7138 for information.

The museum is open 10 A.M. to 5 P.M. daily. Admission is $6 adults, $3 seniors and children 12 to 17, and $1 children 6 to 11.

M. H. de Young Memorial Museum. Refurbished and reorganized, this venerable art museum (started in 1894) concentrates on American art from colonial times to the 20th century. Heart of the show is the acclaimed John D. Rockefeller III collection of paintings, sculpture, furniture, and decorative arts. The country's great artists from Paul Revere to Richard Diebenkorn are represented.

The museum (good cafeteria, gift store) is open 10 A.M. to 4:45 P.M. Wednesday through Sunday. Admission of $4 adults, $2 seniors and children ages 12 to 17, includes the Asian Art Museum (see below) and a same-day visit to the California Palace of the Legion of Honor (see facing page).

Asian Art Museum. Though it's in the same building as the de Young Museum and costs no more to visit, this impressive museum is a separate institution, the largest of its kind outside of Asia. Heart of the collection is the Avery Brundage collection of more than 12,000 works spanning 6,000 years. Note especially the Chinese jades and ancient bronzes.

Japanese Tea Garden. Just west of the M. H. de Young Museum, this lavish display of Oriental landscaping boasts a moon bridge, hand-carved gates, pagodas, a large bronze Buddha, and a teahouse (tea and cookies served from 10:30 A.M. to 4:30 P.M. daily). Spring cherry blossoms peak around April 1, turning the 5 acres into a fairyland. The modest admission is waived on the first Wednesday of the month. The garden is open from 9 A.M. to 5 P.M. daily.

Strybing Arboretum. This self-contained 70-acre world of plants includes 6,000 species from all over the world. Highlights include a fragrance garden for the visually impaired, home demonstration gardens, and a stunning display of California redwoods.

The free gardens, located at 9th Avenue and Lincoln Way, are open weekdays from 8 A.M. to 4:30 P.M., weekends from 10 A.M. to 5 P.M. Guided tours take place at 1:30 P.M. weekdays, 10:30 A.M. and 1:30 P.M. weekends.

Conservatory of Flowers. The atmosphere in this jungle setting (open daily 9 A.M. to 5 P.M.; small admission) is warm and humid. Lush tropical plants include bright crotons, large-flowered hibiscus, rare cycads, graceful ferns, and a variety of orchids. Pathways are lined with tall palms and huge old philodendrons.

The wooden greenhouse, a replica of the conservatory at London's Kew

Gardens, was transported from England around the Horn on a sailing ship and erected here in 1878. The conservatory is off John F. Kennedy Drive in the park's northeast corner.

The western edge

A tumultous meeting of sand and surf, the 4-mile stretch of Ocean Beach alongside the Great Highway is a favorite lookout for tourists and sunset watchers. Like most of the city's beaches, it's not safe for swimming. (Swimmers should head for secluded and often sunny China Beach to the north at 28th and Sea Cliff avenues.)

Overlooking the Pacific at the city's northwest corner, Adolph Sutro opened the elaborate gingerbread Cliff House resort in 1896. It was destroyed by fire in 1907, and the current incarnation, built in 1909, is the third to occupy the site. It houses a restaurant, lounge, and the Musée Mécanique amusement arcade (see page 25).

In those early days people frolicked happily at Sutro Baths, the largest indoor swimming pools in the world, just north of Cliff House. Closed in 1952, the concrete ruins can still be discerned, though the elaborate stained glass, fountains, and gardens are long gone. Offshore, at the foot of Point Lobos Avenue, Seal Rocks are alive with shore birds and stellar sea lions. Bring binoculars for a closeup. On a clear day, you can see the Farallon Islands some 30 miles away.

Other western attractions include Lincoln Park's renowned art museum, the San Francisco Zoo, and an open-air amphitheater for summer music performances.

California Palace of the Legion of Honor. This fine-arts museum commands a heady view from its hilltop site in Lincoln Park near 34th Avenue and Clement Street. Modeled after the Palais de la Legion d'Honneur in Paris, the elegant museum was given to the city in 1924 by the Spreckels family.

A sister museum to the M. H. de Young (see page 32), it was once devoted exclusively to French art but now houses an eclectic collection of European works from medieval days to the 20th century. Auguste Rodin's *The Thinker* graces the entry.

Admission to the museum (open Wednesday through Sunday from 10 A.M. to 5 P.M.) is $4 adults, $2 seniors and children 12 to 17 (free the first Wednesday of the month). Admission entitles you to a same-day visit to the M. H. de Young and Asian Art museums in Golden Gate Park.

San Francisco Zoo. This top-ranking zoo at the edge of Ocean Beach includes snow leopards, koalas, a rare white tiger, and pygmy hippos among its resident species. (Turn inland from the Great Highway at either Sloat Boulevard or Park Road; the entrance is near 45th Avenue.)

Of special interest are the Penguin Island, one-horned rhinos (a gift from the King of Nepal), and the Primate Discovery Center and Gorilla World. A Children's Zoo within the zoo (small separate entrance fee) corrals petting animals and an unusual collection of insects. Kids will also be attracted by the zoo's carousel and trackless train (20-minute guided circuits, small charge).

The zoo is open daily from 10 A.M. to 5 P.M. To hear the lions roar, get there for the 2 P.M. feeding. Zoo admission is $6 adults, $3 ages 12 through 15, free under 12 accompanied by an adult (free for all the first Wednesday of every month).

Sigmund Stern Grove. A wooded open-air amphitheater just east of the zoo at 19th Avenue and Sloat Boulevard is the setting for an annual Midsummer Music Festival. Free musical entertainment, from classical offerings to pops concerts, takes place Sunday around 2 P.M.; come early to reserve a patch of lawn, spread out a blanket, and enjoy a picnic.

Just for Kids

Children love San Francisco at first glance, for the toylike cable cars that swoop down the hills, the bridges, and the array of boats along the waterfront. And the city bulges with other tot-sized delights, from forts to fortune cookies.

Many places described in this chapter appeal to youngsters, especially the Zoo, the children's playground and other attractions in Golden Gate Park, the Exploratorium at the Palace of Fine Arts, Fort Point under the Golden Gate Bridge (cannon is fired at 1:30 and 2:30 P.M.), Hyde Street Pier (sea chantey singalongs on the first Saturday afternoon of the month), and Pier 39's fun zone.

The Josephine D. Randall Junior Museum (199 Museum Way off Roosevelt Way) is an informal place for tykes to experience nature first hand. Among the attractions are a petting corral, a working seismograph, and mineral and fossil displays. The free museum is open 10 A.M. to 5 P.M. Tuesday through Saturday.

For a hands-on approach to art, youngsters can take part in free Saturday programs at the M.H. de Young Museum in Golden Gate Park. For 7- to 13-year-olds, "Doing & Viewing Art" includes a docent-led tour and an art activity. "Big Kids, Little Kids" is geared to ages 3½ to 6 (an adult must accompany). Both programs run from 10:30 A.M. to noon (no reservations needed). Call (415) 750-3658 for details.

If cookies intrigue, head for Chinatown's Golden Gate Fortune Cookies Company, at 56 Ross Alley (1 block west of Grant Avenue, north of Washington Street). You'll see workers deftly placing the fortunes inside.

And at bedtime, youngsters may dial (415) 626-6516 for a story, courtesy of the San Francisco Public Library.

The Bay Area

*T*he San Francisco Bay covers some 900 square miles from its mouth at the Golden Gate. Around its perimeter lie towns that hide a wealth of attractions, some of the state's finest parks, and several top entertainment complexes.

North of the Golden Gate Bridge are upscale Marin County's bayside villages and bucolic parks. East of the Bay Bridge, communities like the port of Oakland and university-oriented Berkeley parallel the shoreline, while new development turns once-sleepy inland towns into burgeoning cities.

The peninsula south of San Francisco is divided into distinctly different regions by its forested mountain ridge. The bay side is lined with cities, while the ocean side from San Francisco to Santa Cruz sports unspoiled beaches and peaceful farmland.

At the south end of the bay, the Santa Clara Valley was known for its orchards before high-tech industries dubbed the area Silicon Valley. San Jose, its largest city, was founded in 1777.

Planning a trip

Weather is no factor when planning a Bay Area trip; the climate is mild, and most locations are at least several degrees warmer than San Francisco. Summers are dry, and spring and autumn days can sparkle.

Getting there. Three international airports serve the Bay Area: San Francisco (14 miles south of the city), Oakland (6 miles south of downtown off Interstate 880), and San Jose (northwest of down-

One of the stars at Marine World/Africa USA, 30 miles northeast of San Francisco at Vallejo, gives a gracious "hand" to an appreciative audience.

town off U.S. 101). Greyhound buses connect area towns, and Amtrak trains stop at Oakland and San Jose.

Major north-south highways are U.S. 101 in Marin and the South Bay, Interstates 880 and 680 in the East Bay, Interstate 280 in the South Bay, and State 1 on the coast. From the east, Interstates 80 and 580 reach the region.

A series of toll bridges links bay communities—Golden Gate and Bay bridges from San Francisco to Marin and Oakland, Richmond–San Rafael from Marin to the East Bay, and San Mateo and Dumbarton bridges from the East Bay to the peninsula.

Several ferry lines serve the North Bay (page 36). Blue and Gold Fleet operates from San Francisco to Oakland/ Alameda; call (415) 522-3300. Red and White Fleet, (415) 546-BOAT, serves Vallejo. Bay Area Rapid Transit (BART) covers the East Bay and dips under the bay to San Francisco (see page 14). Various bus lines provide transbay and regional service, and commuter trains run down the peninsula (see page 12).

Where to stay. Most chain hotels cluster around airports or in main cities such as San Rafael, Sausalito, Oakland, Berkeley, San Mateo, Palo Alto, and San Jose. Small inns and motels are scattered along the coast.

Activities. You can watch professional baseball (Oakland Athletics) and basketball (Golden State Warriors) at the Oakland–Alameda County Coliseum 5 miles south of downtown Oakland on Interstate 880. The South Bay is headquarters for the San Francisco 49ers football team and home of the San Jose Sharks hockey team. Bay Meadows Racecourse in San Mateo and Golden Gate Raceway across the bay in Albany draw crowds for horse racing.

The East Bay has the touted Oakland Ballet and Berkeley Repertory Theater, plus symphony, opera, jazz clubs, and more theater. Call (415) 835-ARTS for Oakland events, (415) 642-9988 for University of California performances. Varied events are staged at Marin County's Veteran's Memorial Auditorium-Theater (San Rafael), Walnut Creek's Regional Center for the Arts, the Mountain View Center for the Performing Arts, and San Jose's Center for Performing Arts. The Concord Pavilion and Mountain View's Shoreline Amphitheatre host summer outdoor concerts.

Contacts

These agencies offer information on attractions and accommodations. See additional contacts throughout this chapter.

NOTE: The telephone area code in East Bay counties will change from (415) to (510) as of October 1991.

Marin County Convention and Visitors Bureau
30 N. San Pedro Rd., Suite 150
San Rafael, CA 94903
(415) 472-7470

Oakland Convention and Visitors Bureau
1000 Broadway, Suite 200
Oakland, CA 94607-4020
(415) 839-9000

San Jose Convention and Visitors Bureau
333 W. San Carlos St., Suite 1000
San Jose, CA 95110
(408) 283-8833 (*information*)
(408) 295-2265 (*activities*)

North Bay

Visitors to the San Francisco Bay Area often find Marin County the surprise treat of their visit. Its bay side is one of the most photogenic shorelines in California. Captivating waterside towns, impressive Mount Tamalpais, and several ancient redwood groves are part of its rich mosaic.

The county's scenic Pacific coast is discussed on page 68.

Arriving by water. Many Marin residents prefer to commute to San Francisco by boat—also a good way for tourists to see the area without a car. Golden Gate Ferries make 10 daily round trips on weekdays and six daily on weekends and holidays from the San Francisco Ferry Building to Sausalito, Tiburon, and Larkspur Landing (north end of the bay near Point San Quentin). For details, call (415) 332-6600.

The Red & White Fleet also has ferry service to Sausalito, Tiburon, and Angel Island from Piers 41 and 43½ at Fisherman's Wharf. For information, call (415) 546-BOAT.

The Tiburon–Angel Island Ferry runs daily in summer, on weekends and holidays the rest of the year. For details, call (415) 435-2131.

Roaming through Marin

Alongside the bay, picturesque Sausalito clings to a hill, while Tiburon includes 10 square miles of salt water in its city limits. Other towns are grouped northward along U.S. 101 or lodged in canyons west of the highway.

En route to these communities, at the northern foot of the Golden Gate Bridge, the former Army garrison of Fort Baker is home for the Bay Area Discovery Museum, a hands-on facility for children 2 to 12 (modest fee).

Sausalito. With a setting reminiscent of a southern European seacoast village, Sausalito has harbors full of small vessels in all sizes and shapes. Shops and restaurants line its waterfront and crawl up the narrow, winding side streets. The most scenic approach by car is Alexander Avenue off U.S. 101 just north of the Golden Gate Bridge.

Sausalito's town center is tidy little Plaza Viña del Mar on Bridgeway. Ferries arrive here, drivers park in nearby lots, and shops and galleries line the blocks on either side. Village Fair at 777 Bridgeway (a multilevel mall with 40 shops and restaurants) has been an opium and gambling den, a gangster hideout, and a Prohibition distillery.

Two historic hotels (Casa Madrona above Bridgeway and Alta Mira on Bulkley Avenue) afford sweeping views. The Alta Mira dining deck is a favorite in nice weather. Waterside restaurants include Horizons, Scoma's, and the Spinnaker.

Sausalito is also home to a working model of San Francisco Bay (see page 14). Visitors are welcome.

Tiburon. On the shore of Richardson Bay at the tip of a peninsula opposite Sausalito (signed exit east from U.S. 101), Tiburon epitomizes the good life. Tourists join locals for alfresco dining at dockside restaurants, shopping on block-long Main Street, or wine tasting at Windsor Vineyards/Tiburon Vintners at 72 Main (10 A.M. to 7 P.M. daily).

On a hill overlooking town, splendid Old St. Hilary's Church is open 1 to 4 P.M. Wednesday and Sunday from April through October. Take Beach Road/Esperanza Street northwest from Tiburon Boulevard.

To the southwest, Beach Road takes you over Belvedere Lagoon past the expensive homes and yacht club of Belvedere. The 1866 China Cabin, formerly the social saloon of a clipper ship, is a free museum (open Sunday and Wednesday from 1 to 4 P.M.).

Trails at the Richardson Bay Audubon Center at the north end of the bay (376 Greenwood Beach Road) meander down to 900 acres of tidelands where birdlife abounds. The center is open Wednesday through Sunday from 9 A.M. to 5 P.M; you can tour its 1876 Lyford House (fee) from 1 to 4 P.M. Sunday, October through April.

Mill Valley. This town got its name from a sawmill that provided lumber for early San Francisco homes. A reconstruction stands in Old Mill Park, just down the street from the town plaza at Throckmorton and Miller. From here, you can see the steeply gabled roofs of homes tucked into the hills.

Sir Francis Drake Boulevard. Marin's most traveled east-west corridor starts at the junction of U.S. 101 and Interstate 580 just west of the Richmond–San Rafael Bridge and threads its way west to the Point Reyes Peninsula. It passes through the towns of Ross (stately homes and an Art and Garden Center at an old estate) and San Anselmo (a center for antique stores).

San Rafael. At 1102 5th Avenue in Marin's largest city, you'll find a replica of Mission San Rafael Arcangel, founded in 1817 (11 A.M. to 4 P.M. daily). A lavish Victorian in Boyd Park (1125 B Street) houses the Marin County Historical Society Museum; call (415) 454-8538 for hours. And the Guide Dogs for the Blind facility at 350 Los Ranchitos welcomes visitors to its kennels and campus; call (415) 499-4000 to arrange a free tour.

Take North San Pedro Road east of U.S. 101 to the bayside China Camp State Park (picnicking, fishing, sailing, camping), which contains the remnants of an 1800s Chinese fishing village. A turn-of-the-century store is now a museum (10 A.M. to 5 P.M. daily).

Nestled in the hills along the highway just to the north is the blue-domed Marin County Civic Center, designed by Frank Lloyd Wright. For a free tour, call (415) 499-7407.

Novato. In the rolling hills of northern Marin County, Novato gives no hint of its Spanish founding, but the town does acknowledge its original settlers with a free Museum of the American Indian (2200 Novato Boulevard, open Tuesday through Saturday from 10 A.M. to 4 P.M., Sunday from noon to 4 P.M.).

Marin parks

From an island in the bay to one of the Bay Area's highest peaks, Marin's parks are a varied lot. The county's climate also varies sharply between east and west, principally because Mount Tamalpais and the high ridges leading up to it form a barrier against fog.

Angel Island State Park. Once called the Ellis Island of the West, this 740-acre wilderness in San Francisco Bay has served as military base, war-prisoner detention center, and immigration camp.

Ferries from Tiburon and San Francisco dock at Ayala Cove on the northwest side of the island. You can sun at the beach, picnic, ride your bicycle around the island on a 5-mile unpaved road, or climb the interior slopes. Free guided tours of Civil War–era military buildings take place in summer.

Mount Tamalpais State Park. Draped across the upper slopes of 2,586-foot "Mount Tam" and reaching down to the sea at Muir Beach, the state park offers a labyrinth of hiking and riding trails. Picnic grounds lie near park headquarters on winding Panoramic Highway; take the State 1/Stinson Beach exit from U.S. 101 and follow the signs. From here you can drive nearly to the summit, 4 miles beyond. There are campsites near headquarters and at East Peak. Stage plays are presented in a hillside amphitheater in May and June; for details, call (415) 388-2070.

Muir Woods National Monument. Cool and green, this 502-acre park named for naturalist John Muir preserves a stand of virgin coast redwoods. The central part of the park and most of the 27 miles of trails are on a relatively level stretch of forest floor, making it accessible by wheelchair. There's also a marked trail for the blind.

To get a map of the park, which is surrounded by Mount Tamalpais State Park, stop by the handsome stone-and-cedar interpretive center. No camping or picnicking are allowed, but there is a coffee shop.

The park is 3½ miles west of Mill Valley, via Panoramic Highway/State 1. The road in is narrow and winding.

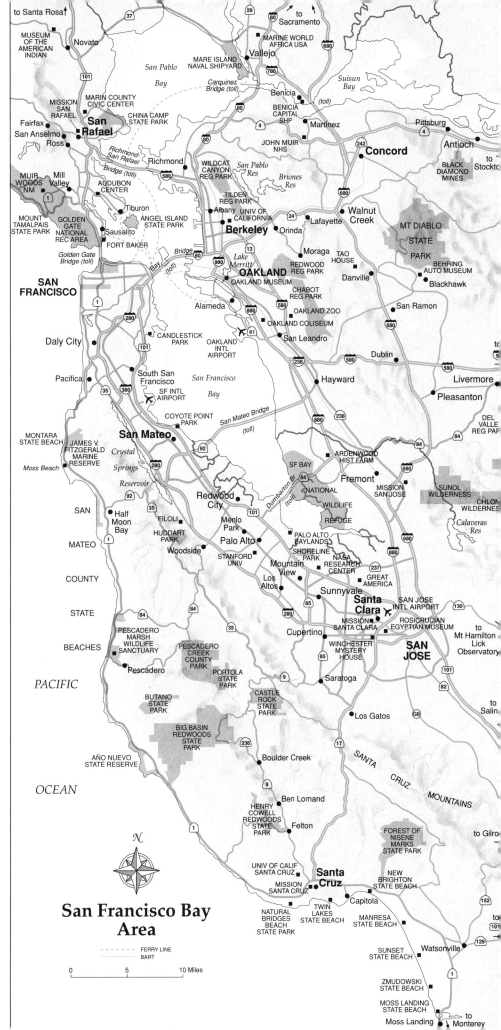

San Francisco Bay Area

FERRY LINE
BART

0   5   10 Miles

East Bay

A long ridge of low hills parallels San Francisco Bay on its eastern side, forming the backdrop for a continuous string of bayside cities. A second tier of communities is a rapidly growing counterpart on the other side of the hills.

This is a region rich in family-oriented attractions and outdoor recreation areas. It also has its share of fine museums and intriguing historic sites.

Regional parklands. In the hills that rise behind the East Bay cities, more than 50,000 acres of countryside have been set aside for recreational use under the aegis of the East Bay Regional Park District. Some parks are small, some large; some are wilderness areas, others highly developed.

You can camp at Chabot (above Oakland/San Leandro), Del Valle (near Livermore), and Sunol Wilderness (near Fremont). For a guide to all the parks, contact the East Bay Regional Park District, 11500 Skyline Boulevard, Oakland, CA 94619; (415) 531-9300.

Dining and shopping. The East Bay is where "California cuisine" was launched in the 1970s, at Alice Waters' Chez Panisse Restaurant in Berkeley (1517 Shattuck Avenue). Subsequently the nearby area, with its upscale food shops and restaurants, has come to be known as "Gourmet Gulch." But the whole East Bay offers a wealth of top-rated dining places.

Among pleasant dining and shopping streets are College Avenue through Berkeley and Oakland (Oliveto Cafe & Restaurant), Oakland's Piedmont Avenue (Bay Wolf Restaurant), Berkeley's 4th Street north of University (Fourth Street Grill), and Solano Avenue through Berkeley and Albany. Berkeley's Telegraph Avenue near the campus has fine bookstores and plenty of local color.

Oakland

Stretched out between the bay and a greenbelt of hilltop parks, the city of Oakland is one of the country's largest container shipping ports. Several attractive redevelopment efforts in recent years have focused on the downtown and waterfront areas, and visitors can take a look during free walking tours at 10 A.M. Wednesday and Saturday from May through October. Call (415) 273-3234 for details.

Oakland Museum. Oakland's acclaimed and handsome museum at 10th and Oak streets presents a different aspect of California in each of its three levels. In the Cowell Hall of California History, vivid displays suggest historical periods. The natural sciences gallery simulates a walk through the state's eight biotic zones, and the Gallery of California Art exhibits more than 550 works. The roof of each level is a garden terrace for the level above.

The museum is at the south end of Lake Merritt, a block east of the Lake Merritt BART Station. It's open Wednesday through Saturday from 10 A.M. to 5 P.M., Sunday from noon to 7 P.M. (closed major holidays). Admission is free, except for some special exhibits.

Around the lake. A 155-acre saltwater tidal basin just east of downtown, Lake Merritt is encircled by a 3¼-mile "necklace of lights" at night and by joggers and strollers during the day.

The country's oldest waterfowl refuge, established in 1870, is at the north end of the lake. Children's Fairyland offers fairytale-based scenes, puppet shows, tot-scaled rides and climbing structures (10 A.M. to 4:30 P.M. daily in summer, Friday through Sunday the rest of the year; modest admission).

Nearby, you can rent boats (daily in summer, weekends the rest of the year) or board the paddle-wheeler *Merritt Queen* for a cruise around the lake (weekend afternoons; modest charge).

At the south end, a rare three-panel Tiffany glass mosaic at Lake Merritt United Methodist Church (1330 Lakeshore Avenue) can be viewed from 2 to 4 P.M. Wednesday (free). Across the lake at 1418 Lakeside Drive, you can tour the elegant 1876 Camron-Stanford House from 11 A.M. to 4 P.M. Wednesday and 1 to 5 P.M. Sunday (small charge).

Downtown. Broadway is Oakland's "main street," cutting through a mixture of ornate early-1900s brick and tile buildings (some seriously damaged in the 1989 earthquake) and modern office towers. At 21st and Broadway is the city's Paramount Theater, a glittery 1931 art deco movie palace that hosts performing arts events. Tours are conducted the first and third Saturday of the month at 10 A.M. (small fee).

The modern-day focal point downtown is the tiered plaza stretching west from Broadway at 13th Street. A sculptural swirl of color called *There* is the city's answer to Gertrude Stein's comment about her Oakland home town, "There is no there there."

The Oakland Museum Sculpture Court at the 1111 Broadway office building is open free from 7 A.M. to 7 P.M. Down the street is downtown's only high-rise hotel, the Parc Oakland, with adjoining convention center.

Two square blocks of restored 1870s commercial buildings west of Broadway between 8th and 10th streets constitute the Old Oakland shopping and office complex. A couple of lunchtime favorites are Pacific Coast Brewing Company brew pub at 906 Washington Street and Ratto's grocery and deli at 821 Washington Street.

Across Broadway to the east, Oakland's Chinatown is concentrated between Franklin and Harrison, 10th and 7th streets. An influx of new Asian residents in recent years has added vitality to this district of food markets, shops, and many fine restaurants.

Waterfront. At the foot of Broadway, the Jack London Square area has restaurants, shops, and a hotel. The First and Last Chance Saloon (50 Webster Street) was once a hangout of author London. You can also peek into a rustic cabin in which London supposedly spent a Yukon winter, reconstructed here.

You can board a ferry to San Francisco from Jack London Square—call

Oakland's Jack London Square provides opportunities for watching waterfront
activities. Giant container-loading cranes loom like harbor mascots; the busy seaport
has the West Coast's largest container facility.

...East Bay

(415) 522-3300 for details—or take a free 1½-hour harbor cruise (every Thursday, May through August); call (415) 272-1188 to reserve. At the foot of Clay Street, take a look at Franklin Roosevelt's former yacht *Potomac*.

Along the hills. Attractions perched above the city would be worth a look if only for the views their hilltop sites afford. Castlelike Claremont Resort Hotel & Spa, built in 1915, straddles the Oakland-Berkeley city line off Claremont Avenue just north of State 13. Equally eye-catching is the Mormon Temple at Lincoln Avenue and State 13 (Warren Freeway). Free tours of its exterior and geneological library are offered daily, 9 A.M. to 9 P.M.

A string of wooded parks borders Skyline Boulevard: Joaquin Miller, Redwood, Roberts, and Chabot.

In the foothills just off Interstate 580, the Oakland Zoo has increased in stature in recent years with the addition of such naturalistic animal enclosures as a 1-acre elephant compound. Eighty species are housed at the zoo, open daily from 10 A.M. to 4 P.M. (moderate admission). Take Golf Links Road east from Interstate 580.

Berkeley

Immediately to the north of Oakland, Berkeley is known both for student activism and culinary preoccupations (see page 38). The University of California at Berkeley provides a lively mix of ideas and slate of events.

University of California. The 720-acre campus is home to more than 30,000 students. Stop at the visitor center in University Hall, University Avenue and Oxford Street, to pick up a map or to join a 1½-hour free walking tour (weekdays at 1 P.M., also Monday, Wednesday, and Friday at 10 A.M.). Take the 50-cent elevator ride up 300-foot Sather Tower for an overview.

Another sweeping view is from the Lawrence Hall of Science, on Centennial Drive above the football field. Inside are all sorts of hands-on science exhibits (10 A.M. to 4:30 P.M. weekdays,

to 5 P.M. weekends; moderate admission). The center's Holt Planetarium has weekend shows at 1, 2:15, and 3:30 P.M. (no children under 6 years).

The free 33-acre Botanical Garden is off Centennial Drive on the way up to Lawrence Hall (9 A.M. to 4:45 P.M. daily).

Also notable are the Lowie Museum of Anthropology (10 A.M. to 4:30 P.M. Tuesday through Friday, noon to 4:30 P.M. weekends; small admission); the free Paleontology Museum (8 A.M. to 5 P.M. weekdays, 1 to 5 P.M. Saturday); and the University Art Museum (11 A.M. to 5 P.M. Wednesday through Sunday, moderate admission).

Tilden Regional Park. One of the East Bay's favorite family playgrounds, this 2,000-acre area in the hills above Berkeley has an antique merry-go-round, pony rides, and a miniature steam train (daily in summer, weekends the rest of the year; small fees). At the free Little Farm, youngsters can pet farm animals, while the adjacent nature center has exhibits about wild ones. There are picnic areas, trails, a swimming lake, a botanic garden, and a golf course.

From Interstate 80, take University Avenue, turn left at Oxford, right at Cedar, and left at Spruce, then continue uphill to cross Grizzly Peak Boulevard and take the first left (Cañon Drive).

Heading south

A trip south to Fremont offers a look at earlier eras, plus a chance to glimpse bayside birdlife.

Ardenwood Historic Farm. Some 20 miles south of Oakland, you can ride a horse-drawn train or wagon, tour a Victorian home, and see demonstrations of turn-of-the-century farm skills.

Ardenwood Farm is open April through mid-November, from 10 A.M. to 4 P.M. Thursday through Sunday; admission is $5 adults, $3 seniors, $2.50 ages 4 through 17. Leave Interstate 880 at State 84 , drive west a mile, and turn right at Ardenwood Boulevard.

San Francisco Bay National Wildlife Refuge. Some 150 different species of birds call at this bayside refuge near the

eastern end of the Dumbarton Bridge. To reach the headquarters, open 10 A.M. to 5 P.M. daily, take State 84 west from Interstate 880 for 2 miles, then turn left onto Thornton Avenue. For a schedule of slide shows, walks, and bird-watching programs, call (415) 792-0222.

Mission San Jose. This 1797 Spanish mission was completely reconstructed in the 1980s. The imposing white structure and the adjacent museum are open daily between 10 A.M. and 5 P.M. (small donation suggested); a 20-minute slide show is presented on the hour. Mission San Jose is at 43000 Mission Boulevard, just south of Interstate 680 (Mission Boulevard exit) or 4 miles east of Interstate 880 (Warren/Mission Boulevard exit).

Carquinez Strait

Fresh and salt water come together in the Carquinez Strait, some 20 miles north of Oakland between Interstate 80 and Interstate 680. Near the western end, Vallejo is home to Marine World/Africa USA (see page 41) and Mare Island Naval Shipyard. For a look at the city's maritime history, stop at the Vallejo Naval and Historical Museum at 734 Marin Street (10 A.M. to 4:30 P.M. Tuesday through Friday, to 4 P.M. weekends; admission by donation).

Benicia. At the eastern end of the strait, the onetime state capital and port of Benicia is now a thriving artists' community. Stop at the Benicia Chamber of Commerce office at 601 1st Street for a walking tour guide.

Founded in 1847, Benicia became California's capital in 1854, a distinction that lasted only 13 months. The restored brick capitol building at 1st and West G streets is operated as a state historic park, generally open Thursday through Monday from 10 A.M. to 5 P.M. (small fee); call (707) 745-3385.

Browse along 1st Street from the waterfront as far as K Street to see a concentration of historic structures, antique stores, and the restored 1882 Union Hotel at 1st and West D streets (notable restaurant). On East H Street, the Yuba Arts Center (600 block) and nearby buildings house the studios of glass blowers and other artisans.

Among the more intriguing structures at the 1851 Benicia Arsenal at the east end of town are sandstone warehouses that once served as camel barns, the aftermath of an Army experiment in using the animals in the Southwest. Now they house a free city museum (weekends from 1 to 4 P.M.).

John Muir Historic Site. South of the strait in the town of Martinez is the elegant Victorian farmhouse where the West's premier conservationist lived from 1890 to 1914. You can take a self-guided tour of the house, orchard, and 1849 Martinez Adobe any day between 10 A.M. and 4:30 P.M. (small admission). John Muir National Historic Site is on Alhambra Avenue just north of State 4.

Over the hills

Across the hills, business parks and suburban housing developments are overtaking pastureland near such burgeoning communities as Concord, Walnut Creek, Livermore, and Pleasanton. Interstate 680 connects towns along this East Bay "sun belt."

Mount Diablo State Park. For an unparalleled view of the Bay Area, head up to the summit of 3,849-foot Mount Diablo. The 15,000-acre state park on the mountain's slopes offers more than 100 miles of trails, a summit visitor center, and a quartet of campgrounds that can sometimes be reserved through MISTIX; call (800) 444-7275.

To get to the park, exit Interstate 680 at Danville (Diablo Road exit) or Walnut Creek (Ygnacio Valley Road to Walnut Avenue).

Black Diamond Mines. A preserve operated by the East Bay Regional Park District offers a glimpse at area mining history and a 1930s underground sand mine. Call (415) 757-2620 to make reservations for the mine tour (expected to reopen in 1992 after repairs; small fee) and to find out about free weekend programs. Take Somersville Road south from State 4 below Antioch.

Danville. This suburban community at the foot of Mount Diablo has a purposefully quaint and countrified downtown and several cultural attractions.

Playwright Eugene O'Neill wrote some of his best-known works while living here from 1937 to 1944. You can tour his Tao House residence, operated as a national historic site, Wednesday through Sunday at 10 A.M. and 12:30 P.M. Call (415) 838-0249 for reservations for the free tour; you'll be picked up in downtown Danville.

In Danville's posh Blackhawk real estate development, the Behring Auto Museum at 3750 Blackhawk Plaza Circle displays more than 60 vintage luxury cars (10 A.M. to 5 P.M. daily except Monday, to 9 P.M. Wednesday and Friday). Admission is $8 adults, $6 seniors, $5 students. Next door, the Museum of Art, Science, and Culture exhibits University of California art and artifacts.

To get to Blackhawk, exit Interstate 680 at Crow Canyon Road and head east 4 miles to Camino Tassajara, then turn right. At the plaza, take a look at FJ's Blackhawk Market, which provides live piano music and cellular phones for the brass-trimmed shopping carts.

Livermore Valley. Interstate 580 cuts through the hills to the Livermore Valley, where nine wineries offer a leisurely approach to wine touring.

Wente Brothers Estate Winery (5565 Tesla Road in Livermore) and Concannon Vineyard (4590 Tesla Road), both founded in 1883, offer tours and tasting. Take Vasco Road south from Interstate 580 to Tesla. Southwest at 5050 Arroyo Road, Wente Bros. Sparkling Wine Cellars has tours, tastings, and the elegant Restaurant, open Wednesday through Sunday.

Pick up a touring map from any winery or from the Livermore Chamber of Commerce at 2157 1st Street.

Livermore is also the home of Lawrence Livermore National Laboratory, known for its nuclear research. A visitor center 3 miles south of Interstate 580 via Greenville Road has scientific exhibits (9 A.M. to 4:30 P.M. weekdays, noon to 5 P.M. weekends); call (415) 422-9797 to visit and to get directions to the lab's computer museum.

Drive east a few miles on Interstate 580 to see a strange landscape of thousands of wind turbines set amidst grazing lands in the Altamont Hills—the world's largest wind-fueled power plant.

Marine World

Where else can you have a tug of war with an elephant and get splashed by a whale on the same day? Marine World / Africa USA, 25 miles north of Oakland at Vallejo, is part zoo, part animal theater, and part elaborate playground.

Highlights of a visit to this 165-acre park are seven shows—killer whales and dolphins, sea lions, tigers, chimpanzees, birds, a wildlife conservation theater, and water-skiing.

The park's Elephant Encounter lets you see elephants in a variety of situations. You can also walk through the steamy tropical Butterfly World, see tidepool activity in an aquarium, observe handlers caring for giraffes, rhinos, and tigers, and glimpse park babies in a glass-walled nursery.

At the Showcase Theater various entertainment is scheduled. And a children's play area offers climbing and scrambling opportunities.

Admission, including all entertainment except elephant rides, is $19.95 adults, $14.95 ages 4 through 12, and $16.95 seniors. Marine World is open daily from 9:30 A.M. to 6 P.M. in summer, Wednesday through Sunday from 9:30 A.M. to 5 P.M. September through May.

From Interstate 80, go west on State 37, then south on Fairgrounds Drive. Or take a Red and White Fleet ferry from San Francisco to Vallejo; a combination ticket includes shuttle to the park.

A favorite family getaway, Santa Cruz lures visitors with wide, sandy beaches and a venerable boardwalk. The wooden Giant Dipper roller coaster, a national landmark, has been thrilling riders since 1924.

Peninsula & South Bay

Geographically, Palo Alto marks the end of the San Francisco Peninsula. But the cities of Mountain View, Los Altos, Sunnyvale, Cupertino, Santa Clara, and San Jose are still considered part of the South Bay.

Separating bayside communities from the pastoral coast are the Santa Cruz Mountains, a spur of the Coast Range, rising 2,000 to 3,000 feet. A string of public parks straddling their spine protects venerable redwood groves.

You can drive from San Francisco to San Jose (some 50 miles) on U.S. 101 (Bayshore Freeway) or Interstate 280 (Junipero Serra Freeway). Skyline Boulevard (State 35) winds along the ridge of the mountains, and State 1 skirts the coast.

Daily commuter trains run between San Francisco and San Jose; call CalTrain, (415) 495-4546, for information. San Mateo County Transit, (415) 761-7000, has bus service as far south as Palo Alto, and Santa Clara County Transit, (408) 287-4210, blankets the southern end of the bay.

Along the Bayshore

U.S. 101 provides the most convenient access to cities, harbors, and parks along the bay. Several major routes connect this highway with Interstate 280, a few miles inland. The two routes join in San Jose.

Bayside parks. Displays and hands-on exhibits at the nature center in Coyote Point Park (Coyote Point Drive exit in San Mateo) provide family fun. Besides the indoor Coyote Point Museum, the indoor-outdoor Wildlife Habitats let you take a look at live animals native to the Bay Area. The center is open Tuesday through Saturday from 10 A.M. to 5 P.M. and Sundays noon to 5 P.M. There's a modest admission along with a $4 per-car park entry fee. Picnic tables around the park offer grand views.

Birding and biking are popular on miles of trails along the levees in Palo Alto Baylands (Embarcadero Road east from U.S. 101). A free nature center is open 1 to 5 P.M. weekends. A 4-mile pathway extends south from here to Shoreline Park in Mountain View, a free 654-acre recreation and wildlife area (Shoreline Park exit from U.S. 101).

Around Palo Alto. This college town is noted for its tree-shaded streets of grand old houses, plus a good range of restaurants and entertainment. Don't overlook the beautifully renovated Stanford Theatre, downtown at 221 University Avenue (1920s Wurlitzer organ, pre-1950s films).

Sunset Publishing Corporation, Middlefield and Willow roads in adjacent Menlo Park, offers free weekday tours of its test kitchens and gardens; call (415) 321-3600 for times. At Arbor Road and Creek Drive in Menlo Park, Allied Arts Guild's shops and dining room inhabit part of an old Spanish rancho. For lunch and tea reservations (closed Sunday), call (415) 324-2588.

Stanford University. In 1891, Leland Stanford opened this private university on his horse farm. You can tour the campus, see the largest collection of Rodin sculptures outside of Paris (on the grounds of Stanford Museum of Art), and ride to the top of the Hoover Tower (small fee) for the view. Hour-long student-led walks start at the stone information booth at the south end of the Oval (end of Palm Drive) at 11 A.M. and 3:15 P.M. daily, except school holidays; call (415) 725-3335. University Avenue leads southwest from downtown Palo Alto into the campus.

NASA Research Center. At Moffett Field naval air station, south in Mountain View, the Ames Research Center offers weekday tours (2½ hours, 2-mile walk) of its wind tunnels and hangars. For reservations, call (415) 694-6497.

Off Interstate 280

En route south from San Francisco, the Junipero Serra Freeway—Interstate 280—passes Crystal Springs Reservoir, which holds San Francisco's water supply. The classic Greek-style Pulgas Water Temple at its southern tip marks the end of the Hetch Hetchy aqueduct, a 162-mile pipeline that begins in Yosemite National Park.

Filoli. This 654-acre estate in Woodside (Edgewood Road exit west to Cañada Road) is reason enough for a drive 25 miles south of San Francisco. The 43-room mansion—featured on TV's *Dynasty*—was built in 1916 by William Bowers Bourn II, who pulled millions in gold out of his Empire Mine in Grass Valley. Its name is a contraction of Bourn's code—Fight, Love, Live.

First-time visitors should join a docent-led tour ($8) of the house (no children under 12) and vast formal gardens (Tuesday through Saturday from mid-February to mid-November). A 3-mile nature hike ($4 adults, $1 children) is offered Monday through Saturday morning. Call (415) 364-2880 for tour reservations.

Stanford Linear Accelerator. Heart of this research center operated by Stanford University for the U.S. Department of Energy (Sand Hill Road exit) is a 2-mile-long accelerator generating high-energy electron and positron beams. Allow about 2 hours for the free guided bus tour. For reservations, phone (415) 926-3300, ext. 2204.

Around San Jose

If you haven't been in downtown San Jose recently, you'll be surprised at the changes. Thanks to major urban renewal, this oldest and biggest of Bay Area cities (population 740,000—the nation's 11th largest) has blossomed into a pleasant melange of old and new.

Downtown. A light-rail system runs along city streets and northeast to Santa Clara's Great America (see page 45). New and renovated hotels (Fairmont, upcoming Hilton, DeAnza, Holiday Inn), restaurants, and shops give visitors a reason to stay downtown.

Hub of the renaissance is the Convention Center (west of San Carlos Street between Almaden and Market) and its attendant cultural complex: Center for Performing Arts (opera, symphony, and ballet companies), Civic Auditorium, and Montgomery Theater (San Jose Repertory).

The new engenders a growing respect for the old. A self-guided history tour (check with the visitors bureau, address on page 35) leads past some of the city's architectural treasures: the Peralta Adobe (San Jose's oldest building), reconstructed St. Joseph's Cathedral, nearby San Jose State College, and the University of Santa Clara (reconstruction and remnants of the Santa Clara Mission, founded in 1777).

Museums of note. The Garage, a high-tech museum named for the scene of several startup Silicon Valley computer companies, will delight both children and adults. Among its displays: a larger-than-life microchip, robots, and the latest computers. The museum, located at 145 W. San Carlos Street, is open 10 A.M. to 5 P.M. (closed Monday). Admission is $6 adults, $4 children over 6 and seniors.

The purple exterior of the Children's Discovery Museum at Guadalupe River Park is your first clue that this lively world of hands-on fun is for kids 2 to 6 or so. Of parental interest: a changing room and a cafe geared to small appetites. The West's largest children's museum, it's open 10 A.M. to 5 P.M. Tuesday through Saturday, from noon Sunday; arrive early to avoid a crowd. Enter on Auzerais Street off Almaden Boulevard; admission is $6 adults, $3 children over 4 and seniors.

To catch a glimpse of turn-of-the-century life, visit 21 original and restored buildings that make up the San Jose Historical Museum in Kelley Park (Story Road exit south off U.S. 101). The museum is open weekdays from 10 A.M. to 4:30 P.M., weekends from noon (separate park entry and admission fees). Elsewhere in the park: a small playground and zoo and a picturesque Japanese garden.

The free San Jose Museum of Art (110 S. Market Street) is best known for its exhibits of post-war modernist and contemporary paintings. Hours are 10 A.M. to 4:30 P.M. Tuesday through Saturday, noon to 4 P.M. Sunday.

The renowned Rosicrucian Egyptian Museum at 1342 Naglee Avenue displays mummies, scarabs, and other artifacts from Egypt, Babylon, and Assyria. Admission fees to the museum (open 9 A.M. to 5 P.M. Tuesday through Saturday, 9 to 11 A.M. Sunday) and the adjacent planetarium are separate. Planetarium shows take place at 11 A.M. and 2 and 3:30 P.M. on weekends.

Across from Santa Clara's City Hall at 1505 Warburton, the stunning Triton Museum showcases turn-of-the-century American paintings, many depicting the Santa Clara Valley. The free museum is open 10 A.M. to 5 P.M. weekdays, noon to 5 P.M. weekends.

Winchester Mystery House. Sarah Winchester, heir to her father-in-law's gun fortune, believed that if she stopped adding rooms onto her house she would die. The 160-room result (Winchester Boulevard and Interstate 280) is a memorial to her obsession. The mansion, gardens, and large gift shop are open daily except Christmas for tours ($10.95 adults, $8.95 seniors, and $5.95 children 6 to 12). Hours vary with the season; call (408) 247-2101.

Lick Observatory. Twenty miles east of San Jose, the narrow and winding Mount Hamilton Road (State 130) climbs up to one of the world's largest telescopes. Visitors get a free look from 10 A.M. to 5 P.M. daily except holidays. The road isn't recommended in bad weather.

Los Gatos and Saratoga. Nestled in the foothills west of San Jose, the neighboring towns of Los Gatos and Saratoga have a well-heeled country village charm. Both are distinguished by an array of boutiques and restaurants. To get there from San Jose, take State 17 west to the Los Gatos exit; Saratoga is 4 miles to the north via State 9.

Tucked into the hills behind Saratoga (follow Big Basin Way west about a mile) are the 15½-acre Hakone Gardens, formerly a private estate, now a city park. The hillside gardens (open 10 A.M. to 5 P.M. weekdays, 11 A.M. to 5 P.M. weekends) feature Japanese plantings, teahouses, and koi ponds.

Through the mountains

South of San Francisco, Skyline Boulevard leads to woodsy communities and some of the area's busiest day-use and overnight parks: Huddart, Sam McDonald, San Mateo County Memorial, and Portola State Park.

From Skyline Boulevard, campers, hikers and sightseers can head south on State 9 to redwood-shaded state parks—Castle Rock, Big Basin, and Henry Cowell—and the charming San Lorenzo Valley towns of Boulder Creek (golf course), Ben Lomond, and Felton.

Roaring Camp & Big Trees Railroad. At Roaring Camp, a simulated 1880s logging town half a mile south of Felton, a narrow-gauge steam train carries passengers on a 6-mile, 75-minute loop through thick redwood groves. For information on this trip and a second route to the Santa Cruz Boardwalk, see page 126.

Along the coast

Though not as spectacular a scenic stretch as the Big Sur coast, the San Mateo County shoreline along State 1 between San Francisco and Santa Cruz reveals many beaches and a few small towns to explore.

Beaches. Your best look at tidepools is from the rocky reef at James V. Fitzgerald Marine Reserve at Moss Beach. A free museum gives you information (collecting is prohibited).

The San Mateo Coast State Beaches, nine narrow strands scattered along 50 miles of the coast (headquarters in Half Moon Bay), are popular for strolling, picnicking, sunbathing, wading, and surf and rock fishing (license required), though the water's not safe or warm enough for swimming.

Año Nuevo State Reserve, a winter breeding ground for elephant seals, is open for docent-led guided tours from December through March. For reservations, call MISTIX, (800) 444-7275.

Towns. An agricultural and fishing center, Half Moon Bay is crowded in mid-October for its annual Pumpkin Festival. The rest of the year it's a good choice for a lazy weekend of fishing, golfing, hiking, or taking in a Sunday afternoon jazz session at the funky Bach Dancing and Dynamite Society. Among lodging choices: San Benito House (noted for its food), Mill Rose Inn, Half Moon Bay Lodge.

Ranches, flower fields, and artichoke farms surround Pescadero, 15 miles south, but most visitors head for nearby beaches, Pescadero Marsh (533-acre wildlife sanctuary), or Butano State Park (hiking, camping), 7 miles inland. Duarte's Tavern, an 1894 landmark, is the place to eat.

Santa Cruz

This seaside town was severely damaged by the 1989 earthquake (the epicenter was in nearby Forest of Nisene Marks State Park). But its visitor attractions, numerous accommodations, and restaurants were almost untouched.

For area details, contact the visitor center at 701 Front Street; phone (408) 425-1234. An information booth on Ocean Street between Water and Soquel is open during summer months.

Attractions. At the long municipal wharf (Center and Beach streets), you can fish, buy souvenirs, and dine at such seafood restaurants as Sea Cloud. Wide white beaches stretch to either side, and the vintage boardwalk (see below) lies at the pier's foot.

Art galleries, museums, wineries, golf courses, and the gravity-defying Mystery Spot (1953 Branciforte Drive, admission fee) are among other choices. You can visit a replica of the 1791 Santa Cruz Mission (126 High Street) or head into the hills to the wooded campus of the University of California at Santa Cruz (take High Street west from State 1).

Along the beach. To watch surfers at Steamer Lane and visit a free surfing museum, follow cove-hugging West Cliff Drive southwest from the pier. The Lighthouse Point museum is open daily except Tuesday from 1 to 4 P.M. in summer, also closed Wednesday the rest of the year.

To the west lies Natural Bridges Beach State Park (migrating butterflies in winter, guided tidepool tours). Nearby Long Marine Laboratory & Aquarium (foot of Delaware Avenue) is open to the public from 1 to 4 P.M. Tuesday through Sunday (free).

Twin Lakes, a day-use beach east of the wharf, is a favorite with local picnickers. One of the park's lagoons is a wildfowl refuge; a second is a yacht harbor.

Southeast of Santa Cruz. South of town are many excellent beach parks popular with swimmers, surfers, and anglers. Water is warmer here than farther north, and the surf is usually gentle.

Campsites are available at Manresa, New Brighton, and Sunset state beaches (see page 121); Seacliff offers trailer hookups, and you can fish from an unusual pier—a 45-foot cement ship. Zmudowski, Moss Landing, and Salinas River are day-use beaches.

Capitola, next door to Santa Cruz, was one of California's first beach resorts, dating back to the late 1880s. Today it sparkles with shops, galleries, eating spots, and begonias—at the Capitola National Begonia Festival in September and at Antonelli Begonia Gardens (2545 Capitola Road). Peak blossom season at the commercial gardens is August and September.

Moss Landing, a former whaling village halfway between Santa Cruz and Monterey, has a hardworking harbor, a bird sanctuary (visitor center and hiking trails inland from the highway), seafood restaurants, and some 25 antique shops.

South Bay Fun Zones

Thrill rides, arcades, and live shows draw crowds to Santa Clara's Great America and the Santa Cruz Beach Boardwalk. Both have acclaimed roller coasters and carousels, but one is a self-contained theme park and the other the last of the West's great beach boardwalks.

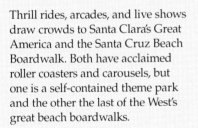

Great America. The plaza of this 100-acre park opens onto five Americana theme areas, each with wild and mild rides, shows, shops, and restaurants. There's even a special zone for tiny tots, with kiddie-sized attractions.

An amphitheater hosts summer concerts, spirited musical revues appear in theaters, and films flicker on the world's largest motion picture screen—7 stories tall, 96 feet wide.

In addition to the Bay Area's largest wooden roller coaster, rides include the West's only stand-up roller coaster, corkscrews, loop rollers, and whitewater rafts.

The park is open daily for Easter vacation and from Memorial Day through Labor Day, weekends only in spring and autumn (closed in winter); call (408) 988-1800 for seasonal hours. Admission is $17.95 adults and children over 6, $10.95 seniors, and $8.95 children 3 to 6. Take Great America Parkway exit north from U.S. 101 at Santa Clara.

Santa Cruz Beach Boardwalk. Since it opened in 1924, this mile-long beach fun zone's most popular rides have been the Giant Dipper wooden roller coaster and the 1911 hand-carved Looff carousel, where you can still reach for the brass (now steel) ring. Both are national historic landmarks.

Other attractions include rides, games, restaurants and snack stands, and an indoor miniature golf course. Rides operate daily in summer, on weekends the rest of the year; seasonal hours vary. Boardwalk admission is free; unlimited ride tickets cost $15.95 (individual tickets available).

Monterey Peninsula

Pristine beaches, surf crashing against craggy rocks, and wave-warped cypresses—along with miles of golf courses—have made the Monterey Peninsula famous around the world. Formed by Monterey and Carmel bays, the peninsula juts into the Pacific Ocean 120 miles south of San Francisco. Here you can explore carefully preserved historic adobes in Monterey; browse through art galleries in carefully quaint Carmel; and drive among grand estates in the dense woods of Del Monte Forest. To the south, Big Sur is one of the state's most spectacular stretches of coast.

Inland lie the caves and peaks of Pinnacles National Monument, picturesque mission towns, a cluster of wineries, and the agricultural center of Salinas, birthplace of author John Steinbeck and site of a top rodeo.

Contacts

These agencies offer information on attractions and accommodations. See additional contacts throughout this chapter.

Monterey Peninsula Chamber of Commerce and Visitors & Convention Bureau
380 Alvarado St. (P.O. Box 1770)
Monterey, CA 93942
(408) 649-1770

Salinas Area Chamber of Commerce
119 E. Alisal St. (P.O. Box 1170)
Salinas, CA 93901
(408) 424-7611

Mexico's last bastion

The peninsula was settled thousands of years ago by the Esselen and later the Ohlone Indians. The first European to sight Monterey Bay was Juan Rodriguez Cabrillo, a Portuguese explorer sailing for Spain, who couldn't land in 1542 because of high seas. Sebastian Vizcaino named the bay on a 1602 visit, but it wasn't until 1770 that the area was settled.

Then Gaspar de Portola and Father Junipero Serra established the first of Spain's four California presidios and the second of the Franciscans' 21 California missions on the south shore of the bay.

Until the middle of the 19th century, Monterey was California's most important settlement. Beginning the century as the Spanish capital of Alta California, it became the Mexican capital in 1822 and the American capital in 1846. After the discovery of gold in 1848 moved the focus north to San Francisco, Monterey turned to whaling, then to fishing and finally tourism.

Planning a visit

The ocean setting conditions the peninsula's weather. Summer months along the coast are likely to be overcast, with early morning and late afternoon fog. Spring and autumn months can be sparkling—warm days, crystal skies. Rain is frequent from December to March, but even January, the wettest month, has occasional crisp, sunny days.

Getting there. Monterey Peninsula Airport, 3 miles east of Monterey on State 68, has daily scheduled flights on some half dozen domestic carriers. Hotel shuttles, local buses, and taxis provide transfers, and rental cars are available.

Salinas is a stop on Amtrak's coastal rail route, and Greyhound has bus terminals in Salinas, Fort Ord, and Monterey. Monterey-Salinas Transit, (408) 899-2555, connects towns within the area (as far south as Big Sur in summer).

If you drive, the most scenic north-south route is coastal State 1. Connecting roads between U.S. 101 (fastest route to inland attractions) and State 1 include State 152 across Hecker Pass from Gilroy, State 156 through the artichoke capital of Castroville, and State 68 between Salinas and Monterey.

Where to stay. The greatest selection of resorts, hotels, motels, and inns is found between Monterey and Carmel; Pacific Grove boasts several beachside Victorian inns. For a list of choices, contact area visitor bureaus. Among the biggest and best-known lodgings in the Monterey-Carmel area are Doubletree, Highlands Inn, Hotel Pacific, Hyatt Regency, Monterey Bay Inn, Monterey Hotel, Monterey Plaza, Monterey Sheraton, Old Carmel Mission Inn, Spindrift Inn, and Tickle Pink Motor Inn.

There are several scenic public campgrounds along the Big Sur coast (see page 54), plus a number of private facilities for RV and tent campers. Other state parks inland from Salinas welcome campers (page 57). For additional details on area camping, turn to page 121.

Fog creeps across the rugged Santa Lucia Mountains along the Big Sur coast. State 1, blasted out of the high bluffs, hugs the shore for some 90 miles between Carmel and San Simeon, site of Hearst Castle.

Monterey Area

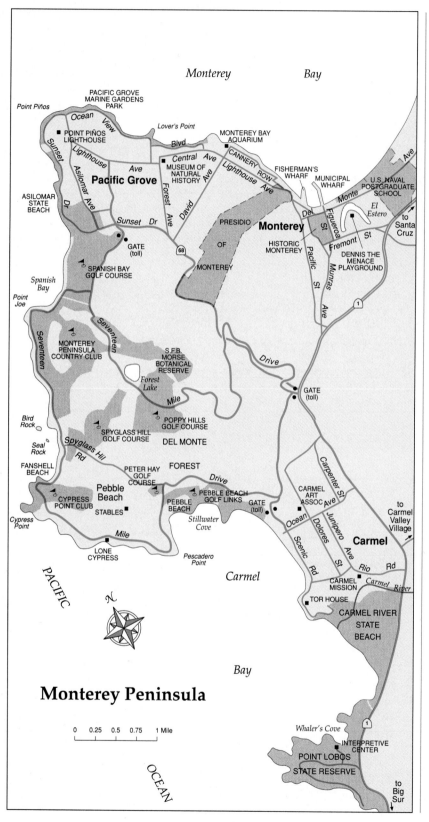

Much of the old Spanish and Mexican village of yesteryear Monterey still stands in the midst of today's modern city of 31,500. Many buildings erected before 1850 are in good repair; about a dozen are preserved in downtown Monterey State Historic Park (see facing page). Stop first at the Custom House Plaza just inland from Fisherman's Wharf for a tour map.

An Adobe Tour each April features other buildings open to the public only for this event. Other events on the peninsula's crowded calendar include the famed Monterey Jazz Festival in September, plus a Bach Festival in July and a Dixieland celebration in March. Golf tournaments are also major events—the area is Northern California's golf capital (see page 123).

Monterey has a compact downtown area, easy to navigate on foot if you have a good map. Pedestrian walkways provide access to its most scenic areas. Parking in 2- and 4-hour metered public lots near Fisherman's Wharf is convenient, albeit crowded on summer weekends.

For the younger set, the free Dennis the Menace Playground downtown on Pearl Street at El Estero Lake makes a nice break from sightseeing. Cartoonist Hank Ketcham, creator of the comic strip character, designed the unusual playground.

A waterfront stroll. A popular Recreation Trail for strollers and cyclists follows the waterfront east for 5 miles from Lover's Point in Pacific Grove (Ocean View Boulevard and 17th Street), through Monterey's Cannery Row and Shoreline Park, past Fisherman's Wharf and Custom House Plaza, and along the Window on the Bay waterfront park and Del Monte Beach. Eventually the linear park will stretch to Castroville, 18 miles away.

Municipal Wharf. Monterey's Municipal Wharf extends into the bay from the foot of Figueroa Street. Here you'll see commercial fishing boats unload anchovies, cod, halibut, salmon, shark,

Scattered around downtown Monterey are good examples of a distinctive architecture still called "Monterey style." Some of these balcony-fronted two-story adobes are preserved and maintained as the Monterey State Historic Park. Others, operated independently, are included on a walking tour map of the city.

Start at the Custom House Plaza near Fisherman's Wharf. At the visitor center, you pay a single admission ($3.50 adults, $2 children 6 through 17) to visit all the following buildings except for Colton Hall, a free museum operated by the city. Most buildings are open 10 A.M. to 5 P.M. daily in summer, to 4 P.M. in winter.

Custom House. At 1 Custom House Plaza stands the Pacific Coast's oldest government office; one section dates back to 1827. Here the U.S. flag was officially raised for the first time in 1846. A collection center for revenue from foreign shipping until 1867, the restored building (free admission) displays 1840s goods.

Pacific House. This two-story structure on the Plaza dates back to 1847. First used for military offices and storage and later as a tavern, it now contains historical exhibits and Indian artifacts.

Boston Store. This building at Scott and Olivier streets, named Casa del Oro because it was supposedly a gold depository at one time, is again operated as a store (closed Monday, Tuesday, and Sunday morning).

Old Whaling Station. The garden of this former boarding house near the corner of Pacific and Scott streets is open for touring.

First Brick House. Next door stands the area's first brick structure, home to a pioneer family.

First Theater. At Scott and Pacific streets, the building that housed the state's first theater was originally a tavern and lodging house for sailors. Plays are still presented on weekends; call (408) 375-4916 for reservations.

Casa Soberanes. This well-preserved house at 336 Pacific was built in 1830. Period antiques decorate its interior.

Colton Hall. On Pacific Street facing Friendly Plaza, this impressive building (free admission) was where the state's first constitution was written in 1849. A second-floor museum displays early government documents. An old jail adjoins.

Larkin House. The two-story adobe at Jefferson Street and Calle Principal was built by Thomas Larkin, American Consul from 1843 to 1846. You

see original furnishings on the guided tour (daily except Tuesday).

Cooper-Molera Adobe. The restored Victorian home at the corner of Polk and Munras (closed Wednesday) belonged to Captain John Cooper, a trader and entrepreneur, who married General Mariano Vallejo's sister.

Stevenson House. Named for Robert Louis Stevenson, who lived here in 1879, the restored and well-furnished house at 530 Houston Street is open for tours daily except Wednesday.

Royal Presidio Chapel. Founded by Father Junipero Serra in 1770 and rebuilt in 1794, San Carlos Cathedral (Church Street at Figueroa) has been in use ever since.

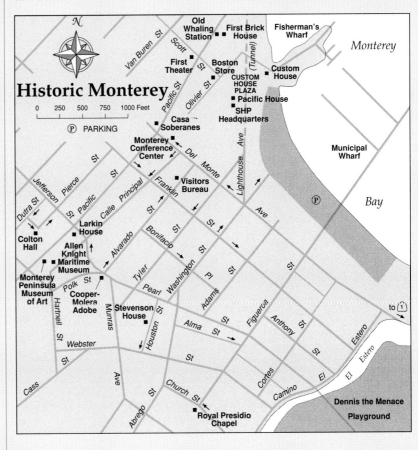

Historic Monterey

On a tour of the Monterey Bay Aquarium, visitors pause at fish-eye level in front of kelp forest exhibit. The world-famous undersea museum on Cannery Row in Monterey houses more than 6,500 sea creatures.

50

...Monterey Area

sole, squid, swordfish, and tuna at processing plants. If you don't mind getting your feet damp, you can watch from doorways as workers clean and pack fish. This is also the best place for pier fishing (licenses are sold at Joe's Boat Hoist on the pier).

Fisherman's Wharf. Built in 1846 as a pier for trading vessels bringing goods around Cape Horn, this wharf (4 blocks west of Municipal Wharf) was home to whaling vessels and sardine boats before its metamorphosis into a pier filled with fish markets, shops, and restaurants (Domenico's is a favorite).

Sportfishing, sightseeing, and whale-watching boats line the wood-planked pier, offering first-hand enjoyment of the bay (see page 125). Seals, sea lions, and otters provide daily entertainment along the length of the wharf.

Near the wharf's expansive plaza sprawls the city's convention center, a handsome three-level complex at One Portola Plaza. It's flanked by two large hotels and a shopping plaza. Other hotels and restaurants lie nearby.

Cannery Row. The row of canneries and warehouses John Steinbeck described as "a poem, a stink, a grating noise" still stands to the north of Fisherman's Wharf, a monument to the sardines that vanished abruptly from the bay in 1948. But the street is very different from the one portrayed in Steinbeck's novel *Cannery Row*.

The old buildings now house restaurants, antique stores, art galleries, shops, hotels, and the area's showcase, the innovative Monterey Bay Aquarium. There are several wine-tasting rooms: Bargetto, Monterey Peninsula, Roudon-Smith, and the striking glass-fronted Paul Masson facility at 700 Cannery Row (small museum, free film). Downstairs from Paul Masson, Steinbeck's Spirit of Monterey Wax Museum covers 400 years of area history (9 A.M. to 10 P.M. daily; admission). Across the street, a turn-of-the-century carousel delights children.

A few reminders of Steinbeck's novel do remain. A private club inhabits Doc Rickett's Western Biological Laboratory at 800 Cannery Row; Lee Chong's Heavenly Flower Grocery across the street is now a shop (free museum at back); and La Ida's Cafe (one of the novel's houses of ill repute) serves food.

At 125 Ocean View Boulevard, around the corner from the row, rises the American Tin Cannery. Once a factory, the refurbished building is now home to 45 discount outlets.

Several parking lots, including a big garage on Foam Street between Hoffman and Prescott, are within easy walking distance of attractions.

Military touches. Founded by Portola in 1770, Monterey's Presidio is a subpost for the U.S. Army's 22,000-acre Fort Ord nearby, a language institute, and a training center. A free museum (open Thursday through Monday from 9 A.M. to 4 P.M.) exhibits military items from Spanish days to the present. The main gate is at Pacific and Artillery streets, near Vizcaino's original 1602 landing site.

Just east of downtown Monterey along State 1 lies the Del Monte Hotel, an early-day seaside resort and now the Naval Postgraduate School. Visitors may stroll around its lushly landscaped acres daily from 9 A.M. to 4 P.M. From State 1, exit onto Aguajito Road and turn right on 3rd Street to reach the main entrance.

Other downtown museums. The Allen Knight Maritime Museum (550 Calle Principal) boasts a large nautical collection, including scale models of ships and the Point Sur light. In summer, the free museum is open Tuesday through Sunday from 10 A.M. to 4 P.M.

The Monterey Peninsula Museum of Art (559 Pacific Street) exhibits paintings, photography, graphics, and ethnic art. The museum welcomes viewers Tuesday through Saturday from 10 A.M. to 4 P.M. and Sunday from 1 to 4 P.M. (donation suggested). The museum also operates tours of the 22-room La Mirada Adobe (720 Via Mirada) on Wednesday and Saturday at 1, 2, and 3 P.M. A $5 donation is suggested.

Pacific Grove

Each October thousands of orange and black monarchs (*Danaus plexippus*) congregate in the pretty town of Pacific Grove just northwest of Monterey, earning it the title of "Butterfly City, USA." Most of these winter visitors prefer the 6-acre grove of trees at the end of Lighthouse Avenue; signs mark the route.

Bay Aquarium

At the edge of Monterey Bay sprawls one of the world's largest and finest aquariums. Some 6,500 marine creatures are dramatically housed in the rambling Monterey Bay Aquarium complex at the west end of Cannery Row.

With its multilevel roofs, boiler stacks, and corrugated walls, the aquarium manages to retain the waterfront feeling that inspired novelist John Steinbeck.

Sea life is displayed here in more than 100 display tanks—including an above-and-below-water sea otter world and a 3-story mature kelp forest.

A 90-foot-long tank, complete with deep reefs, a sandy ocean floor, and old wharf pilings, replicates life in the bay. Several species of large sharks cruise here among other bay denizens.

One end of the building is devoted to touchable displays—bat rays to pet and feed, for example, and tidepools to explore. A stunning walk-through aviary is home to marsh and shore birds.

Admission to the aquarium (open daily except Christmas from 10 A.M. to 6 P.M.) is $8 adults, $5.75 teens and seniors, and $3.50 children. Ticketron sells advance tickets.

...Monterey Area

It was Methodists, not butterflies, who founded Pacific Grove in 1875 when they held the first of many seashore camp meetings here. Incorporated in 1889, the town was corseted with ordinances regulating dancing, drinking, and public bathing.

Nowadays the city at the northern gate of the 17-Mile Drive is better known for its ornate Victorian houses and inns and its 3-mile stretch of rocky coast. Three annual events draw crowds: the Victorian Home Tour in April, the Feast of Lanterns festival in July, and the Butterfly Parade in October. For information on these and other activities and attractions, stop by the Pacific Grove Chamber of Commerce offices in the little blue Victorian at Forest and Central avenues, or call (408) 373-3304.

Museum of Natural History. Across the street from the chamber of commerce at 165 Forest, this little museum is a gem. Of particular interest are its "touchable" collections of native plants and animals. On an area relief map, you get an idea of the great chasm of Monterey Bay, some 8,400 feet deeper than the Grand Canyon. The free museum (donations welcomed) is open daily except Monday from 10 A.M. to 4 P.M.

Pacific Grove Marine Gardens Park. A walking and cycling path runs the length of Ocean View Boulevard, providing plenty of places to stop and enjoy the view. A white sand "pocket" beach offers good tidepooling (don't disturb the creatures), and Lover's Point (Ocean View at 17th) is a good place for picnicking, birding, and watching scuba divers.

Point Piños Lighthouse. The lighthouse just north of the intersection of Lighthouse and Asilomar avenues has stood at the entrance to the harbor since 1855. The West Coast's oldest continuously operating lighthouse, the Cape Cod–style structure is now a museum (see page 77).

Asilomar State Beach. A boardwalk lets you explore the rolling sand dunes between Point Piños and Asilomar State Beach without harming the plants. Asilomar Conference Center, inland from Sunset Drive, welcomes individuals as well as large groups; for information, call (408) 372-8016.

17-Mile Drive

One of the state's most beautiful roads, the 17-Mile Drive winds through the Del Monte Forest between Pacific Grove and Carmel. It takes less than an hour to tour the area, but you'll want to linger longer to savor the views of dramatic coastline and impressive homes, enjoy a beachside picnic lunch, overnight in a famed resort, or play a round on one of the golf courses overlooking the ocean.

The privately-owned road (part of Ben Hogan Properties) can be entered through several gates. There's one at Pacific Grove (off Sunset Drive), a marked exit off State 1 midway between Monterey and Carmel, and another in Carmel (west end of Ocean Avenue).

Entrance fee of $5.75 per car includes a map of the area. The gate charge is waived for golfers with tee times, hotel guests, and restaurant patrons with advance reservations. Cyclists enter free but must sign a liability release; biking is permitted daily except when special events are scheduled.

Seaside sights. From the Pacific Grove Gate, skirt the Inn and Links at Spanish Bay (resort and golf course), veering west along the shore at the road's fork. After passing Spanish Bay, you reach Point Joe, site of many early-day shipwrecks. The fury of colliding offshore currents can be seen even on calm days.

Sea lions and birds bask within viewing distance on Bird and Seal rocks. Neighboring Fanshell Beach boasts a nearly perfect crescent of white sand. For best views of the Pacific coastline and Point Sur Lighthouse (20 miles south), stop at the Cypress Point Lookout.

All along the rocky shore, weathered Monterey cypresses cling to the bluffs, their branches and foliage dramatically distorted by the wind. Lone Cypress, the most famous, stands by itself on a rocky outcropping above the surf. You'll see the eerie bleached white form of the Ghost Tree near Pescadero Point.

Activities. Overnight camping isn't allowed, but you can picnic at Spanish Bay and Seal Rock and fish from Fanshell Beach north. Access to Stillwater Cove (popular with divers) is through the Beach & Tennis Club parking lot; to reserve one of the limited number of parking spaces, phone (408) 625-8507.

The Pebble Beach Equestrian Center on Sombria Lane offers assorted rides on 36 miles of bridle trails through Del Monte Forest; for information, call (408) 624-2756. The adjacent Collins Polo Field hosts major West Coast equestrian events.

The area's golf courses are famous. For information on 18-hole public courses, see page 123. Scenic Cypress Point and Monterey Peninsula Country Club courses are not open to the public.

Resorts. Lingering for a fine meal or perhaps an overnight stay at one of the two deluxe resort hotels allows time to enjoy the area's beauty. The Lodge at Pebble Beach first opened its doors to guests in 1919. The Inn at Spanish Bay was added in 1989. Both have an array of shops.

Carmel Area

Celebrated by poets, writers, and photographers, Carmel has been home to such diverse personalities as poet Robinson Jeffers, photographer Ansel Adams, actress Kim Novak, and actor and former mayor Clint Eastwood.

Carmel prides itself on remaining a simple village by the ocean. Houses have no street numbers and no mail delivery; its 5,000 residents meet at the post office. Downtown there are no billboards, no neon signs, no stoplights, and almost no street lights. Side streets have no curbs and no sidewalks.

This very lack of commercialism, however, acts as a drawing card, attracting far too many tourists in summer. The sidewalks are crowded and the main street, Ocean Avenue, is jammed with cars almost every weekend. For maximum enjoyment, time your visit for a weekday out of season.

Plenty of motels, inns, and cottages line Carmel's streets, but there are only two hotels downtown—Pine Inn and La Playa. Restaurants—dozens of them—are small and run the gamut from tea shops to elegant establishments serving haute cuisine.

Shopping. Carmel is a village of shops, more than 150 of them, mostly small. Dozens of galleries displaying artists' works are scattered around town; the largest concentration is near the Carmel Art Association gallery on Dolores Street between 5th and 6th.

Along the shore. Carmel's classically beautiful beach at the foot of Ocean Avenue is ideal for strollers and, in good weather, sunbathers. It's unsafe for swimming, but most bathers find the water too cold anyway.

Scenic Road offers fine views along the shoreline. Robinson Jeffers' stone home, Tor House, faces Scenic Road at Carmel Point; you can tour the house Friday and Saturday from 10 A.M. to 3 P.M. Call (408) 624-1813 for advance reservations; on tour days, call (408) 624-1840. Admission is $5 for adults, $1.50 high school students (no younger children admitted).

South of the village limits, at the end of Scenic Road, is Carmel River State Beach, a gentle and usually sunny stretch of coast. It's a good place to picnic.

Carmel Mission. South of town, the second California mission founded by Franciscan Father Junipero Serra provides one of the most authentic and picturesque links to early California history. Father Serra is buried inside the Basilica San Carlos Borromeo del Rio Carmelo, established here in 1771 after being founded the previous year along Monterey Bay.

The mission is fully restored, and you could spend several hours wandering through the chapel, museum (donations encouraged), gardens, and cemetery (final resting place for some 3,000 Indians). You can visit from 9:30 A.M. to 4:30 P.M. Monday through Saturday and from 10:30 A.M. to 4:30 P.M. Sunday. To get there, turn west from State 1 at Rio Road; or follow Junipero Avenue south from downtown Carmel.

Point Lobos State Reserve. "Strange, introverted, and storm-twisted beauty"—so poet Robinson Jeffers described Point Lobos, the promontory jutting into the Pacific 4 miles south of Carmel. For many visitors, the reserve's 6-mile-long coastline represents nature at its most magnificent.

The 1,500-acre park (per-car entrance fee) offers a place to hike, picnic, look at rich tidepools, sun on the beach, scuba dive, watch birdlife, and fish. Pick up a map (small fee) at the entrance or at the information station at the Sea Lion Point parking lot. The interpretive center at Whaler's Cove on the north shore is a restored Chinese frame cabin built in 1851. Inside, artifacts trace cabin—and area—history from whaling days to movie fame.

Reserve hours are 9 A.M. to 5 P.M. daily. In summer, parking lots fill up quickly, so plan to arrive before 11 A.M. on weekends. Dogs are not permitted.

Scuba divers can reserve one of the 15 diving permits issued daily by calling MISTIX at (800) 444-7275 up to 28 days in advance. Unreserved slots are distributed by lottery at the entrance station each morning at 8:30 A.M. Divers must show proof of certification.

Carmel Valley

Just south of Carmel, Carmel Valley Road (County G16) heads inland from State 1 along the Carmel River. You turn onto the road at Carmel Rancho shopping center, which fronts the beautifully landscaped Barnyard shopping mall, location of the acclaimed Thunderbird Bookshop (also a restaurant).

Driving through the valley, you pass artichoke fields, fruit orchards, nurseries, strawberry fields, small shopping centers, and elegant resorts with golf courses. The Begonia Gardens, about 6 miles into the valley, are at their peak bloom in July and August. Chateau Julien (8940 Carmel Valley Road) offers wine tasting and touring daily from 10:30 A.M. to 2:30 P.M. Laid-back Carmel Valley Village lies about 12 miles southeast of State 1 on the Carmel Valley Road.

Recreational playground. When fog hangs over the rest of the Monterey Peninsula, the Carmel Valley is usually sunny, making it an ideal setting for some of the area's premier resorts and recreational sites. John Gardiner's first tennis ranch is here, as are three championship golf courses. The Carmel River holds an abundance of trout, and steelhead fishing is excellent in season.

Just beyond Carmel Valley Ranch Resort (about 8 miles inland from State 1), the 540-acre Garland Ranch Regional Park has hiking and equestrian trails, and a visitor center where you can pick up maps and brochures. You can camp at Riverside Park and Saddle Mountain Recreation Park.

Valley lodging. Carmel Valley's resorts and small lodges all offer interesting activities. For a list of accommodations, write to the Carmel Valley Chamber of Commerce, P.O. Box 288, Carmel Valley, CA 93921; or call (408) 659-4000.

Big Sur Coast

The 90-mile drive along the Big Sur coast on State 1 from Carmel to San Simeon, site of Hearst Castle, takes several hours. The two-lane road (built in the 1930s) dips and rises, clinging precariously to the seaward face of the Santa Lucia Mountains as it follows the rugged coastline.

One dramatic vantage point is just a few miles southwest of Carmel at Bixby Creek Bridge, 260 feet above the creek bed. Park your car and walk out to an observation alcove for a view of the surf, beach, and headlands. In winter, you'll often see California gray whales on their annual migration south to Baja California.

Along the route you'll pass other lookouts, too: cliff-perched eating places like Rocky Point, Nepenthe (where Henry Miller lived and wrote and Rita Hayworth and Orson Welles honeymooned), and Ventana Inn (an exclusive hideaway resort).

The village of Big Sur has several rustic resorts, grocery stores, restaurants, and shops. The Coast Gallery (center for local artisans) maintains two showrooms.

For additional information on area attractions, hotels, and activities, contact Big Sur Chamber of Commerce, Box 87, Big Sur, CA 93920; (408) 667-2156.

Parks along the way

Some of the finest meetings of land and water occur in four state parks along this coast. Two offer camping, but you have to walk in to one of them. For state park campsite reservations, call MISTIX, (800) 444-7275. For information on wilderness area camping sites in Los Padres National Forest, call (408) 385-5434.

Point Sur State Historic Park. Point Sur Lighthouse, rising on a headland of rock high above the surf, was completed in 1889. Guided tours (small fee) take place on Saturday and Sunday, weather permitting. For tour details, call (408) 625-4419. Parking at the lighthouse is limited; only 15 cars are admitted at a time.

Tours take 2 to 3 hours and include a half-mile hike with a 300-foot climb; for additional information, see page 77.

Andrew Molera State Park. You have to park your car along the road and hike into this 2,088-acre park along the lower section of the Big Sur River. Somewhat primitive campsites (chemical toilets, no showers) are available on a first-come, first-served basis (small fee). Fire-control roads make it easy to get around this preserve of redwoods, rocky bluff, meadowland, and sandy beach.

Pfeiffer Big Sur State Park. Though it isn't large (821 acres of river flats and canyons in the middle of Big Sur), this is one of the state's most popular nonbeach parks. In summer, you'll need advance reservations for its 218 riverside campsites (no hookups). For additional details, see page 121.

The most scenic public ocean beach in the Big Sur area is 2-mile-long Pfeiffer Beach (not part of the park), accessible from Sycamore Canyon Road just to the south.

Julia Pfeiffer Burns State Park. Among the attractions of this day-use park are a dramatic waterfall, redwood groves, and vantage points for viewing gray whales during their winter migration. You'll also find 2 miles of scenic coastline and upcountry canyons laced with trickling creeks.

Nearly 2 miles north of the park, a small parking area marks the entrance to Partington Cove. On your walk down the hill you cross a footbridge and pass through a 50-foot solid-rock tunnel. Scuba diving is popular at the cove, but you need a permit; check with the ranger at Pfeiffer Big Sur State Park (above).

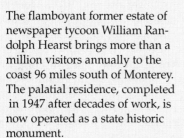

Hearst Castle

The flamboyant former estate of newspaper tycoon William Randolph Hearst brings more than a million visitors annually to the coast 96 miles south of Monterey. The palatial residence, completed in 1947 after decades of work, is now operated as a state historic monument.

Hearst Castle crowns a hillside above the town of San Simeon on State 1. Four guided tours award glimpses of a lifestyle that once rivaled those of the media mogul's celebrity guests.

Tour 1, best introduction to the 123-acre estate, covers the gardens, guest house, pools, and main floor of Hearst's residence.

Tour 2 covers the main building's upper floors, including Hearst's private quarters and libraries, guest rooms, and kitchen.

Tour 3 takes in the guest wing, a guest house, gardens, pools, and home movie theater. From April through October, another tour visits the wine cellar, pools, underground vaults, and bowling alley.

The castle is open daily except New Year's, Thanksgiving, and Christmas. Each tour costs $12 ($6 children), lasts about 2 hours, and requires considerable walking and climbing.

Some tickets are available on a first-come, first-served basis, but advance reservations are recommended. Call or visit any MISTIX outlet; in California, the toll-free number is (800) 444-7275; from out of state, phone (619) 452-1950.

Perched on a cliff overlooking the Big Sur coast, Nepenthe restaurant is a favorite watering hole for locals and tourists. It was built in 1944 as a honeymoon cottage for Orson Welles and Rita Hayworth.

In & Around Salinas

Salinas, the heart of the valley dubbed the "salad bowl of the world," is also the birthplace of Nobel and Pulitzer prize–winning novelist John Steinbeck (1902–1968). The city and surrounding valley provided local color for Steinbeck novels such as *East of Eden.*

Visit the John Steinbeck Library, 110 W. San Luis Street, to learn about the writer's life and works. The library is open 10 A.M. to 9 P.M. Monday through Thursday, from 10 A.M. to 6 P.M. Friday and Saturday. Steinbeck's home, a gracious two-story Victorian at 132 Central Avenue, has been restored and opened as a luncheon restaurant and gift shop; for reservations, call (408) 424-2735.

Historical museums. Two of the city's oldest buildings contain county artifacts and photographs. The Boronda Adobe (open weekdays from 9 A.M. to noon and weekends from 1 to 4 P.M.) stands at the intersection of Boronda Road and Calle del Adobe in northwest Salinas; take Laurel Drive exit from U.S. 101. Admission is free.

The Harvey-Baker House (home of the city's first mayor) at 238 E. Romie can be toured from 1 to 4 P.M. the first Sunday of each month. For more information, call the Monterey County Historical Society, (408) 757-8085.

Rodeo. The wild West is alive and well in Salinas when the California Rodeo comes to town the third weekend in July. More than 700 competitors participate in the state's largest rodeo, culmination of a week-long celebration with thoroughbred racing, parades, barbecues, and hoedowns. For tickets and schedule information, contact the California Rodeo Office, P.O. Box 1648, Salinas, CA 93902; (408) 757-2951.

Three missions

Three of California's original Spanish missions are short detours off U.S. 101 in the Salinas Valley. Popular Mission San Juan Bautista is north of Salinas; Soledad and San Antonio de Padua lie to the south.

San Juan Bautista. About 21 miles north of Salinas, 3½ miles east of U.S. 101, is the town of San Juan Bautista, where Father Fermin Lasuen founded a mission in 1797. Its success was due largely to the energy and zeal of two other friars. Father Felipe del Arroyo, a linguistic whiz, preached to the Indians in seven dialects and even taught them the writings of Plato and Cicero. Father Estevan Tapis was an ebullient musician; by depicting different musical parts in brightly colored notes, he formed Indian choirs that continued his legacy for 40 years.

Restored mission buildings still overlook the valley, but the frame structures that stand shoulder-to-shoulder along 3rd Street in the old town—a state historic park since 1933—now house shops, galleries, and other attractions. To add to the ambience of the mid-1860s, power lines have been laid underground and vintage lighting installed. On the first Saturday of every month, state park personnel don period attire.

Among the historic sites open for touring are the 1840 Castro-Breen adobe, the Plaza Hotel (built in 1858), the two-story Plaza Hall (formerly a combination residence and dance hall), the Plaza Stable (blacksmith's shop, carriages, and wagons on display), the jail, and an early settler's cabin. Several of the buildings charge admission.

Soledad. Some 25 miles south of Salinas stands Mission Nuestra Señora de la Soledad, California's 13th mission, founded by Father Fermin Lasuen in 1791.

This mission reached its peak in 1820, but life was hard in this remote area, and by the 1830s the mission personified its name, "loneliness." When Father Vicente Francisco de Sarria died in 1835, the mission was officially closed. Winds and rain later reduced the adobe structure to crumbling ruins, but the chapel and the wing where the friars resided have been rebuilt.

The mission is west of U.S. 101 near the junction of Mission and Fort Romie

roads. You can visit between 10 A.M. and 4 P.M. daily except Tuesday.

San Antonio de Padua. Father Serra founded this mission near King City in 1771. Though somewhat isolated in the middle of a military reservation, it's a rewarding place to visit. Some of the original tiles still top the roof of the restored mission. Besides the chapel, you'll see a water-powered grist mill, a tannery, an original wine vat, and early artwork.

To get to the mission, turn south from U.S. 101 at the Jolon Road (County G14) exit; it's about 18 miles farther.

Winery trails

Stretching along U.S. 101 from Morgan Hill to Greenfield and west along State 152 between Gilroy and Watsonville across the Hecker Pass, wineries cluster like so many grapes on the vine. Not all are open for tours, but most offer daily tasting.

Monterey Vineyard at Gonzales has good tours of its sprawling facilities. But what makes it an interesting stop is the gallery housing Ansel Adams' *Story of a Winery*, photographs shot in Monterey and Santa Clara counties between 1960 and 1963.

The winery is open from 10 A.M. to 5 P.M. daily, with tours on the hour from 11 A.M. to 4 P.M. Exit U.S. 101 on Gloria Road and go west to Alta; turn north to the winery.

State 152 from Gilroy (not recommended for trailers and RVs) is a gateway to scenic sites and picnic grounds. Just after passing A. Conrotto Winery, you'll come to Goldsmith Seed Company's test fields, a brilliant sight from late spring through summer. Due west the D'Arigo Cactus Pear Farm comes into view (no tours).

Wineries along State 152 include Fortino (excellent Italian deli), Hecker Pass, Thomas Kruse, Kirigin, Live Oak, and Sarah's Vineyard. All have pleasant tasting rooms and picnic grounds. At the top of the pass, Mount Madonna County Park (day-use fee) is another option; from Mount Madonna Inn you can see to the ocean.

Two state parks

Among nearby camping spots is Fremont Peak State Park, a rich historic and botanical area 11 miles south of San Juan Bautista on the San Juan Canyon Road (day-use and overnight fees). A winding road leads up to an observatory, open to the public on selected Saturdays for viewing through a 30-inch telescope; call (408) 623-4255.

Henry W. Coe State Park, 14 miles east of Morgan Hill on East Dunne Avenue, is little known and usually uncrowded (fee). The park headquarters occupy old ranch buildings perched at 2,600 feet. When wildflowers bloom, scores of would-be Monets flock to the park's rolling, grassy hills, their paints and canvases in hand. You'll find picnic tables and a few campsites.

Pinnacles National Monument

Laced with a surprising variety of trails, Pinnacles National Monument's spectacular spires and crags rise to 1,200 feet above the canyon floors, presenting a sharp contrast to the surrounding countryside. Below the ground lies a chain of caves.

This rugged territory, a remnant of ancient volcanic action, is a magnet for mountain climbers, hikers, and spelunkers (carry your own flashlight or buy one at the visitor center). A brochure showing the trail network (15 cents) is a good investment.

There are two entrances to the park, but no through roads. The best way to get there is from the east on State 25 through Hollister, then turn west on State 146 to the privately owned Pinnacles Campground; call (408) 389-4462 for reservations. The park's east entrance and visitor center lie just beyond.

To reach the west entrance, visitor center, and more primitive park-operated Chaparral Campground, exit U.S. 101 at Soledad and drive east on State 146 (too narrow for RVs). For information on campsites, turn to page 120.

Summer at the monument is *hot*.

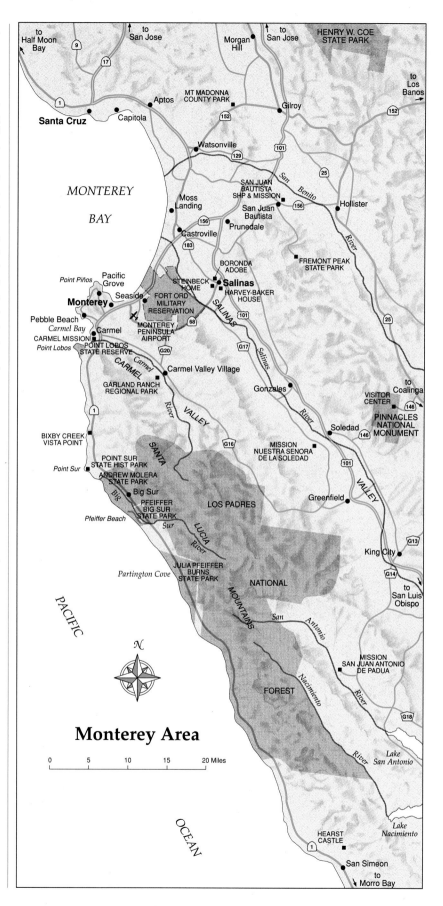

Monterey Area

Wine Country

North of San Francisco lie the valleys and hills synonymous with California wine. Some 3 million people visit the bucolic Napa and Sonoma valleys each year, primarily to watch the winemaking process and sample the results. This venerable wine district contains most of the state's best-known cellars and attractions, although Sonoma County's Alexander Valley and Russian River areas and the emerging Mendocino and Lake county districts are challengers.

The whole area abounds with other activities, too, from mud baths and swimming pools to quiet fishing lakes and flat viney byways ideal for cycling. You can ride in a hot-air balloon, tour by train, and browse through a multitude of intriguing galleries and shops.

Geography and climate combine in the Napa and Sonoma regions to create ideal grape-growing conditions. Wine was produced in the area as early as 1780 by Franciscan monks who planted cuttings from European grape stock. But it is Hungarian winemaker Agoston Haraszthy, who in 1857 introduced a number of European varietals at his Buena Vista Winery in Sonoma, who is widely credited as being the father of the state's wine industry.

Planning a trip

You *could* visit 20 cellars a day. But you would miss the details—and details are what make wine. Experienced travelers limit themselves to three, or at most four stops a day.

This chapter mentions major wineries and others with outstanding archi-

You have to get up early for this bird's-eye view of Napa Valley vineyards. Hot-air balloons lift off shortly after dawn.

tecture, gardens, or another particular reason to visit. For a complete list of visitable wineries, check with the tourist bureaus listed at right. The Sunset book *Wine Country California*, a guide to all the state's wineries, makes a valuable companion.

Getting there. Napa and Sonoma lie only some 15 miles apart, about 1½ hours from San Francisco. Napa County sandwiches neatly between U.S. 101 to the west and Interstate 80 to the southeast. State Highways 12, 29, 37, 121, and 128 connect the valley in various ways to the two freeways.

U.S. 101 also serves as entrée to Sonoma wineries. Sonoma and Napa valleys combine easily via State 12/121, through the Carneros Valley, and State 128, through Alexander and Knights valleys.

. There's Greyhound bus service to both Napa and Sonoma valleys, and to towns along U.S. 101.

Dining and lodging. The wine country lends itself to lazy lunches; bring along a picnic basket or stop at bakeries, delis, and cheese shops along the way. Many wineries offer picnic sites; several have dining rooms. Virtually all have wine for sale. A wealth of intimate inns and romantic—and highly acclaimed—dining spots make it possible to extend wine forays.

When to go. A wine country visit can be rewarding at any time of the year. Spring is the most picturesque season, autumn (the time of the crush) the most dramatic. In winter, vintners may have more time to explain the steps from vine to wine. And, though summer temperatures can soar, that's when you'll find the most visitor activities.

Most wineries are open daily year-round. To avoid crowds, schedule a midweek visit and include cellars off the main highways.

Touring & tasting

Wineries vary in size from tiny family-run cellars requiring advance appointments to large operations with formal tours, tasting rooms, and gift shops. Old-line cellars with developed tours make good targets for newcomers to wine touring. Some wineries discourage visits due to size and staff limitations or remote location.

Touring and tasting used to be almost synonymous. Now, with many wineries often swamped with visitors, tasting is no sure bet. Where it is offered, visitors sample only two or three vintages, and there's often a fee to sip at Napa Valley cellars.

Contacts

These agencies offer information on attractions and accommodations. See additional contacts throughout this chapter.

Napa Valley Conference & Visitors Bureau
1556 1st St.
Napa, CA 94559
(707) 226-7459

Sonoma Valley Visitors Bureau
453 1st St. East
Sonoma, CA 95476
(707) 996-1090

Sonoma County Convention & Visitors Bureau
10 4th St., Suite 100
Santa Rosa, CA 95401
(800) 326-7666; (707) 575-1191

Napa Valley

Cradled between the redwood-forested Mayacamas Mountains to the west and the oak- and pine-studded Vaca Range on the east, the Napa Valley is only 30 miles long and 3 miles across at its widest point. Yet the little valley boasts some 220 wineries, many open for touring or tasting. A 24-hour hotline gives up-to-date information on wines and events; call (707) 963-1112.

The greatest concentration of wineries flanks State 29 north from Napa to Calistoga. To avoid the traffic that fills this main thoroughfare, knowledgeable travelers use the Silverado Trail, a scenic, winery-lined parallel road along the eastern edge of the valley. Crossroads among the vineyards connect the two arteries.

Though the city of Napa is by far the largest (53,000), each of the valley towns has its charms. In Calistoga you find spas and geysers; St. Helena claims many of the region's best dining and lodging choices as well as a wine library and the Silverado Museum; and Yountville offers dozens of shops, eating spots, and galleries, many tucked into a great brick winery.

Outside of these towns lie more wineries, markets, inns, quiet picnic spots, and historic parklands.

Plotting your route. Most visitors start a winery tour from the south end of the valley; you might consider reversing the order. Beginning in Calistoga gives you an opportunity to visit cellars such as Sterling, Chateau Montelena, and Clos Pegase that you might miss if you're here for only a day.

An alternative tour option, though you only clickety-clack past wineries, is the Napa Valley Wine Train, beautifully refurbished albeit controversial (residents resent its intrusion). See page 126 for details.

For yet another view, go aloft in one of the colorful hot-air balloons that brighten the sky above the valley vineyards. Balloon companies operate out of several valley towns; check with the Napa Valley Conference & Visitors Bureau (address on page 59).

Napa & Carneros region

The city of Napa is skirted by major highways and often passed unnoticed by motorists. A century ago, when the Napa River served as a main transportation route to the valley, it was a bustling port. The Napa Riverboat Co. lets you see the area as the oldtimers did—from the water (see page 125).

A walk down Napa's Main Street gives you a look at the refurbished historic downtown. Near the riverside park at 2nd Street, you can sip gourmet coffee or enjoy an alfresco lunch. For self-guided walking tours or to arrange a guided walk (small fee), stop at Napa County Landmarks (1144 Main Street), open Monday, Wednesday, and Friday from 8 A.M. to 5 P.M. To learn about valley history, go by the free historical society museum at 1219 1st Street, open noon to 4 P.M. Tuesday and Thursday.

Wineries. Just west of Napa, the Carneros district on the northern shores of San Pablo Bay is the first wine-growing region you pass if you're coming from San Francisco on State 12/121. The showplace of the region, Domaine Carneros (1240 Duhig Road), was built by the Taittinger sparkling wine people. You tour and taste (fee) in a replica of a Loire Valley chateau. Handicapped access avoids the steps from the parking lot.

The Hess Collection Winery (4411 Redwood Road) lies in the mountains 8 miles northwest of Napa. It's worth the trip to take a self-guided tour of this handsome winery, a former Christian Brothers novitiate, and multilevel modern art gallery. An excellent 20-minute wine film is shown in a small theater. Tasting is extra.

Yountville area

Named for George Yount, Napa Valley's first white settler, Yountville is chockful of quaint shops, lodging choices (Napa Valley Lodge and Vintage Inn are the largest), and historic sites. Vintage 1870, housed in on old brick winery, has be-

come a rural Ghirardelli Square shopping complex (shops, restaurants, bakery, tasting room). Two other specialty shopping areas lie just off the highway nearby, as do such trend-setting restaurants as Domaine Chandon (within the winery of the same name), French Laundry, Mustards Grill, Piatti, and the Diner.

Historic sites. Yount's final resting place is in the Pioneer Cemetery off Jackson Street, hard by the land in which he planted the valley's first vines in the 1850s. A free museum in the century-old Veterans Home west of the freeway is open noon to 2 P.M. Wednesday through Sunday.

Wineries. Architecture is one reason to visit historic Trefethen Vineyards (reached via Oak Knoll Avenue south of town) and Monticello Cellars (just east on Big Ranch Road). Trefethen's redwood winery was built a century ago, while Monticello, a replica of Thomas Jefferson's home, is a relative newcomer. Both wineries are open daily from 10 A.M. to 4:30 P.M.

French-owned Domaine Chandon (1 California Drive, just west of State 29) offers hourly tours explaining the manufacture of sparkling wine. Also at the sophisticated facility are a tasting center (fee), a restaurant (reservations usually required), and a small museum.

On the Silverado Trail east of Yountville, stop by S. Anderson (at Yountville Cross Road) to tour wine-aging caves carved from volcanic rock. Across the street, a huge red metal sculpture marks the entrance to Robert Sinskey Vineyards.

Oakville & Rutherford

Grand wine estates in this wide, flat part of the valley make the landscape around these two crossroads particularly impressive. You get a good look at the valley floor from Auberge du Soleil, an elegant inn and restaurant at 180 Rutherford Hill Road east of the

Silverado Trail. The Oakville Grocery (on State 29) offers the area's best one-stop shopping for picnic supplies.

Wineries. One of the best overviews of the wine-making process is given at Robert Mondavi Winery (west of State 29 at Oakville). Avoid this popular stop on weekends, when you need an advance reservation to tour. The winery's handsome artwork includes a Beniamino Bufano sculpture.

Other worthwhile winery stops along State 29 include historic Inglenook, venerable Beaulieu, and Franciscan's tasting center. East of the highway between Oakville and Rutherford, St. Supéry boasts both a state-of-the-art winery and a restored Queen Anne Victorian containing a wealth of Napa Valley history.

Guided tours of Mumm's extremely pleasant Napa Valley facility (8445 Silverado Trail) give a good look at sparkling wine production. Tasting takes place on an enclosed porch overlooking the vineyards.

St. Helena

The 1890s look of St. Helena's Main Street is proudly maintained by the city's 5,000 residents, and so is the town's century-old emphasis on wine. A small hotel, Meadowood resort (off Silverado Trail), and many inns offer lodging. Bay Area travelers often come just to dine in such eateries as Terra, Trilogy, and Tra Vigne. You can buy picnic fixings at the Model Bakery on Main Street, the Olive Oil Company (835 McCorkle Avenue), and V. Sattui Winery's deli (1111 White Lane). The latter also offers underground caves to tour and shady picnic sites.

Attractions. A major collection of wine literature, assembled by the Napa Valley Wine Library Association, takes up part of the town library 2 blocks west of Main on Adams Street. A separate wing of the library contains the free Silverado Museum, a large display of Robert Louis Stevenson memorabilia (noon to 4 P.M. daily except Monday).

The peripatetic author honeymooned in an abandoned bunkhouse of the defunct Silverado Mine on Mount St.

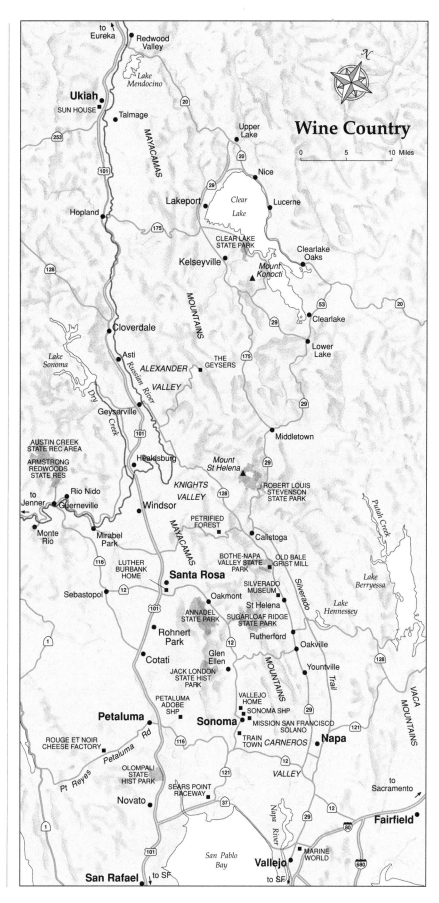

...Napa Valley

Helena in 1880–81. He recounted that experience in *Silverado Squatters*.

Wineries. Beringer, Christian Brothers, and Charles Krug, three romantic old wineries on State 29 north of town, offer complimentary tours and tastings. Even if you're only marginally interested in wine, you'll enjoy the historic structures. South of St. Helena on State 29 lie Louis M. Martini (tours and tasting) and Heitz (tasting only). Spring Mountain Vineyards (2805 Spring Mountain Road west of town) is the winery of *Falcon Crest* television fame.

Calistoga

The town situated at the foot of looming Mount St. Helena has long been famous as a center for health and relaxation. Thousands of tourists slither into mud baths and slide into mineral pools here every year. They've been arriving ever since millionaire entrepreneur Samuel Brannan built the first local spa in 1859. The unique Sharpsteen Museum at 1311 Washington Street gives you a free look at those early days. It's open 10 A.M. to 4 P.M. in summer, noon to 4 P.M. the rest of the year.

Lodging choices include bed-and-breakfast inns and the refurbished Mount View Hotel. A glider port, one-of-a-kind shops, and dozens of restaurants invite lingering. Calistoga Mineral Water and Crystal Geyser bottling plants downtown welcome visitors during working hours. For information on other attractions, contact the Calistoga Chamber of Commerce, 1458 Lincoln Avenue, (707) 942-6333.

Diversions. The Old Bale Grist Mill, off State 29 just south of Calistoga, takes visitors back to 1846, a time when wheat, not grapes, was the basis of the local economy. The 1-acre historic park (admission fee) is open daily from 10 A.M. to 5 P.M.; the immense overshot waterwheel actually grinds corn weekends at 1 and 4 P.M.

California's "Old Faithful" geyser spews steam and vapor skyward at about 40-minute intervals. The geothermal field on Tubbs Road about 1½ miles north of town (turn east from State 128) is open daily (small charge).

Wineries. Sterling Vineyards (1111 Dunaweal Lane east of State 29) provides an aerial tram ($5) to get up to its hilltop winery. Self-guided tours show winery works; the tasting room overlooks the upper Napa Valley.

Down the road, striking Clos Pegase winery's entrance leads you through an atrium; self-guided tours include a gallery and aging caves. Drop in for tours and tasting at longtime favorite Hanns Kornell Champagne Cellars (1091 Larkmead Lane east of State 29), and explore Vintners Village (west side of the highway), a collection of premium winery tasting rooms, shops, restaurants, and picnic grounds.

Hiking & camping

Hiking and cycling are good ways to get around the valley floor; heading up into the encircling hills provides plenty of exercise.

Bothe–Napa Valley State Park. About 4 miles north of St. Helena, this vast parkland with more than 1,000 acres of broad-leafed trees and second-growth redwoods extends west into the hills from State 29. Facilities include hiking trails and a swimming pool. For campsite reservations (April to October), phone MISTIX, (800) 444-7275.

Robert Louis Stevenson State Park. Eight winding miles north of Calistoga, this 3,000-acre undeveloped site sprawls along the eastern slopes of Mount St. Helena. A fire trail leads to the remnants of the author's cabin and the old Silverado Mine, continuing 4 miles to the 4,334-foot summit.

A Trio of Lakes

Three of the wine country's largest bodies of water attract anglers, water-skiers, and boaters.

Clear Lake. Anglers looking for trophy-sized bass head for Clear Lake in the spring, but a summer water temperature of 76° brings flocks of water-skiers and boaters to the 110 miles of shoreline at the state's largest lake (Tahoe is larger but is shared with Nevada). You can rent boats at resorts.

Clear Lake State Park on Soda Bay Road northeast of Kelseyville makes a good first stop. The center has geology exhibits, slide shows, and an aquarium. Kelsey Slough, a lush inlet snaking through the park, offers secluded bank-fishing sites and a remarkable array of birds. Four campgrounds accommodate tents and recreational vehicles; see page 121. The most direct route from the Bay Area (about 120 miles) is State 29 through Napa Valley.

Lake Berryessa. A popular year-round fishing hole in the dry hills separating the Napa and Sacramento valleys, Berryessa is best explored by boat. Launches are spaced at close intervals from Markley Canyon near the dam up to Putah Creek. In summer, anglers give way to skiers and motorboats.

All of the modest development, ranging from campsites to motels, lies along 12 miles of the west shore. Call (707) 966-2111 for information. Easiest access with a boat or camper is from Interstate 80.

Lake Sonoma. About 11 miles northwest of Healdsburg, massive Warm Springs Dam created the Lake Sonoma Recreation Area. A visitor center (open daily in summer, Thursday through Monday the rest of the year) gives a good overview of this fishing, boating, and swimming haven. Tent and RV camps and boat-in sites are on a first-come, first-served basis. A private marina offers boat rentals.

The most direct route from U.S. 101 is Canyon Road from Geyserville.

Picturesque Hop Kiln Winery in the Russian River area near Healdsburg recalls an era when Sonoma County was known more for growing hops than grapes. The 1905 stone kiln is a state historic landmark (tasting daily, tours by appointment).

Valley of the Moon

Historically, Sonoma is one of the state's most interesting towns. Site of Mission San Francisco Solano, last and northernmost of the 21 missions founded by the Franciscans in California, the Sonoma pueblo was also headquarters for General Mariano Vallejo, the Mexican administrator at the time of the Bear Flag Revolt in 1846.

Sonoma is also where Agoston Haraszthy laid the groundwork for some premium California wines at his Buena Vista winery. And it was the last home of author Jack London, who gave the valley its romantic "Valley of the Moon" name.

Sonoma Valley lies 45 miles north of San Francisco. From U.S. 101, take State 37 east to an intersection with State 121, which heads north toward the town of Sonoma. One more turn onto State 12, clearly marked, leads you right to the town plaza.

The main approach from the north is State 12, cutting inland from U.S. 101 at Santa Rosa. Coming from the east on Interstate 80, you turn west onto State 12 and follow the signs.

Sonoma Valley wineries

Two separate clusters of wineries are open to visitors. One begins in Sonoma town and stretches a mile or two east. The other lies north toward the head of the valley. In or near Sonoma: Sebastiani (sizable, with tours and tasting), Buena Vista (tours and tasting), Gundlach-Bundschu (tasting), and Haywood and Hacienda (tasting, picnic areas). Gloria Ferrar's champagne center (tours and tasting) lies southeast of town off State 121.

To the north, from Glen Ellen to Kenwood: Valley of the Moon (old-line family cellar), Glen Ellen (self-guided tour), Smothers Brothers, St. Francis, and Grand Cru. The Wine Gallery in Kenwood offers tastings of Caswell and Las Montanas vintages. Chateau St. Jean (self-guided tour, tasting, picnic sites) has a free "Wineline" reporting on valley grape crops and specific releases; call (800) 332-WINE.

In & around Sonoma

Historic sites, hotels, restaurants, and craft and food shops surround the town's central plaza. Of several annual events staged on the plaza, the Vintage Festival in September and the Ox Roast in June are the most famous.

Pick up a walking tour map from the Sonoma Valley Visitors Bureau office on the plaza. Parking is behind the Sonoma Barracks; turn in from 1st Street East just beyond Spain Street.

Dining and lodging. Two restored city hotels, El Dorado and Sonoma, face the plaza. Nearby are bed-and-breakfasts, motels, and the upscale Sonoma Mission Inn & Spa (north on State 12 in Boyes Hot Springs).

Dining choices in town include popular La Casa (across from the mission) and the two hotel restaurants. Out of town, head to the spa for an elegant meal or to the historic Grist Mill Inn, off State 12 in Glen Ellen.

Stroll around the plaza to assemble picnic fixings from the French Bakery, Sonoma Sausage Co., Sonoma Cheese Factory (or Vella Cheese Factory on 2nd Street East), and Wine Exchange.

History and trains. Across from the plaza's northeast corner stands the Sonoma Mission, founded July 4, 1823. Now part of Sonoma State Historic Park, it contains an outstanding museum collection (10 A.M. to 5 P.M. daily).

Several other park buildings can be toured for the single admission fee: the Sonoma Barracks, the servants' wing of Casa Grande (Vallejo's first home, mostly destroyed by fire in 1867), and General Mariano Vallejo's home (2 blocks west and north of the plaza on 3rd Street West). The adjacent warehouse (now a museum) was built in 1852 from timber and bricks shipped around Cape Horn.

Other historic buildings on the plaza include Blue Wing Inn (a gambling hall in the gold rush era), the Toscano Hotel, Swiss Hotel (now a restaurant), and the home of Salvador Vallejo.

Train Town, on State 12 about a mile south of the plaza, provides a change of pace. A 20-minute ride on a scale model railroad carries you through 10 acres of landscaped grounds with a stop at a replica of an old mining town. The park (admission charge) is open daily from 10:30 A.M. to 5:30 P.M. in summer, weekends from Labor Day to mid-June.

Into the hills

In the upper end of the valley, several state parks invite visitors to picnic, hike, and ride. Sugarloaf welcomes campers. In April and May these open spaces are carpeted with wildflowers.

Jack London State Historic Park. In the hills west of Glen Ellen, the House of Happy Walls, built by London's wife Charmian after his death in 1916, is a museum of the author's life (10 A.M. to 5 P.M. daily). At the end of a ¾-mile trail from the museum loom the rock walls of Wolf House, which burned before the couple could move into it. Nearby are London's grave, the ruins of his winery, his cottage, and several barns.

To reach the 803-acre park, open dawn to dusk daily, follow State 12 north about 6½ miles to Glen Ellen, then follow signs. There's a per-car admission.

Sugarloaf Ridge State Park. North of Kenwood, follow Adobe Canyon Road northeast from State 12 for 2 miles to a mountainous 2,500-acre park that was once a cattle ranch. Some 25 miles of trails crisscross the park, which has 50 campsites; reserve through MISTIX (800) 444-7275. There's a day-use fee.

Annadel State Park. First Pomo Indian land, then part of a Spanish rancho, this free 5,000-acre retreat boasts 35 miles of trails. The 3-mile hike to Lake Ilsanjo (no swimming or boating) is the most popular.

To reach the park, follow State 12 toward Santa Rosa; turn south on Los Alamos Road. At Channel Drive turn left and follow the signs.

Other Wine Valleys

Some of the most visitor-friendly wine districts stretch north from Santa Rosa to Ukiah alongside U.S. 101. Here, too, are the recreation-rich Russian River Valley, redwood groves, and charming towns. Backroads are good sources of fresh farm produce, Christmas trees, and handicrafts. For a free guide, write to Sonoma County Farm Trails, P.O. Box 6675, Santa Rosa, CA 95406.

Stops along U.S. 101

Santa Rosa and Healdsburg are gateways to the Russian River, Dry Creek, and Alexander Valley wine regions. Petaluma, to the south, is a quintessential small town, its setting used in such movies as *Peggy Sue Got Married* and *American Graffiti*.

Petaluma. Though it's now known for farms, Petaluma was once one of the country's foremost carriage-building centers. Prosperous times left an architecturally wealthy downtown; pick up a walking tour guide from the chamber of commerce (215 Howard Street). An old waterfront mill (6 Petaluma Boulevard) is now a warren of shops.

Four miles east of town at Adobe Road and Casa Grande Avenue lies Petaluma Adobe State Historic Park (open 10 A.M. to 5 P.M. daily; small admission), the restored headquarters of General Vallejo's old ranch. Nine miles southwest of town stands the venerable Rouge et Noir Cheese Factory (take C Street, which becomes the Pt. Reyes Petaluma Road). You can tour (10 A.M. to 4 P.M.), buy snacks, and picnic.

Santa Rosa. Sonoma County's largest city and county seat has an array of accommodations and good dining choices, such as John Ash & Co. next to the Vintners Inn amid the vineyards at the north end of town. Railroad Square, the restored and antique-filled historic district just west of the freeway, is worth a detour; browse along 4th and 5th streets west to the restored 1907 La Rose Hotel and the landmark 1870s-era stone train station.

Other highlights include the home and gardens of horticulturalist Luther Burbank. Guided tours of his furnished home (corner of Santa Rosa and Sonoma avenues) take place from 10 A.M. to 3:30 P.M. Wednesday through Sunday from April through mid-October (small fee). The free gardens are open daily from 8 A.M. to 5 P.M.

One block west, at 492 Sonoma Avenue, a chapel built from a single redwood appropriately houses the "believe it or not" Robert Ripley Museum of oddities (11 A.M. to 4 P.M. Wednesday through Sunday, small fee).

Healdsburg. Wineries, bed-and-breakfast inns, and a downtown plaza that almost rivals Sonoma's mark the town of Healdsburg, 14 miles north of Santa Rosa. Shops, restaurants, the Downtown bakery (don't miss the sticky buns), and small hostelries attract tourists and locals. You get a good idea of the town's past at a free museum at 221 Matheson Street, open noon to 5 P.M. except Sunday and Monday.

Russian River region. Northern Californian vacationers have long swarmed to the 12-mile stretch of river from Mirabel Park to Monte Rio to canoe, raft, splash, and sun. Today they also tour wineries.

The region (a popular gay vacation retreat) extends west to Jenner at the river's Pacific mouth. It has no one center, but Guerneville is its traditional hub, with most of the lodging and dining choices. You can make a leisurely loop trip on Eastside and Westside roads, which run on either side of the river from Healdsburg to Guerneville. The quickest approach to the river is to pick up River Road 4 miles north of Santa Rosa.

Canoeing. With a durable canoe or kayak, you can float between Asti/Healdsburg (canoe rentals) and Guerneville. The season runs from about April to October. Trips can last from 4 hours to 2 days. Take along food, water, and sun protection.

Parks. Two miles north of Guerneville sprawl the side-by-side Armstrong Redwoods State Reserve (a forest of ancient giants) and Austin Creek State Recreation Area (a 4,000-acre meadowland with springs and a fishing lake). Picnic sites nestle among the trees at Armstrong. Austin Creek has primitive campsites and an equestrian camp; for information on pack trips, call (707) 887-2939.

Wine touring

Several Russian River wineries offer tours, including Piper Sonoma (daily picnic lunches), Korbel, Mark West, and Rodney Strong. Others welcome tasters and provide picnic sites. Foppiano (near Healdsburg) is the area's oldest.

From Healdsburg north to Cloverdale, the tour roster includes William Wheeler, White Oak, Simi, and Chateau Souverain (noted restaurant). Trentadue and Geyser Peak (tasting only) have nice picnic facilities. West of U.S. 101 near Healdsburg lie Dry Creek, Robert Stemmler, and Lambert Bridge. Northwest of Cloverdale, Anderson Valley offers more wineries (page 76).

For another scenic setting, head southeast from Healdsburg on State 128 to the Alexander Valley, noted for its cabernet wines. Alexander Valley Fruit & Trading Co. (picnic baskets), Johnson's Alexander Valley, Alexander Valley Vineyards (gardens), and Field Stone (unusual architecture) are some taste choices.

Ukiah Valley boasts several easily visited wineries, among them Parducci (patriarch of Mendocino County cellars), Cresta Blanca, and Weibel. South at Hopland, don't miss Fetzer Vineyards' winery, gardens, and respected Sundial Grill.

A walker's guide to Ukiah's old homes is available at the Sun House, 431 S. Main Street. Once the home of painter Grace Carpenter Hudson, the building now contains her paintings and Indian artifacts (10 A.M. to 4 P.M. Wednesday through Saturday, noon to 4:30 P.M. Sunday; donations requested).

North Coast

Stretching almost 400 miles from San Francisco Bay to the southern border of Oregon, the virtually unspoiled North Coast delights sightseers. Sheer cliffs, pounding waves, rocky headlands, and photogenic offshore rocks characterize much of its shoreline. A national seashore, pocket beaches, and secluded coastal inlets invite visitors.

State 1, often termed the state's most beautiful highway, passes by Fort Ross (a former Russian fur-trading outpost), old fishing and logging ports, and weathered farmsteads and fences. Mendocino, an artists' mecca, is physically reminiscent of New England, while Eureka, a Victorian lumber town on U.S. 101, provides entrée to sheltered Humboldt Bay. And just to the north lies the soaring stillness of magnificent Redwood National Park.

A wealth of activities

It's near-impossible to list all the attractions of this stretch of Northern California. Anglers tussle with fighting steelhead where mighty rivers empty into the sea; campers choose between parks in sandy dunes or dense forest; and crowds of urbanites flock to unique rural festivals.

The charms of Mendocino and its bustling fishing and lumbering neighbor, Fort Bragg, rank high. To the north, trails through groves of mighty coast redwoods tempt hikers and backpackers, who pass fern-choked waterfalls, tranquil lagoons, and herds of Roosevelt elk munching in grassy meadows.

Planning a trip

To thoroughly explore the North Coast, you need a car. Only Eureka and Crescent City have regularly scheduled air service, and bus travel is similarly limited. It's easiest (and usually less expensive) to pick up a car in San Francisco; other areas may have no rental agencies.

Greyhound bus service is available to cities along U.S. 101, and from Cloverdale to Fort Bragg via State 128. Golden Gate Transit offers scheduled bus service from San Francisco to Point Reyes National Seashore.

Getting there. Heading north across the Golden Gate Bridge from San Francisco, you follow U.S. 101 (an inland route until it meets the ocean at Humboldt Bay) or take the slower, coast-hugging State 1. Backcountry roads connect these two parallel highways before they join at Leggett, just south of the redwood-lined Avenue of the Giants.

When to visit. Oddly enough, weather is usually foggy and cold along the coast during the summer, but winter often brings clear, warm days. The most sparkling days can occur in spring and autumn. Weekends are crowded almost year-round. For the most elbow room, time your visit for weekdays.

Where to stay. Historic hotels and charming bed-and-breakfast inns (many in Victorian residences) dot the coastline and are sprinkled around many interior towns (see page 72). Most motels congregate along U.S. 101, but you'll also find a number along State 1 near Point Reyes National Seashore, Tomales Bay, Bodega Bay, and from Mendocino to Fort Bragg.

For complete listings of lodging, contact the visitor bureaus listed at left. The California Office of Tourism also publishes a free guide to bed-and-breakfast inns; its address is on page 4. The American Automobile Association also puts out a guide to California inns for members.

Campers find a variety of sites throughout the region; for additional details, see pages 120 and 122. Advance reservations are required almost everywhere in summer and are recommended at any time of year.

Contacts

These agencies offer information on attractions and accommodations. See additional contacts throughout this chapter.

Marin County Visitors Bureau
30 N. San Pedro Rd., Suite 150
San Rafael, CA 94903
(415) 472-7470

Mendocino County Convention and Visitors Bureau
P.O. Box 244
Ukiah, CA 95482
(707) 462-3091

Redwood Empire Association
785 Market St., 15th Floor
San Francisco, CA 94103
(415) 543-8334

Sonoma County Convention and Visitors Bureau
10 4th St., Suite 100
Santa Rosa, CA 95401
(707) 575-1191

You'll descend three ramps and 307 steps (and then climb back up) to visit the squat iron tower of Point Reyes Lighthouse, in winter a popular whale-watching site.

Marin Beaches

As far as mariners are concerned, the Marin County shore from Point Reyes to the Golden Gate has little to recommend it. For them it's a treacherous obstacle to reaching San Francisco, composed of sea fogs, howling winds, reefs, and shoals.

But for shorebound creatures, it means something else: good rock-fishing, wave-watching, rockhounding, and clamming. In its shallow bays, the hardy even enjoy swimming. Only one remote beach is more than an hour from San Francisco, and some of the shore is barely 15 minutes away.

In spite of its proximity to the city, Marin's coast has not been subjected to any permanent overcrowding, because the terrain rises sharply skyward in many places. Development has also been discouraged by the creation of parks along all but a handful of miles of shoreline.

Marin's shores from the north end of the Golden Gate Bridge are practically all open to the public as part of the Golden Gate National Recreation Area, which extends as far north as Olema. The land is a mixture of former army forts, ruggedly undeveloped open areas, and once-private ranch lands.

Marin Headlands

Just minutes north of San Francisco, the Marin Headlands are now part of the Golden Gate National Recreation Area. Plummeting from bare-crested hills to deep water all along their length, the headlands stretch west from the Golden Gate Bridge to Point Bonita. The region offers protected coastal valleys, windswept beaches, former army forts, abandoned artillery bunkers, and magnificent views of San Francisco, the Golden Gate Bridge, and the Pacific Ocean.

For solitude, take a hike. The Miwok, Coast, and Tennessee Valley trails begin in the headlands and traverse the coastal hills. Kirby Cove (a pocket beach in the shadow of the bridge) and Rodeo Beach (a broad beach near the California Marine Mammal Rescue Center, opposite Bird Island) offer fine spots for a picnic. These beaches afford sweeping ocean views, but their waters are not safe for swimming.

To reach the headlands from San Francisco, take the Alexander Avenue exit off U.S. 101 and turn left, following the GGNRA signs toward Forts Baker, Barry, and Cronkhite. From the north, take the last exit before reaching the Golden Gate Bridge and follow the signs.

You loop through the area by following Conzelman Road along the bluffs beyond Point Bonita to Bunker Road. (A left turn on Bunker Road leads to the ranger station, for maps and information.) Bunker Road heads back from Rodeo Valley through a tunnel to U.S. 101.

A hostel at Fort Barry offers overnight facilities for a slight fee; call (415) 331-2777 for information.

Point Bonita light station. The old lighthouse perched on the eroding tip of the headlands is now open for weekend tours; for information, see page 77.

A prime weather station and warning point for the bay, it's a reliable gauge of the comings and goings of the summer fog bank. The islands in the distance are the Farallons, now protected as a national wildlife refuge.

The first sounding device installed at Point Bonita in 1856 to help befogged mariners was an army sergeant charged with firing a muzzle-loading cannon at half-hour intervals whenever the weather demanded. At the end of two months he was exhausted, and had to petition for relief.

Fort Cronkhite. This outermost of three sentinel forts on the north side of San Francisco Bay welcomes visitors. Reasons for making the trip are many: rockhounds roam the gravelled shore in search of jadeite and jasper (especially good pickings in winter); the summer crowd comes to bask in the lee of bluffs that offer some protection from the prevailing westerlies; and people who like to watch seabirds have a superior arena.

Along the coast

State 1 leads to Marin County's west coast. Earthquake damage in 1989 closed a section of the highway south of Stinson Beach, rerouting traffic via the Panoramic Highway on the shoulder of Mount Tamalpais (see page 37).

If you're going to Point Reyes and Tomales Bay, State 1 is best reached from U.S. 101 via Sir Francis Drake Boulevard (exit west at Greenbrae). Or you can take Lucas Valley Road from U.S. 101 north of San Rafael west past Nicasio, then west 6 miles farther on the Point Reyes–Petaluma Road.

Stinson Beach. This is the name not only of a small town but also of a day-use park that's now part of the Golden Gate National Recreation Area. Anglers do well fishing for ling cod, cabezone, and blenny at several rocky points toward the park's southern boundary.

Just opposite the town's entrance is a 4,500-foot-long swimming beach, its waters warmed by the shoal of Bolinas Bay. Swimming is permitted from late May to mid-September, when lifeguards are on duty and the weather is most temperate.

Audubon Canyon Ranch. About 3 miles north of Stinson Beach on State 1 lies a 1,000-acre bird sanctuary. On weekends and holidays from March through July 4, rookery outlooks (open 10 A.M. to 4 P.M.) afford close-up views of flocks of great blue herons and egrets. The birds nest in trees overlooking the Bolinas Lagoon.

Bolinas. Sitting just across from Stinson Beach on the mouth of a small lagoon, the artists' haven of Bolinas tries hard not to attract visitors (residents tear down direction signs)—but it gets them anyway. To get there, turn left at the foot of the lagoon, then left again immediately. Follow the road to the other side of the lagoon and make another left.

Duxbury Reef, a principal cause of the town's popularity, creates ideal conditions for surfing, tidepooling, clamming, and rock-fishing. Each end of the town's east-west main street dips down to a beach access. The one nearest Stinson Beach serves bass anglers and surfers; the westerly end is closest to the foot of Duxbury Reef.

Tomales Bay

Headquarters for the Point Reyes National Seashore (see right) is Bear Valley Visitor Center, about a half-mile west of Olema. Tomales Bay, north of the park, is a tranquil alternative.

En route to the 13-mile-long bay, State 1 passes through the small town of Point Reyes Station (an arts and crafts center). Just south of town, it crosses Sir Francis Drake Boulevard, which leads to Inverness (marina, restaurants, inns) on the west side of the bay.

About 1½ miles north on State 1, a parking lot marks one entrance to the bay's eastern edge. Walk west about a mile to the shore for good picnicking spots (no facilities) and views of the bird life in the marshland sanctuary below.

Tomales Bay State Park. Pierce Point Road leads into the park (small fee) and to protected Heart's Desire Beach, where you can spread a picnic blanket or take a half-mile marked nature trail to learn how native Miwok Indians used plants and dug for oysters around the bay. In addition to its shoreside charms, the park is a preserve for Bishop pines.

A county boat launch lies just south of the point where State 1 bends inland toward the town of Tomales. Beach areas all along the bay are accessible for cockling or fishing during the winter run of herring. You can buy oysters from one of the commercial growers in the tiny town of Marshall or enjoy a casual lunch at a cafe perched over the bay.

Dillon Beach. This raffishly charming summer village at the mouth of the bay is almost due west of Tomales on a spur road. Clamming for gapers on a low-tide island, fishing, and swimming (for the hardy only) are popular sports.

Point Reyes

Like a wild land apart, the windswept, triangular-shaped Point Reyes Peninsula juts into the Pacific Ocean 50 miles northwest of San Francisco. Its pine-forested hills, rolling pasturelands, and rocky, wave-battered beaches are all part of the 66,000-acre Point Reyes National Seashore.

Geologically speaking, Point Reyes is really an island of land (on the Pacific plate) divided from the mainland (on the American plate) by the San Andreas Fault that runs through the Olema Valley. Olema was the epicenter of the 1906 San Francisco earthquake, during which the Point Reyes Peninsula moved 20 feet northwestward.

Point Reyes is easily reached from U.S. 101 via Sir Francis Drake Boulevard or from State 1. It's about a 1½-hour drive from San Francisco.

U.S. Weather Bureau statistics cite Point Reyes as the foggiest and windiest spot, bar none, between Canada and Mexico. That goes for summer, too—so bring warm clothing. Ideal months for active outings are August, September, and October. From February through July, colorful wildflowers carpet the land.

Exploring the park. Begin your exploration at the Bear Valley Visitor Center (open 9 A.M. to 5 P.M. daily) off State 1 on Bear Valley Road, a short drive west of Olema; phone (415) 663-1092. Here you can get maps, trail guides, nature books, and schedules of nature programs.

You'll also find dioramas depicting the area's natural and cultural history. Nearby points of interest include two short hikes, the Earthquake Trail along the San Andreas Fault and the Woodpecker Nature Trail; a replica of a coastal Miwok Indian village; and a Morgan horse–breeding ranch.

Several paved roads lead to other sites within the park. Bear Valley is the gateway to more than 100 miles of trails, providing access to the park's remote beauty for hikers, bicyclists, and horseback riders. Horses can be rented at Five Brooks Stables, 4 miles south of Olema on Highway 1, and at Stewart's Horse Camp, on State 1 a quarter-mile north of the Five Brooks Trailhead.

No fees or permits are required for day use, but there are a few rules: don't bring dogs or other pets on trails, carry your own water, and stay back from the cliffs.

Wave-watching. This park's grandeur owes much to its varied seashore, popular for picnicking, strolling, beachcombing, and whale watching. Before beginning a beach walk, check the tide tables at the visitor center. Be alert for unexpectedly large waves and falling rocks from the steep cliffs.

A number of beaches dot the protected, curving crescent of Drakes Bay, considered by many historians the site of the first landing on this continent by an English explorer. Some claim that Sir Francis Drake arrived here in 1579 aboard his ship, the *Golden Hinde.*

Two Drakes Bay beaches of note are Limantour and Drakes, where you'll find the Kenneth C. Patrick Visitor Center, Drakes Bay Cafe, and sheltered picnic tables.

On Point Reyes Promontory, at the end of Sir Francis Drake Boulevard, stands Point Reyes Lighthouse and the Lighthouse Visitor Center (see page 77).

Bird-watching. Point Reyes Bird Observatory is the only full-time ornithological field research station on the continent. Here you'll see land birds, shorebirds, and waterfowl the year around. Located on the south end of the peninsula, the station is reached by Mesa Road from Bolinas.

Visitors tour the sturdy stockade at Fort Ross, a 19th-century North American outpost for Russian fur traders on the Sonoma Coast.

Sonoma Coast

Shorter and less developed than the Mendocino coast, its more famous neighbor to the north, the Sonoma coastline begins at Bodega Bay and runs north to the mouth of the Gualala River. Its principal attractions are a series of beach parks, awesome scenery, and Fort Ross, the last surviving sign of the 19th-century Russian settlements in California.

The Sonoma coast divides into three distinct parts: two lengths of coastal shelf divided by a file of steep hills marching into the sea. The shelves extend from Bodega Bay to Jenner on the south and from Fort Ross to Gualala on the north.

Getting there. State 1 continues north from Marin County through Mendocino County. More direct routes to the Sonoma coast from U.S. 101 are State 116, which winds along the Russian River from Guerneville through the re-created town of Duncans Mills to Jenner, or State 12, through the apple country around Sebastopol to the coast below Bodega Bay.

Lodging. Overnight accommodations are becoming more numerous along this scenic coastal stretch, though most still cluster around Bodega Bay and Jenner. It's wise to make reservations in advance. For a list of facilities, contact the Sonoma County Convention and Visitors Bureau (address on page 66).

Around Bodega Bay

The Bodega Bay-to-Jenner segment is the most developed and easiest to view. A gently sloping shelf permits State 1 to skirt a series of sandy beaches only 1½ hours from San Francisco.

Bodega Bay. Discovered by Spanish explorers in 1775, this harbor provides the only protected small-boat anchorage of any size between San Francisco and Noyo in Mendocino County. Both charter and commercial boats operate out of Bodega, chasing salmon from May to October and bottom fishing when salmon are scarce. If you're there in the early afternoon, watch a party fishing boat unload the day's catch at Spud Point Marina.

Perch feed in the lagoon shoals, especially along the western shore. Some gaper clams lurk along the shore, but most are clustered offshore on a low-tide island.

Outside the lagoon, surfers ride toward the spit, starting at a point 400 yards east of the breakwater. Rock fishers work the jetties and the exposed side of Bodega Head, a high, treeless knob at the northern end of the bay that's now part of the Sonoma Coast State Beach park. It's a good place to sight migrating gray whales from mid-December to mid-April.

Active children can romp endlessly in the rolling dunes that run all the way from the head north to Salmon Creek. A state campground at Bodega Dunes has more than 100 sites.

For information on shops, galleries, parks, restaurants, golf links, sport-fishing vessels, and lodging, contact the Bodega Bay Chamber of Commerce, 555 Coast Highway, Box 146, Bodega Bay, CA 94923, or call (707) 875-3422.

Sonoma Coast State Beach

Small coves, rocky headlands, and massive offshore rock stacks characterize Sonoma Coast State Beach. This collection of beaches and bays extends along State 1 from Bodega Bay to the mouth of the Russian River—over 14 miles of uninterrupted shore.

Beachcombers and anglers find this stretch fascinating. For a park brochure, stop at the entrance to Bodega Dunes or at park headquarters at Salmon Creek Beach.

Salmon Creek. About 1½ miles north of the town of Bodega, Salmon Creek forms an inviting summer wading pond. After autumn rains break down the sand bar, it becomes a spawning stream for salmon and steelhead. Lo-cal surfers, night smelters, and surf fishers use the outer beach. Sand dunes roll away to the south, crisscrossed by foot and bridle paths.

Duncan's Landing. A sign on this dangerous section of coast warns that a number of people have been swept to their deaths in a pounding sea by unexpectedly high waves. Yet there's plenty of safe rock fishing in other spots en route.

On sandy beaches, surf fishing and dip-netting for smelt are good. Duncan's Cove, just in the lee of the point, is one of the most productive day smelt beaches in the region.

Wrights Beach. North of Duncan's Landing, this beach is another camping unit for the state beach. It's also a favorite with picnickers, as much for its broad, sandy strand as for its facilities.

Goat Rock Beach. This site combines a protected cove with a long, sandy beach (which reaches out to form the mouth of the Russian River) and a sandy length of riverbank. Its northern end is a popular daytime beach with good smelt fishing in summer and steelheading in winter. The beach road forks off of State 1 near a long upgrade crest and descends across nearly a mile of meadows to sea level.

A Russian fort

Fort Ross is about 13 miles north of Jenner, where State 1 finally winds down from elevations that are either awe inspiring or terrifying, depending on the density of the sea fog and how you feel about steep dropoffs. You see the stout wooden buildings set high on the headlands before you reach them. The parking lot turnoff is just beyond the park.

The fort was originally the North American outpost for 19th-century Russian fur traders. Later, loggers and ranchers used the site. The Russians and Aleuts arrived in 1812 and stayed 30 years. During their sojourn these

Mellow old inns along the coast offer a warm welcome to travelers. From south to north, our sampling focuses on bed-and-breakfasts housed in vintage facilities from former farmhouses to a hospital. Rates vary (from $50 to more than $150 for two), depending on location and season. Prices include breakfast and other extras.

Book well in advance in summer and weekends year-round; most inns require 2-night stays on weekends. For a complete list of B & Bs, check with the county visitor bureaus and the California Office of Tourism (address on page 4). The American Automobile Association also publishes a free guide to B & Bs for members.

Bear Valley Inn, 88 Bear Valley Rd., Olema, CA 94950; (415) 663-1777. Two-story Victorian ranch house close to Point Reyes; full breakfast; 3 rooms (2 share bath).

Ten Inverness Way, Inverness, CA 94937; (415) 669-1648. Turn-of-the-century inn near national seashore; hot tub; 4 rooms.

Heart's Desire Inn, 3657 Church St., Occidental, CA 95465; (707) 874-1311. Mid-Victorian country residence; complimentary sherry; wheelchair accessible; 6 rooms, 1 suite with fireplace.

Murphy's Jenner Inn, 10400 State 1, Jenner, CA 95450; (707) 865-2377. Early Sonoma coast inn; ocean views; hot tub; complimentary aperitifs; 9 rooms, 3 suites, and 1 cabin, some with deck and fireplace.

Old Milano Hotel, 38300 State 1, Gualala, CA 95445; (707) 884-3256. Historic hotel opened in 1905; restaurant; hot tub; ocean views; 9 rooms (some share bath).

Coast Guard House, 695 Arena Cove, Point Arena, CA 95468; (707) 882-2442. Cape Cod–style house (1901) overlooking lighthouse; ocean or canyon views; continental breakfast; 6 rooms, (some share bath).

Elk Cove Inn, 6300 S. State 1, Elk, CA 95432; (707) 877-3321. Bluffside Victorian home and 4 ocean-view cottages with private beach access; 6 rooms, 2 with fireplace.

Harbor House, 5600 S. State 1, Elk, CA 95432; (707) 877-3203. Oceanside inn with private beach; full breakfast; 9 rooms, each with fireplace.

Fensalden Inn, 33810 Navarro Ridge Rd., (P.O. Box 99), Albion, CA 95410; (707) 937-4042. Restored 1860s stagecoach station 7 miles south of Mendocino; free hors d'oeuvres; 8 rooms, 6 with fireplace.

Glendeven, 8221 N. State 1, Little River, CA 95456; (707) 937-0083. New England–style farmhouse and converted barn; art gallery; 10 rooms and suites (2 share bath), 6 with fireplace.

Victorian Farmhouse, 7001 N. State 1, Little River, CA 95456; (707) 937-0697. Early Victorian near Mendocino and state parks; complimentary sherry; continental breakfast in room; 10 rooms, 6 with fireplace.

Agate Cove Inn, 11201 N. Lansing St., Mendocino, CA 95460; (707) 937-0551. Nineteenth-century farmhouse and cottages with sea views; complimentary sherry; 10 cottages, 9 with fireplace.

Brewery Gulch Inn, 9350 State 1, Mendocino, CA 95460; (707) 937-4752. Farmhouse (more than 130 years old) on 10 acres near town; full breakfast; 5 rooms (most share baths), 2 with fireplace.

John Dougherty House, 571 Ukiah St., Mendocino, CA 95460; (707) 937-5266. Cape Cod–style home in midst of the village; complimentary wine and chocolates; 6 rooms, 2 suites (2 with fireplace).

Joshua Grindle Inn, 44800 Little Lake Rd., Mendocino, CA 95460; (707) 937-4143. Two acres surrounding 1879 Victorian; full breakfast; 10 rooms, 6 with fireplace.

Gray Whale Inn, 615 N. Main St., Fort Bragg, CA 95437; (707) 964-0640. Large 1915 redwood building in heart of town near Skunk train depot; lounge; TV and game rooms; 14 rooms, 2 with fireplace, 4 overlooking ocean, 1 with jacuzzi and sun deck.

Bowen's Pelican Inn, 38921 N. State 1, (P.O. Box 35), Westport, CA 95488; (707) 964-5588. Turn-of-the-century hotel; restaurant and bar; 8 rooms (3 share bath).

Gingerbread Mansion, 400 Berding St., (P.O. Box AA40), Ferndale, CA 95536; (707) 786-4000. Well-photographed Queen Anne Victorian; English garden; afternoon tea; bicycles; 9 rooms, 3 with fireplace.

Shaw House Inn, 703 Main St., Ferndale, CA 95536; (707) 786-9958. Large yard surrounds 1854 gabled Gothic-style house; complimentary tea; 5 rooms (3 share bath).

Old Town Bed and Breakfast Inn, 1521 3rd St., Eureka, CA 95501; (707) 445-3951. Antique-furnished 1871 home in historic area; evening social hours; 5 rooms (2 share bath).

The Plough and The Stars, 1800 27th St., Arcata, CA 95521; (707) 822-8236. Midwestern-style 1860 farmhouse in suitable setting; croquet and horseshoes; 5 rooms (2 share bath), 1 with fireplace.

hunters, helped by their American and British rivals, wiped out the sea otter herds to the point of extinction.

Painstakingly restored and reconstructed after the 1906 earthquake and several later fires, the fort, which includes a tiny chapel, looks much as it must have originally. A modern visitor center's artifacts and displays illustrate the fort's colorful history, and the gift shop sells authentic Pomo basketry.

Free audio wands in the Rotchev house, the only Russian-built structure still standing in the compound, let visitors tune into the period simply by pointing at numbered listening posts.

The fort is open from 10 A.M. to 4:30 P.M. daily except Thanksgiving, Christmas, and New Year's; a small day-use fee is charged. Two holidays— Living History Day, July 22, and Ranch Day, on the last Sunday in September—attract many visitors. For more information, contact Fort Ross State Historic Park, 19005 Coast Highway 1, Jenner, CA 95450; phone (707) 847-3286.

A paved loop walk takes you to the bluff. From here, you can view rock fishers and rockhounds. The well-situated campground (see page 122) has redwoods and splendid views.

North to Gualala

From Fort Ross to Mendocino, the coastal shelf is narrow but gently sloping, sometimes wooded but mostly covered by meadow grass. Take along a picnic basket; restaurants are scarce. Immediately north of Fort Ross is the Timber Cove development. Walk around the seaward side of the hotel to look at sculptor Beniamino Bufano's last finished work, *Peace*.

Stillwater Cove County Park. Some 3½ miles north of Fort Ross is a day-use park much favored by scuba divers. Features include picnic tables, a canyon trail, and the old Fort Ross schoolhouse.

Salt Point State Park. Midway between Jenner and Stewarts Point, this park's rich environment makes it worth a stop. The strange offshore formations are sandstone columns eroded by

waves. The park has open and secluded campsites (see page 122), miles of hiking trails, an underwater park for scuba divers, small stands of pygmy pines and redwoods, and deer and other wildlife. For picnicking, head for Fisk Mill Cove.

Kruse Rhododendron State Reserve. This large preserve on Plantation Road 22½ miles north of Jenner is at its best from April to June, the peak blossom period. Sorry, no picnic tables.

Sea Ranch. The architectural contrast between the weathered buildings of tiny Stewarts Point (general store and schoolhouse) and this private development just up the road is striking. Built in 1868, Stewarts Point's general store is one of the oldest buildings along this stretch of coast; it has picnic food, tackle sales and rentals, bait, and eclectic oddities.

At modern Sea Ranch, award-winning houses, designed to blend into the landscape, are scattered around more than 5,000 acres of grassy beachlands and forested slopes. Sea Ranch Lodge has 20 rooms with fireplaces or ocean views, plus a restaurant. Many of the trend-setting residences also can be rented.

Six marked trails (Black Point is the most dramatic; Walk-On is wheelchair accessible) lead the public to the beaches. Note that the trails are open for day use only (small fee), and that parking lots are tiny (holding four to six cars and no RVs). No parking is allowed along State 1 or on Sea Ranch streets.

Gualala Point Regional Park. This 75-acre park just beyond the northern boundary of Sea Ranch occupies the headland and spit that form the south side of the Gualala River and mark the northern boundary of Sonoma County. You can camp beside the river in which Jack London liked to cast for steelhead, visit a small nature center (open weekends from Memorial Day to Labor Day), and scramble out along the often-windy point for ocean views.

St. Orres, a renowned restaurant and inn a few miles north of Gualala, is vaguely reminiscent of Fort Ross in its Russian-inspired architecture.

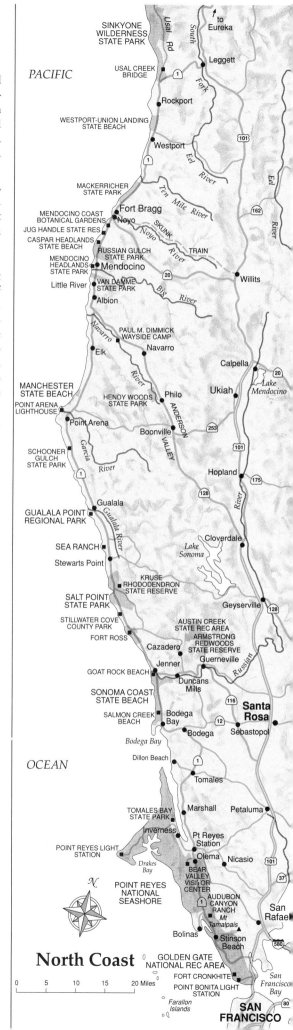

North Coast

0   5   10   15   20 Miles

Mendocino Coast

Summer fog doesn't daunt the thousands of annual visitors who come to enjoy the 19th-century charm and scenic beauty of Mendocino's splendid coast. Urbanization doesn't threaten yet either, thanks to environmental activism and the narrow, crooked roads. Towns are still small and spaced well apart.

Blue sea and white surf contrast with the area's deep green forests and weathered gray barns. In the 100 miles from Gualala to Rockport, the mood changes around every headland, making this stretch a photographer's paradise: even the gap-toothed fences are appealing.

For most visitors the heart of this rugged coast is the short distance between the art colony of Mendocino and Fort Bragg, terminus for the strangely named Skunk trains. At either end of this 11-mile stretch, you'll find less deep-sea fishing, Victoriana, and tourism, but more expansive beaches for strollers, driftwood hunters, and surf fishers.

Logging opened up the coast between Point Arena and Fort Bragg in the 1850s, and mill towns and ports sprang up along the ragged coastline. In the 1940s nearly 50 sawmills worked this stretch of coast; now sheep graze the once-forested beachlands.

Getting there. Most visitors feel they need at least 3 days to linger in comfortable old inns, browse among shops and galleries, and picnic on pebbly beaches.

The county's southern boundary is only 125 miles north of San Francisco, its northern one 250. And yet following sinuous State 1 from San Francisco to Fort Bragg takes about 6 hours.

If perusing Mendocino's art and charm is your goal, there's a delightful alternative route. Head north on U.S. 101 as far as Cloverdale, then take State 128 through the Anderson Valley, a 57-mile sequence of rolling hills parting around a tunnel of towering redwoods. It's about a 3½-hour drive from the Bay Area.

To the north, State 20 also offers coastal access, heading west from Willits. It parallels the route of the Skunk trains through 34 miles of fine stands of redwood and Douglas fir, and joins State 1 just south of Fort Bragg.

Accommodations. Most lodging is around Mendocino and Fort Bragg, though you'll find historic hotels or upscale inns at Gualala, Point Arena, Elk, Albion, Little River, Noyo, and Westport. Some choices are listed on page 72.

Reservations are essential in summer and are advisable all year. For a complete list of facilities, contact the Mendocino County Convention and Visitors Bureau (see page 66) or the Fort Bragg–Mendocino Coast Chamber of Commerce, P.O. Box 1141, Fort Bragg, CA 95437; phone (707) 964-3153.

Beach parks

Public beaches are scattered along the coast from Gualala to Fort Bragg. Ranging from flat, sandy coves to tunneled headlands, most offer fine camping or picnicking facilities and abundant scenery. For park information, write to Department of Parks and Recreation, Mendocino Area State Parks, P.O. Box 440, Mendocino, CA 95460. Reservations are made through MISTIX, (800) 444-7275. For more camping details, see page 122.

Schooner Gulch State Park. Newest and southernmost of the county's state beaches, Schooner Gulch is a little more than 11 miles north of the Gualala River. Picnickers can descend a trail to the driftwood-littered sands or climb to the top of the bluffs for a fine view.

Manchester State Beach. The last generous sand stretch south of Fort Bragg, this park's 7 miles of wide shore span most of the distance between Garcia River and Alder Creek. Middling good for sand castles, the beach is far roomier than the minimally developed campground, which is sheltered behind sand dunes from frequent winds. To the south lies Point Arena Lighthouse (see page 77).

Van Damme State Park. The beach side of this park on scenic Little River makes a pleasant wayside stop, but the main section (with campsites) is on the inland side of the highway. Activities include reasonably safe (but cold) swimming, skin diving, and cycling and hiking trails. One trail leads to an ancient forest of stunted conifers in the southeast quarter of the park (wheelchair access via Little River Airport Road).

Mendocino Headlands State Park. Beginning as a sandy beach at the mouth of Big River, this splendid park becomes a wall of rock looping west beneath the bluffs and then broadens to cover the flat fields of the headlands as well as their wave-swept edge. Heeser Drive, a loop road west of town, circles along the bluff's edge and extends down to the beach. Public fishing access is from the road's northern end.

This highly sculpted shore abounds with wave tunnels, arched rocks, narrow channels, and even a few lagoons. Skin divers fare well; tidepoolers should take a look-but-don't-touch attitude. For details, stop by the Ford House visitor center on Main Street.

Russian Gulch State Park. This parkland, which looks back at Mendocino across a broad bay from the next headland to the north, is a compacted replay of the sheltered beach at Van Damme and Mendocino's exposed headlands. A creek cutting out of the gulch pauses in a low, sandy spot, seemingly so that children can splash around in safety, and then slips into the sea in the lee of a craggy, lofty headland. A blowhole just north of the main overlook performs during storms.

From this dramatic boundary, the park runs deeply inland; protected campsites nestle in the mouth of a canyon. It's an easy hike upstream to a lacy waterfall set amidst a forest underlaid with beds of ferns.

Dining on the Noyo River at the southern end of Fort Bragg guarantees your "catch of the day" to be right off the boat.

MacKerricher State Park. North of Fort Bragg, where Pudding Creek empties into the sea, this versatile park (three campgrounds) includes headlands, beaches, heavily forested uplands, and a small lake for fishing and boating.

A road wanders down to the shore between a rocky beach to the south and a sandy one to the north. The chief reasons for heading out along the dunes are smelt fishing or driftwood hunting. You can get to the Ten Mile River end of the beach from an old logging road off State 1.

Mendocino

Startlingly in contrast to its time and place, this small cluster of wooden towers and carpenter's Gothic houses contains a contemporary society of artists and artisans. When you amble through the town's galleries, you'll see how they've translated the stunning setting into artworks.

Mendocino's top galleries may be the sprawling Mendocino Art Center (45200 Little Lake Street) and its offshoot, the Mendocino Art Center Showcase (560 Main Street). Both combine studios with rotating exhibits by local and international artists. Another good choice is Gallery Glendeven (next to the Glendeven Inn on State 1 about 1½ miles south of town).

Settled as a mill town in 1852 by timber baron Henry Meiggs, Mendocino may look like a Cape Cod relic (and indeed is a stand-in for Cabot Cove on the TV series *Murder, She Wrote*), but its weathered buildings are bursting with life: cleverly named shops, studios, restaurants, and inns.

You can drive around it in 10 minutes, but it's best to park your car and walk, picking up the free map available at most stores. The terrain is also easily covered by bike. But perhaps the best way to learn about town history is to stop by the Kelley House Museum, 45007 Albion Street. Besides being a repository of memorabilia, it serves as an unofficial tourist center.

A number of area restaurants soothe hunger pangs. Town dining ranges from the homey Sea Gull Restaurant (10481 Albion Street) to the highly respected MacCallum House (45020 Albion Street) and the acclaimed Cafe Beaujolais (961 Ukiah Street). Other favorites (Ledford House and Little River Restaurant) are a few miles south.

Anderson Valley

State 128 through the Anderson Valley is a scenic drive popular with travelers heading to and from the Bay Area. At the beginning of its route from the coast, the highway parallels the Navarro River, with big redwoods rising between road and river.

Paul M. Dimmick Wayside Camp, a 12-acre park, makes a handy base for trailer and tent campers. Nearby Hendy Woods State Park has two camping areas, a stream for summer swimming and fishing, and fine redwood stands.

About 30 miles from the coast, amid vineyards, orchards, and quiet ranchland, lies Boonville, settled in the 1850s. For many years, its claim to fame was "Boontling," a tongue-in-cheek dialect.

Now it's a good place to overnight (at Anderson Creek Inn and The Toll House, or Philo Pottery Inn in nearby Philo), eat (New Boonville Restaurant and Boont Berry Farm are two choices), or assemble a picnic. Between Philo and Boonville, fruit and juice stands thrive in season. Wineries (tasting rooms) cluster around Philo, and the Anderson Valley Brewing Company in Boonville produces several beers.

North to Fort Bragg

The beaches at two state parks (Caspar Headlands and Jug Handle) are good picnic spots en route to Fort Bragg. At Jug Handle, an "ecological staircase" (a series of terraces formed by wave action and varying sea levels) gives you a cram course on a half million years of natural history. Pick up a map from the vending machine (small charge) at the top of the stairs.

Mendocino Coast Botanical Gardens. A lavish display of flowers covers 47 acres of bluffs 2 miles south of Fort Bragg. It's at its best in spring, when the rhododendrons bloom. The reserve is open daily year-round; there's a small charge to visit.

Fort Bragg. As you enter Fort Bragg, you cross a bridge high over the Noyo River. The harbor east of the highway is home port to a big commercial fishing fleet. Visitors charter fishing boats or enjoy seafood restaurants.

Fort Bragg, the largest town on the coast (about 6,000 people), was settled as an army post in 1857, then resettled as a lumber town when the first sawmill was built in 1885. Paul Bunyan Days (Labor Day weekend) bring big crowds to watch loggers compete.

Visitors can pick up a walking tour map at the chamber of commerce office, 332 North Main Street (closed Wednesday and Sunday), visit the Guest House Museum (a former lumber company house filled with displays illustrating logging and shipping history), hop aboard the Skunk train for a trip through the redwood groves to Willits on U.S. 101 (see page 126 for details), or go beachcombing at Glass Beach, just north of town.

To the Lost Coast

Beyond Fort Bragg the coastal shelf narrows to next to nothing. Highway 1 suddenly veers inland above Rockport, unable to engineer its way along the formidable coastal terrain. Its failure results in a ruggedly unspoiled stretch known as the Lost Coast.

Westport. Weathered Westport's New England–style houses have changed little since the heyday of lumbering. The tiny town has only a couple of inns (one of them the rustic Cobweb Palace Inn) and restaurants.

Shore fishing is productive at Westport–Union Landing State Beach and at South Kibesillah Gulch Coast Angling Access Area, where a pair of parking lots provide access to several hundred yards of vertical shoreline.

Sinkyone Wilderness State Park. Access to the southern part of this skinny, 7,400-acre coastal preserve is only mildly difficult, at least in dry weather. A 6-mile dirt road (no RVs or trailers) departs State 1 about 13 miles north of Westport. The northern entrance is off U.S. 101 near Garberville. For details, call (707) 446-2311 or (707) 986-7711.

Not-so-lonely Lighthouses

Romanticized and treasured, the West Coast's surviving lighthouses have become as popular as they once were lonely. Some of these shoreline landmarks have been preserved and opened to the public as museums, hostels, and even a bed-and-breakfast inn.

Many of the beacons are on coastal promontories of stunning scenic beauty; others stand in or near parks or wildlife refuges. So your visit may also include beach-combing and driftwood collecting (check area regulations), tidepool-ing, camping, and wildlife watching (especially for gray whales).

We list, from north to south, 10 you can visit along the Northern California coast. Another, south of Mendocino at Point Cabrillo, is now part of the Coastal Conservancy and scheduled to open soon. For a free list of all state lighthouses, send a self-addressed stamped envelope to the U.S. Lighthouse Society, 244 Kearny Street, San Francisco, CA 94108.

Battery Point (1856). Topping a wave-washed rock nearly engulfed at high tide, this tiny Cape Cod–style stone lighthouse at Crescent City was among the first along the coast. You reach it at low tide via a 200-yard spit; the hike is an adventure. Visit a fine museum, climb into the 45-foot tower, picnic, and whale-watch. From April to October, the light is open Wednesday through Sunday from 10 A.M. to 4 P.M. Admission: $2 adults, 50 cents children under 12. For access times and directions, call (707) 464-3089.

Point Arena (1870). The 1906 quake toppled the first lighthouse on this long peninsula, 65 miles north of Point Reyes. You'll find a museum here and three bungalows to rent ($80 to $110 a night). Steps wind up into the 115-foot tower. The light is

open 11 A.M. to 2:30 P.M. daily, except December, and 10 A.M. to 3:30 P.M. summer weekends. Admission: $2 adults, 50 cents children under 12. For information, call (707) 882-2777.

Point Reyes (1870). A squat, 16-sided iron tower sits three ramps and 307 steps below the bluff. Foggy, barren, beset by storms, it was one of the West's least desirable locations; many keepers quit or went mad. Open Thursday through Monday 10 A.M. to 4:30 P.M., the light station is now part of a national park. Whale-watchers crowd it on winter weekends; go early in the day. The second and last Saturday evening of the month you can watch the lens being relighted; call (415) 669-1534 for reservations. Admission: free (park entry fee).

Point Bonita (1877). Clinging to a basalt outcrop northwest of the Golden Gate Bridge, the low iron tower (part of the Golden Gate National Recreation Area) is reached by trail, tunnel, and 180-foot steel suspension bridge; children under 12 are not permitted. The light is open 12:30 to 4 P.M. weekends, with guided tours at 1 P.M. For directions and to reserve monthly moonlight tours, call (415) 331-1540. Admission: free.

East Brother Light Station (1873). On a 1-acre island off Point Richmond in San Francisco Bay, a bed-and-breakfast inn ($295 a couple including dinner, breakfast, and transportation; book 6 months ahead) occupies the restored Victorian buildings. For overnight reservations or day visits ($10, minimum 4 people), call (415) 233-2385.

Point Montara (1875). After two cargo steamers piled up on a shallow ledge offshore, a fog signal was built at this spot, 20 miles south of San Francisco. The light tower, atop 70-foot cliffs, was added later. Restored buildings house a hostel ($10 a night).

Lodging is bunk-bed style, and you help with chores. For information, call (415) 728-7177 from 7:30 to 9:30 A.M. and 4:30 to 9:30 P.M.

Pigeon Point (1872). This station 30 miles north of Santa Cruz is named for a ship that broke up on nearby rocks in 1853. Weekend tours are hourly from 11 A.M. to 2 P.M. by reservation and 3 to 4 P.M. without. Admission: $2 adults, $1 children. There's also a dormitory-style hostel ($10 a night). For information, call (415) 879-0633.

Santa Cruz (1967). A snug brick structure on W. Cliff Drive, Mark Abbott Memorial Lighthouse was built on the site of an 1860s light by parents of a surfer who drowned nearby. The museum (historical surfing artifacts) is open daily except Tuesday from 1 to 4 P.M. in summer, also closed Wednesday the rest of the year. Admission: free.

Point Piños (1855). The oldest continuously operating lighthouse on the West Coast, this New England-style Pacific Grove structure operated for more than 40 years by women, is now a museum. Its tower rises over a cozy red-roofed house filled with period furniture and marine artifacts. The museum, on Asilomar Avenue at Pacific Grove, is open weekends from 1 to 4 P.M. Admission: free (donations accepted).

Point Sur (1889). This lighthouse 20 miles south of Carmel was recently acquired by the state parks department, which offers 2½-hour tours of keepers' homes, storehouses, and the lighthouse (includes a steep ½-mile hike). Tours take place on weekends, weather permitting. For information and parking directions, call (408) 625-4419. Admission: $2; no small children allowed because of hazardous site conditions.

Rhododendrons brighten this sequoia grove in Redwood National Park. These giant redwoods grow naturally nowhere else in the country except this coastal region.

Redwood Country

Before the gold rush brought a surge of new population to Northern California, a vast forest of the world's tallest trees—the coast redwood or *Sequoia sempervirens*—blanketed an area up to 30 miles wide and 450 miles long. Magnificent redwood groves extended from the Santa Lucia Mountains south of Monterey northward into a corner of Oregon. The oldest known coast redwood had reached the age of 2,200 years before being cut in the 1930s.

Civilization's demands have left only small parts of the forest primeval. The majority of the remaining redwoods are located along U.S. 101 from Leggett (where it merges with State 1) north to Crescent City.

Getting there. Via U.S. 101, it takes between 4 and 5 hours to drive from San Francisco to the southern edge of redwood country. Garberville, the northern entrance to the Sinkyone Wilderness State Park on the Lost Coast, is a favorite overnight stop. Most of the air service is to the Eureka/Arcata area, though some flights reach Crescent City. Rental cars are limited at airports. Greyhound also connects the region. Year-round 2- and 3-day sightseeing trips are also offered by several companies.

Accommodations. The supply of rooms in this region is often exceeded by the demand, especially in summer. A cluster of motels around Garberville and Miranda is your best bet in the south. Stop for a meal or just to take a look at the Tudor-style Benbow Inn, even if you're not planning to stay.

Farther north, Eureka and Arcata have the largest number of motels and inns. It pays to make reservations. Without them, you'll have better luck finding a place in Orick, Klamath, or Crescent City.

Weather. Climate in redwood country is changeable. The finest season is autumn, when crowds thin out, the air turns brisk, and a seasonal show of color brightens the countryside. Wild-flower season extends from March into August, but peaks from April to June. You may encounter rain even in summer; redwoods flourish in moist climates.

Avenue of the Giants. North of Garberville a 33-mile alternative scenic route (State 254) roughly parallels U.S. 101. Winding leisurely through a cathedral-like aisle of 300-foot-high trees, it offers a closer view of these "ambassadors from another age." Staying on U.S. 101 saves half an hour, but you'll miss grand groves, public campgrounds, picnicking and swimming spots, and an interesting mill town.

The avenue's entrance is at Sylvandale; it ends about 5 miles north of Pepperwood, which is 30 miles south of Eureka. Numerous turnouts and parking areas allow for neck-craning; trails lead through tranquil glens and along the Eel River.

Scotia. Pacific Lumber Company operates the world's largest redwood mill; mill tour permits and brochures are available at its office on Main Street. (In summer, get tickets at the company museum across the street; the mill is closed the first week in July.) Hours are 7:30 to 10:30 A.M. and 12:30 to 2:30 P.M. weekdays.

For a bit of luxury, stay at the Scotia Inn (11 antique-furnished rooms); call (707) 764-5683 to reserve. The dining room is open Wednesday through Sunday evenings. For information on other area lodging and dining choices, call the Rio Del–Scotia Chamber of Commerce at (707) 764-3436.

Pick a park

Some of the best remaining coast redwoods are preserved in Redwood National Park and several state parks along U.S. 101. Parks are busy throughout the summer, offering informative naturalist programs, nature hikes, and evening campfires.

South of Eureka, scenic attractions and the highway play tag with the South Fork of the Eel River. Sprawling Humboldt Redwoods State Park is the main attraction, but there are other good spots for campers.

Standish-Hickey State Recreation Area, just north of Leggett, has plenty of camping but only one mature redwood among its dense forest. Picnicking is popular at Smithe Redwoods State Reserve, a little farther north. You can hike to a waterfall or take a footpath down to the Eel River. The Benbow Lake State Recreation Area, south of Garberville, features picnic and limited camping facilities.

For details on these parks, write to California Department of Parks and Recreation, District 1 headquarters, 3431 Fort Avenue, Eureka, CA 95501. For camping details, see page 122.

Richardson Grove State Park. You can't miss this relatively small park: the highway runs right through its 800 acres. Swimming holes, highly developed campgrounds, and 10 miles of trails make it a popular choice. Though it can be wet and chilly in winter, it's open year-round. In winter, silver and king salmon and steelhead trout attract many anglers.

Humboldt Redwoods State Park. Scattered along most of the length of the Avenue of the Giants, this park was acquired piece by piece and now consists of more than 70 memorial groves. It begins unobtrusively at the Whittemore Grove across the river from the highway; take Briceland Road at Redway.

At Burlington, in a dark copse of second-growth trees, an all-year campground adjoins the park headquarters and museum. Rangers have information on camping and picnic facilities in other parts of the park; in autumn they'll tell you where to see the best color.

Park highlights include the Founders Tree, for many years considered the world's tallest (364 feet before a broken top brought the figure down to 347); the solemn depths of the Rockefeller

...Redwood Country

Forest; the wide pebble beach of the Eel, where you can stand back and look at redwoods from top to bottom instead of being encircled and overwhelmed; and Bull Creek flats, site of the present tallest tree.

Grizzly Creek Redwoods State Park. This small, secluded area along the Van Duzen River (18 miles east of U.S. 101 on State 36) is highly prized by picnickers and campers for its climate, which is often warmer and less foggy than parks right along the coast. Its 234 acres include a virgin redwood grove, more than a mile of river front, hiking trails, and improved campsites—but no grizzlies. Summer trout fishing is fair to good; steelheading is good from mid-February to mid-April.

In & around Eureka

Lumbering and fishing made Eureka, and they're still its main industries. Located midway between San Francisco and Portland, this city of some 25,000 is the North Coast's largest, and a perfect place to break up your drive. Sniff the air: the odors come from docks along Humboldt Bay or pulp mills south of town.

A cache of historic homes, hotels, and saloons, many dating from the late 1800s, and a fine harbor are hidden behind the blur of motels, gas stations, and coffee shops that line U.S. 101.

For an accommodations guide (Carter House, Hotel Carter, and the imposing Eureka Inn are among your choices) and brochures on attractions, stop by the Eureka Chamber of Commerce (2112 Broadway; open 8:30 A.M. to 5 P.M. weekdays).

In summer, the chamber offers a 5-hour narrated bus tour of the area, including lunch and a bay cruise. The price is around $15, and reservations are a must. For more information, call (707) 442-3738.

Old Town. It was once a collection of raucous bars and bordellos along the harbor. Now Old Town (1st and 2nd streets, just off U.S. 101) is a renovated shopping center with restored buildings that house shops, restaurants, and vintage museums. Stop by the Clarke Memorial Museum at 240 E Street (open noon to 4 P.M. Tuesday through Saturday; donations) to see Indian artifacts. The free Humboldt Bay Maritime Museum at 1410 2nd Street (open daily 11 A.M. to 4 P.M.) exhibits historical marine paraphernalia.

Victorian-sighting. A brick-lined promenade with old-fashioned street lamps leads up 2nd Street to the flamboyant and much-photographed Carson Mansion, called the "queen of Victorians." Now a private men's club, the mansion looks much as it did when completed by lumber baron William Carson in 1886. The smaller house across the street was also built by Carson, as a wedding gift for his son.

Fort Humboldt State Historic Park. Constructed in the 1850s and abandoned as a military post in 1865, the partly restored fort (open daily 9 A.M. to 5 P.M.) is a half-mile off U.S. 101 on the southern edge of town; follow signs on Highland Avenue, east of U.S. 101.

A small museum gives a brief history, including the time Ulysses S. Grant spent there prior to his resignation from the army. But most of the fort is now devoted to documenting logging life. Peek into a logger's cabin, see steam engines used to haul logs, and ride on a steam train (third Saturday of the month). Donations are welcome.

Sequoia Park. A woodland oasis at Glatt and W streets in the heart of Eureka contains one of the region's best forests. Here you can walk leafy trails past ferns and streams, stop at a zoo and children's playground, or feed ducks the remains of your picnic lunch.

Humboldt Bay. Just beyond the waterfront section of downtown Eureka and almost concealed from the highway is Humboldt Bay, the largest deepwater port between Portland and San Francisco. You can explore the harbor on an old ferry (see page 124), study birdlife, and go boating, fishing, or beachcombing along great stretches of land guarding the harbor.

Samoa. Following State 255 northwest across the Samoa Bridge takes you over Woodley and Indian islands. Marshy Indian Island, part of the Humboldt Bay National Wildlife Refuge, is the northernmost egret and heron rookery on the Pacific Coast. Roosting birds look like a feathery white cloud.

A sign marks the turnoff to the Samoa Cookhouse (open 6 A.M. to 9 P.M. daily), where you dine family-style in a barnlike structure that served loggers from a nearby lumber mill from 1890 until the 1950s. A hearty breakfast or lunch costs about $5; dinner is around $10. A museum displays antique cookware that matched lumberjacks' appetites.

Arcata. From Samoa you can continue along the North Spit across Mad River Slough to Arcata, where a self-guided architectural tour takes you back to the time of Bret Harte and the heyday of gold mining. Jacoby's Storehouse, an original one-story stone building on the plaza (791 8th Street), has been enlarged to include shops and restaurants. At Humboldt State University's Natural History Museum (1315 G Street), some of the plant and animal artifacts date back 500 million years.

Azalea reserve. A few miles north of Arcata on State 200 (accessible from U.S. 101 and State 299), the 30-acre Azalea State Reserve bursts into bloom around Memorial Day. Trails lead you through masses of colorful overhanging blossoms.

Trinidad. Settled in 1850, this small fishing village 22 miles north of Eureka is one of the North Coast's oldest towns. As you enter its Main Street from U.S. 101, turn left onto Trinity Street and park by Memorial Lighthouse. The harbor, dotted with colorful boats, lies straight ahead.

At Edwards and Ewing streets, Humboldt State's marine lab aquarium (free tours; open 8 A.M. to 4 P.M. weekdays and 1 to 5 P.M. Saturdays) contains pettable local critters. Below the lab, Edwards Street leads to Trinidad State Beach, a good place for picnics or beachcombing. To your left is Trinidad Head. A pleasant 1½-mile trail leads around the dramatic promontory.

Patrick's Point State Park. A forest- and meadow-covered headland, this 625-acre park lies 6 miles north of Trinidad. Its surprisingly varied area contains a beachful of agates, trees that stand on octopuslike arms, sea stacks, and even a tiny museum. The 2-mile Rim Trail leads through the forest and along the jagged shoreline.

A valley loop. A 73-mile road loops through pastoral Mattole Valley to the sea and back into the redwoods. You can begin at the refurbished town of Ferndale, about 15 miles south of Eureka. Here you'll find some of the coast's best-preserved Victorians, from small white cottages to intricate gingerbread mansions (several are now quaint bed-and-breakfast inns; see page 72).

Stop at the Ferndale Museum (3rd and Shaw streets; small admission) to look at the memorabilia and pick up a self-guided walking tour. Two houses, known locally as "butterfat palaces" because they were built by wealthy dairy farmers, also invite touring.

For information on 28-room Fern Cottage on Centerville Road, call (707) 786-4835. Linden Hall, a 15-room mansion at Bush Street and Port Kenyan Road, is surrounded by lovely grounds; call (707) 786-4908 for details.

From Ferndale, the Mattole Road heads south over Bear Ridge to the ocean and then sneaks inland past the little hamlets of Petrolia, site of California's first oil wells, and Honeydew, one of the state's smallest towns. The latter consists of a general store, gas station, and post office—all under one roof.

Redwood National Park

A representative segment of old-growth redwoods and some outstanding coastal scenery have been protected in a 106,000-acre park 330 miles north of San Francisco. Eight miles of shoreline roads and more than 150 miles of trails afford close-ups of magnificent trees and the abundant plant and animal life they nurture.

Included within its boundaries are three long-established state parks (Prairie Creek, Del Norte Coast, and Jedediah Smith), sites for most camp-

ing; for details, see page 120. Motels are found in Orick and Crescent City, to the north. Klamath, at the mouth of the Klamath River, is known for fine salmon and steelhead fishing, and for white-water rafting (see page 125) and jet boat tours. Paul Bunyan greets visitors at the Trees of Mystery (admission fee) just beyond town.

Visitor information. A visitor information center on the highway south of Orick provides park information and handles tickets for summer shuttles to the Tall Trees Grove (the loftiest giant is 367.8 feet high). The center is open daily from 9 A.M. to 5 P.M. (to 6 P.M. in summer) except Thanksgiving, Christmas, and New Year's. For more information, call (707) 488-3461.

The main park headquarters is located in Crescent City at 1111 2nd Street; phone (707) 464-6101. Information on area attractions is also available across the street from the chamber of commerce; phone (707) 464-3174.

Prairie Creek Redwoods State Park. A favorite of many campers, Prairie Creek has more than its share of special wonders: a handsome creek, a herd of native Roosevelt elk, the wide expanse of sand at Gold Bluffs Beach (tent campsites), and scenic Fern Canyon. Hiking its more than 100 miles of trails (including one for the blind) is the best way to explore. Lady Bird Johnson Grove, reached by a short trail off Bald Hill Road, has a cluster of giant trees.

Del Norte Coast Redwoods State Park. A drive through the park lets you enjoy both rugged inland forest and fine Pacific Ocean vistas. The Damnation Creek Trail leads through dense forest to the sea, where giant redwoods grow almost to the shore. From April to July, you'll see outstanding displays of rhododendrons and azaleas.

Jedediah Smith Redwoods State Park. At the northern end of the national park (9 miles northeast of Crescent City), Jed Smith presents views of skyline ridges still tightly furred with giant redwoods. The highway runs through two of the 18 memorial groves and then out to a flat, where the most imposing trees soar.

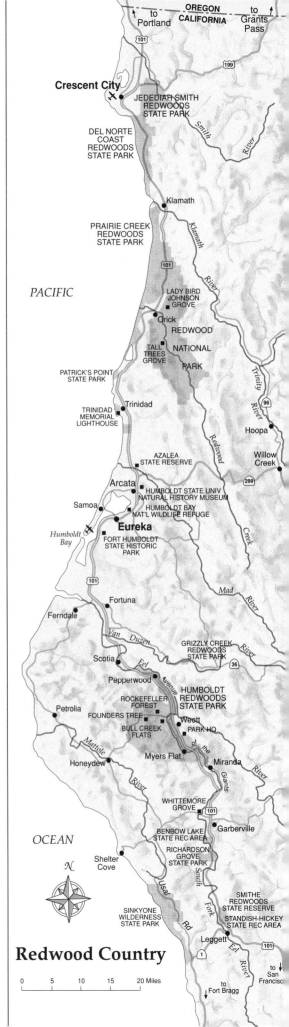

Redwood Country

0   5   10   15   20 Miles

Shasta-Cascade Region

*S*plashing streams, towering snow-covered peaks, snug valleys encircled by forested slopes, miles of deep blue waters, and some of nature's most unusual attractions make up the Shasta-Cascade region, an area stretching from the Coast Range east to Nevada and from the upper Sacramento Valley to the Oregon border.

In this vast land (about the size of Ohio) lie six national forests, eight national and state parks, the Trinity Alps, and the California Cascade range, which includes two gigantic glaciated volcanoes: the dormant 14,162-foot Mount Shasta and the still-active 10,457-foot Mount Lassen.

Though the gold rush here was never as well chronicled as the one in the Sierra Nevada, millions in ore were extracted by miners who thronged north in the 1850s.

A bonanza of recreation

This scenic northern wonderland offers plenty of open space in which to unwind and unlimited outdoor recreation to pursue, from leisurely sightseeing to adventurous mountain climbing. You can fish and raft along the Klamath River, waterski on Whiskeytown Lake, steer a houseboat around Lake Shasta and Trinity Lake, ride horseback through magnificent wilderness, sail across Eagle Lake, and camp among piney forests beside clear mountain streams.

Mountain lakes and streams offer good catches all year, making the region an angler's paradise. It's also salmon and steelhead country, boasting chinook of up to 55 pounds. Before you wet your line, check the regulations and restrictions on limits, size of hooks, types of lures, and stream closures.

Lava Beds National Monument and Lassen Volcanic National Park showcase unusual geologic formations, while Lake Shasta Caverns provide an underground look at equally impressive landscapes. Several hundred miles of the Pacific Crest National Scenic Trail (a route extending 2,600 miles from Canada to Mexico) traverse the region.

Planning your trip

This chapter covers only the most popular wilderness retreats. To reach them or other, more secluded areas in this far-flung empire, you'll need a car. Interstate 5 is the main north-south route through the northern mountains, State 299 the main east-west highway. U.S. 395 runs along the northeastern corner.

Rental cars are available at Redding, a destination of several intrastate airlines. Amtrak train stations are located at Redding and Dunsmuir (near Mount Shasta). Greyhound buses reach the largest towns.

When to visit. A popular summer vacation site, Shasta-Cascade is most active from May to October. Though Redding and Red Bluff can be sweltering in midsummer, the region's plentiful lakes provide cooling retreats. And in the nearby high country, you'll sleep under a blanket.

An autumn drive through the mountains offers a spectacular display of color. This season is also a good time to greet the wintering clan of bald eagles arriving at Tule Lake.

Many visitor attractions close in winter and heavy snowfall limits backroad driving, but Shasta and Lassen parks host skiers, snowshoers, and dogsled racers.

Where to stay. Redding, the area's largest city (population 65,000), offers the widest choice of lodging. The biggest motor lodges line Interstate 5. Other accommodations can be found in town along major highways.

A wealth of public and private campgrounds welcomes tourists throughout the region. Particularly popular is the Whiskeytown-Shasta-Trinity National Recreation Area, a 243,000-acre vacationland northwest of Redding.

Majestic Mount Shasta (14,162 feet) dominates the surrounding landscape for more than 100 miles. This view is from Grass Lake, off U.S. 97 to the north.

Contacts

These agencies offer information on attractions and accommodations. See additional contacts throughout this chapter.

Shasta-Cascade Wonderland Association
1250 Parkview Ave.
Redding, CA 96001
(916) 243-2643 *(for entire region)*

Redding Convention & Visitor Bureau
777 Auditorium Dr.
Redding, CA 96001
(800) 874-7562

Lassen Volcanic National Park
Box 100
Mineral, CA 96063
(916) 595-4444

Redding Area

Located at the junction of Interstate 5 and State 299, 4 hours from San Francisco and 3 hours from Sacramento, Redding makes a good base from which to explore the surrounding region. Majestic Mount Shasta looms to the north, and many other natural and man-made attractions lie within a 70-mile radius.

River walk. Taking full advantage of its picturesque setting on the Sacramento River, the city has developed a 5-mile nature walk along its banks. The starting point is from the Diestlehorst Bridge at Benton Drive.

Town museums. Caldwell Park along the river contains two museums. The Carter House Science Museum (small fee), open 10 A.M. to 4 P.M. Tuesday through Sunday, has natural history displays and a small collection of live animals.

A free city museum exhibits artwork, historical mementos, and Native American artifacts. From June through August, it's open Tuesday through Sunday, 10 A.M. to 5 P.M. The rest of the year, it's open Tuesday through Sunday afternoons and all day Saturday (closed major holidays).

Red Bluff

Named for the area's colored sand-and-gravel cliffs, this small city (population 13,000) 30 miles south of Redding is noted for its Victorians—and for the adobe ranchhouse of California's only president.

William B. Ide Adobe. Ide, a carpenter from Massachusetts, led a small band of settlers against the Mexican authorities in the so-called Bear Flag Revolt of 1846. He was elected president of the short-lived California Republic.

His restored ranch house and outbuildings are now part of a 4-acre state park on Adobe Road, east of Interstate 5. Picnic facilities and natural valley oaks make this park on the west bank of the Sacramento River a shady oasis. It's open daily from 8 A.M. to 5 P.M.

Kelly-Griggs House Museum. To see a classic resentative of the city's fine collection of Victorians, tour the two-story Kelly-Griggs house (311 Washington Street). Though there's no charge to visit the well-furnished mansion, donations are encouraged. Hours are 2 to 4 P.M. Thursday through Sunday (to 5 P.M. in summer).

Salmon viewing. At Diversion Dam south of State 36, underwater cameras record the action of salmon climbing fish ladders on their way upstream to spawn. The best viewing takes place between September and April. The area (open daily from 8 A.M. to 8 P.M.) offers picnicking, camping (fee), and boat-launching facilities.

Shasta Lake

Nine miles north of Redding soars Shasta Dam, an enormous structure holding back the bright blue waters of Shasta Lake, the state's largest man-made lake and part of a vast three-lake national recreation area. With a spillway three times the height of Niagara Falls, the 602-foot-high dam is a popular visitor attraction. Open daily, the visitor center offers historical and geological exhibits and a film on the dam workings. There are no tours of the dam itself.

Activities. Long popular for its houseboating, waterskiing, swimming, and fishing, the four-pronged lake is big enough (30,000 surface acres, with 365 miles of shoreline) to offer plenty of secluded anchorage for its houseboat armada. The Shasta-Cascade Wonderland Association (address on page 82) has boat rental and resort information.

The calmer waters of the Pit River arm and Jones Valley area are best for skiing. A waterskiing show takes place on summer evenings near Bridge Bay.

Of the 22 species of fish found here, bass, catfish, and crappie are the most prevalent in summer. Trout go deep when the water warms, but you can try for them in front of the dam or in the cold waters farther up the McCloud

River. Bass fishing is at its best on the Pit River.

Accommodations. Motels line Interstate 5 at Bridge Bay (south side of the lake) and Lakehead (north end). You can camp anywhere on shore with a fire permit, or in one of 1,200 Forest Service campsites, the most private and scenic of which are accessible only by boat. Your best chance of a quiet camp is on the McCloud, Pit, or Squaw arms.

Lake Shasta Caverns. The deep, complex limestone caves overlooking the McCloud River arm of Shasta Lake are fun to explore; just getting there is an adventure. You travel by boat and then transfer to a bus for the spectacular 800-foot ascent to the cavern entrance, a deceptively normal-looking door into the mountainside.

The 2-hour tour (including boat and bus ride) takes you through well-lighted tunnels and up and down stairs to see geologic formations possibly a million years old. Bring a sweater, as temperatures average 58°.

The caverns are open daily except Thanksgiving and Christmas. From April through October tours take place on the hour from 9 A.M. to 4 P.M.; service is reduced to three daily trips (10 A.M., noon, and 2 P.M.) the rest of the year.

To reach the caves, take the O'Brien–Lake Shasta Caverns exit off Interstate 5 about 15 miles north of Redding. Follow the signs for about 2 miles to the visitor center. If you're boating, you can dock at the landing on the east side of the McCloud arm. Admission is $12 adults, $6 ages 4 to 12; call (916) 238-2341 for specifics.

Whiskeytown Lake area

The other units that make up the Whiskeytown-Shasta-Trinity National Recreation Area lie off State 299 west of Redding. For detailed information on this recreation area, write to the Shasta-Cascade Wonderland Association or the Redding Convention & Visitors Bureau (addresses on page 82).

Shasta State Historic Park. Shasta, 6 miles west of Redding on State 299, is a mere ghost of its former lusty self. On a self-guided tour (modest park admission), you'll see the courthouse and jail (now a museum) and a refurbished general store. The museum is open daily March through October (except major holidays), closed Tuesday and Wednesday the rest of the year.

Whiskeytown Lake. Some of Northern California's most beautiful scenery surrounds this reservoir 8 miles west of Redding. A number of hiking and riding trails climb high enough to afford sweeping views of the lake's wooded islands. The National Park Service visitor center is on the east side of the lake adjacent to State 299.

The 36-mile-long cove-indented shoreline has plenty of room for waterskiing, scuba diving, swimming, and boating—it offers some of the region's top sailing waters. Fishing is good for trout, kokanee, bass, and bluegill, especially in autumn and early spring.

Two marinas—Oak Bottom and Brandy Creek—provide services; boats launch from the Whiskey Creek picnic area north of the highway. Other picnic and camping areas (some close to the beach) are marked; for more informa-tion, see page 120. No fires are allowed on the beach.

Trinity Lake. Though Clair Engle Lake is its official name, Trinity County residents still call this 16,500-surface-acre impoundage Trinity. Anglers come for good trout and smallmouth bass trophy fishing. An irregular shoreline creates many secluded hideaways for small boats and houseboats.

You can launch your own boat from five ramps or rent fishing boats or houseboats from four marinas. Motels and campgrounds (some with sandy swimming beaches) stretch along the Stuart Fork Arm.

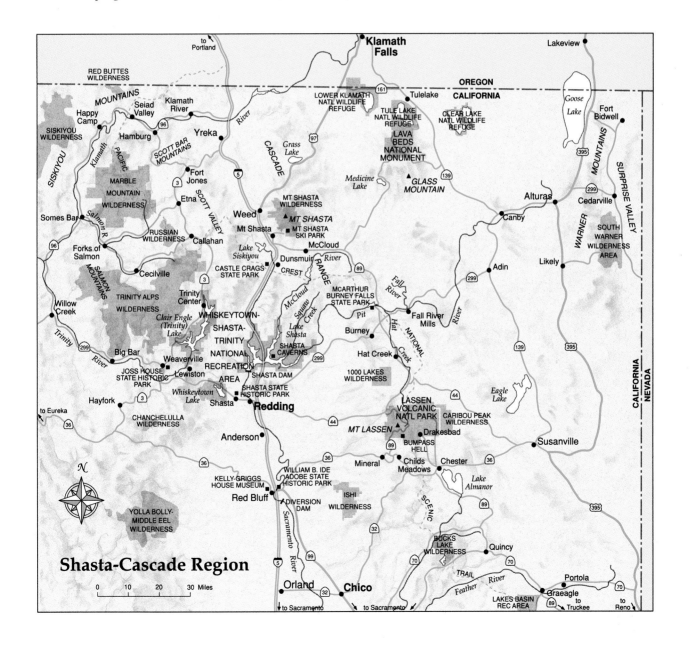

Shasta-Cascade Region

Rainbows often form in the mist at the foot of Burney Falls, once described by Theodore Roosevelt as "the eighth wonder of the world." Downstream lies Lake Britton, a popular water sports site.

Into the Wilderness

The Shasta-Cascade Region contains many of the state's wilderness areas. These uniquely scenic and undeveloped spots are roadless, open only to hikers, horseback riders, packers, and campers. Fishing and hunting are permitted in many locations. We sample only a few. For specific area maps ($2 each), contact the Office of Information, U.S. Forest Service, 630 Sansome Street, Room 529A, San Francisco, CA 94111; phone (415) 705-2874. Several areas require a free entry permit; campers need a free fire permit.

Few roads lead into the heart of the northern mountains where three large ranges—Klamath-Scott (including the Trinity, Salmon, and Marble mountains), Cascades, and Warner—contain beckoning wilderness areas. Here, trails rise steeply to high peaks; the timberline is low (7,000 feet), so you quickly reach alpine terrain.

It's easy to sample the fringes by car and even to take day hikes into some regions. Isolated towns on the perimeter provide overnight lodging, and some remote mountain resorts offer lodging, meals, and pack trips.

Trinity Alps

Rugged and sawtoothed, the Trinity Alps are camouflaged by lower mountains. You scarcely notice them from Interstate 5, and even their easy approach from State 299 has never brought them heavy traffic.

You need a wilderness permit even for day hikes. Call the Forest Service in Redding, (916) 246-5222, for maps and permits. Before heading out, ask about trail conditions at ranger stations in Weaverville, Big Bar, or Coffee Creek.

Three roads form a circle around the Trinity Alps, linking old gold towns. The main road, State 299, parallels the Trinity Trail, famous as an Indian path, pioneer trail, and gold rush road; State 3, from Weaverville to Callahan and Yreka, was part of the old California-Oregon Wagon Road; and the third links Salmon River settlements on the mountains' west and north slopes.

Weaverville. Gateway to the Trinity Alps and Trinity County seat, this former boomtown at the junction of State 3 and State 299 came to life in the 1850s, when gold brought a flood of miners—including some 2,500 Chinese immigrants.

Brick facades and exterior spiral stairways remain almost unchanged on Main Street. The Weaverville Drug Store (founded in 1854) displays early remedies and potions, and the free J. J. "Jake" Memorial Museum (closed from December to April) contains mementos of the town's gold roots, including a stamp mill.

At Joss House State Historic Park (Oregon and Main streets) the Chinese left a lovely legacy in the form of an 1874 temple. Tours are offered from 10 A.M. to 5 P.M. The temple is closed Tuesday and Wednesday.

Into Scott Valley. From Weaverville, State 3 roams along the edge of Trinity Lake, over a mountain pass into peaceful Scott Valley, and north to meet Interstate 5. Several bed-and-breakfast inns open sporadically in the valley, but your best lodging bets are at Weaverville and Yreka.

The Scott Museum (open most of the year) at Trinity Center gives you an idea of how it was to live in the early mining days. And block-long Callahan, a former trading center for miners and ranchers, still has century-old buildings lining its boardwalks.

Tiny Etna, 13 miles to the north, appears almost a metropolis by contrast. The Native Daughters of the Golden West Museum is usually open summer afternoons, and you shouldn't miss the drugstore (sodas, antiques, and gifts).

Noted for its fine museum of Indian crafts (open Memorial Day to October 1), Fort Jones, 12 miles up the road, was the site of an old army outpost.

Wild West lawlessness, Chinese tong wars, and an 1871 fire were not enough to destroy Yreka. Though the area is booming, some fine old restored 1850-era survivors can be found along Miner Street. The Siskiyou County Court-

house exhibits nugget and placer gold, and a free history museum (910 S. Main Street) contains other exhibits.

Marble Mountains

A loop road (State 96 on the west and north and good, partly gravel roads to the east and south) encircles the 280,000-acre Marble Mountains. The best way to approach them from Interstate 5 is to turn west onto State 96 some 10 miles north of Yreka. From Hamburg (35 miles to the west) a winding road follows the Scott River to Fort Jones and Etna and continues down the North Fork of the Salmon River to the tiny towns of Sawyers Bar, Forks of Salmon, and Somes Bar, all wilderness entry points.

The Marble Mountains are easier to get around in than the Trinity Alps to the south. The Sky High Lakes are almost in the center of the wilderness. From here, trails radiate in all directions.

Cascades

Extending all the way from British Columbia through Washington and Oregon, the Cascade Range ends at Lassen Volcanic National Park. Two wilderness areas around Lassen are popular with backpackers and anglers.

Thousand Lakes Wilderness. About 12 miles north of Lassen Park, four major trails lead into the heart of the wilderness. All are demanding, but the scenery and number of lakes in the valley compensate for the rigors of the hike. Cyprus Camp Trail, the easiest route, leads to large Lake Eiler. You can drive to the area on several unimproved roads from State 89; check with the ranger at Hat Creek. Bunchgrass Campground lies to the south.

Caribou Peak Wilderness. A series of lakes with good trout fishing and easy access from Silver Lake in Lassen County make Caribou popular. To reach the lake, take County A21 eastward 11 miles from State 44. Several campgrounds lie nearby.

Guest Ranches & Resorts

Whether it's for a get-away-from-it-all vacation or a family reunion, consider a guest ranch for a relaxing change of pace in a friendly western setting. You can even select your favorite area of Northern California, as ranches are sprinkled throughout the northern mountains, the Sierra Nevada, the coastal valleys, and the high northeastern desert.

While most ranches cater specifically to guests, a few are working ranches with guest activities. We also include two upscale resorts with stables.

Typically, ranches include lodging, all meals, and activities in the daily price; horses may be extra. Accommodations vary from rustic tent cabins to deluxe suites, and daily rates range accordingly: from $300 a week to $300 a day.

Canyon Ranch Resort, P.O. Box 6, Sierraville, CA 96126; (916) 944-3340. Fishing (both creek and lake), hunting, and hiking are the lures of this year-round resort in Sierra Valley. It also boasts a swimming pool, hot tub, and stocked trout pond. Riding is available nearby. Meals are extra.

Coffee Creek Guest Ranch, Star HC 2, Box 4940, Trinity Center, CA 96091; (916) 266-3343. Located in the Trinity Alps northwest of Redding, this rustic and friendly resort offers horseback riding (extra charge), fishing, canoeing, riflery and trap shooting, square dancing, and special children's programs.

Drakesbad Guest Ranch, Warner Valley, Chester, CA 96020 (June through September) or California Guest Services, 2150 N. Main St., Suite 7, Red Bluff, CA 96080 (off-season); (916) 529-1512. The only lodging in Lassen Volcanic National Park, this comfortable (and all-too-

popular) resort boasts a spring-heated pool, nearby fishing, and plenty of hiking and riding (extra fee).

Flying "AA" Ranch, Ruth Star Rte., Box 700, Bridgeville, CA 95526; (707) 574-6227. Guests at this site east of Fortuna stay in motel rooms, tent cabins, or mobile homes. On hand are a swimming pool, tennis, volleyball, horseshoe courts, and a tots' playground. Meals and horses are additional.

Greenhorn Creek Guest Ranch, P.O. Box 7010, Spring Garden, CA 95971; (916) 283-0930, (800) 33-HOWDY. Daily maid service in the cabins and a two-story lodge pamper guests on this 840-acre ranch east of Quincy. Among the activities are horseback riding, fishing, and evening singalongs.

JH Guest Ranch, 8525 Homestead Ln., Etna, CA 96027; (916) 467-3468. At this Christian retreat in Scott Valley, take your choice of white-water rafting (extra), mountain climbing, backpacking trips, horseback riding (extra), swimming, or fishing. A western rodeo tops your week.

Josephine Creek Lodge, Star Rte. 2, Box 5703, Trinity Center, CA 96091; (408) 353-1663. This adult hideaway lies deep in the Trinity Alps, 30 miles north of Coffee Creek. Guests are tucked away in cabins; meals are provided in the main lodge. Activities include fishing and hiking.

Spanish Springs Guest Ranch, P.O. Box 70, Ravendale, CA 96123 or Information Center, 1102 2nd St., San Rafael, CA 94901; (800) 272-8282 (in California), (800) 228-0279 (out of state). This 70,000-acre working cattle ranch in Lassen County is open year-round. Guests are housed at the main ranch or in other refurbished historic homesteads and participate in cattle drives, brandings, wild horse tours,

pack rides, and trail rides. Winter fun includes sleigh rides, sledding, cross-country skiing, and ice skating. The ranch is not set up for children.

Stonepine, 150 E. Carmel Valley Rd., Carmel Valley, CA 93924; (408) 659-2245. Built as a getaway by the Crocker family, this small, elegant resort bears little resemblance to a ranch, but its stables are one of its main attractions. Others are a swimming pool and tennis courts. You'll feel like you're visiting a private mansion.

Timberhill Ranch, 35755 Hauser Bridge Rd., Cazadero, CA 95421; (707) 847-3458. Though the exterior of this inn and working ranch may look rustic, the interiors are beautifully decorated and the meals are gourmet, not pork and beans. Tennis, swimming, horseback riding, and picnic lunches at the beach are just some of its features. Leave the children at home for this stay.

Trinity Alps Resort, Star Rte., Box 490, Lewiston, CA 96052; (916) 286-2205. This large, family-oriented resort (restaurant and lounge) on Trinity Lake, with more than 40 cabins along the Stuart Fork River, is open summers through September. The facility offers swimming, fishing, horseback riding (extra), and tennis, volleyball, and badminton courts.

Trinity Mountain Meadow Ranch, Star Rte. 2, Box 5700, Trinity Center, CA 96091; call (408) 353-1663 for information. Despite its wild setting 28 miles north of Trinity Lake, this well-appointed, comfortable ranch has a heated pool and volleyball and badminton courts. Hiking trails lead into the Trinity Alps for fishing; adults can rent mountain bikes (no horses).

Shasta Country

The most massive cone volcano in the Cascade chain, Mount Shasta juts up abruptly from the landscape just north of Redding, dominating the region 100 miles around it. Eight glaciers mantle the 14,162-foot peak and Shastina, the 12,330-foot cone that rises from its western flank.

Here climbers tackle mountain slopes, wilderness hikers and campers head for the 37,000-acre wild area around the peak or the 7,300-acre Castle Crags Wilderness (abutting the state park) to the south, and anglers have a choice of good rivers and lakes. In winter, Mount Shasta Ski Park (at the 5,500-foot level) hosts downhill skiers (see page 124). The Forest Service also offers Nordic skiing and snowmobiling at areas around Mount Shasta.

The big mountain is off Interstate 5 about 5 hours from San Francisco. From the freeway, you can head east to more parks, fishing streams, and small towns. The area is sparsely populated—its towns slow paced and its high lakes and streams uncrowded—even in midsummer.

Hiking. Each year 7,000 hikers attempt Shasta's summit. If you're determined to try, contact the Forest Service in Mt. Shasta at 204 West Alma Street—(916) 926-4511—for information.

Day hikes on Shasta's shoulders are an easier option. Carry plenty of liquids and dress in layers (cold winds can pick up). A 2-mile trail from Bunny Flat, on the southwest slope at a cool 6,800 feet, to Avalanche Gulch rewards hikers with fine valley views. The trailhead is 11 miles east of the city of Mt. Shasta, on the Everitt Memorial Highway.

Lodging. Bustling Mt. Shasta is a good base for exploring the mountain and nearby Castle Crags State Park. It has over a dozen hotels and inns and twice that many restaurants. Because the mountain is considered sacred by many people, a dozen or more religious sects flourish around town.

Historic Dunsmuir, a few miles south, faded when railroad jobs dwindled, but a number of motels and a half-dozen restaurants make it a convenient stop. Railroad Park Resort, just off the freeway, is a train buff's dream. You can lodge in a caboose, dine in a railroad car, and admire the 1927 Willamette Shay engine and other rolling stock. Camping and RV facilities are nearby.

Castle Crags

A landmark off Interstate 5 near Dunsmuir, the gray granite outcroppings of Castle Crags are carved into snaggle teeth. Easy access makes this state park a popular place to camp (no hookups) from about the first of April to the end of October.

Fishing, swimming, inner tubing, and picnicking take place along the Sacramento River, a 2-mile stretch of which meanders through the park. If you're in shape, try the short (2½ miles), steep Crags Trail up to the rocks. The 8,544-foot formations perch in the wilderness area beyond.

Lake Siskiyou

This 430-acre lake on the Sacramento River was constructed solely for recreation. Facilities include 50 picnic areas, 299 campsites (with hookups), and a broad, sandy beach. Besides swimming, wind surfing, and boating (from a launch ramp and marina), the lake offers year-round fishing for brown and rainbow trout and bass. From Interstate 5, the lake is 4 miles southwest of Mt. Shasta town, off Barr Road.

Around McCloud

Queen of the lumber mill days, gaslit McCloud (10 miles east of Interstate 5 on State 89) was a company town founded in 1827. The mill workers were paid in scrip, spent it at the company store, and lived in houses made of the pine they had milled. Today, the 1890s Mercantile Building on Main Street contains a hardware store and a cafe with great milkshakes.

The Dance Country Restaurant, at 424 Main, serves up lumberjack meals. Up the hill, the beautifully restored 1907 McCloud Guest House is now a small bed-and-breakfast inn and restaurant.

South of town lies the Nature Conservancy–protected McCloud River Preserve, a 6-mile corridor of prime wild trout stream. Take Squaw Valley Road 9 miles to Lake McCloud, follow signs on a dirt road 9 miles to Ah-Di-Na camp, and then go 1 mile to the road's end. From there, it's a half-mile hike to the preserve cabin. (Check on road conditions first with the Forest Service at (916) 964-2184.)

McArthur-Burney Falls

One of the state's most scenic waterfalls is the chief attraction of this park near the junction of State 299 and State 89. A short nature trail brings you to the base of the misty 129-foot falls.

The 565-acre state park (open year-round) includes 6 miles of hiking trails and a portion of Lake Britton, a popular 9-mile-long reservoir. A grocery store and snack bar are open from mid-April to mid-October. The town of Burney offers a few motels and restaurants, groceries, and fly-fishing shops.

Two top streams

Several streams on Shasta's east side are renowned for their trout. Angling is at its best in September—cooler weather and fewer mosquitoes. Double-check fish and game regulations; they can vary on the same stream.

The icy, spring-fed waters of Hat Creek and Fall River, two meadow streams full of wily rainbow and brown trout, present a challenge even to experienced anglers. One good access point on Hat Creek is a PG&E day-use area off State 299, some 9 miles northeast of Burney. You can only get to Fall River from Cal Trout's Island Bridge, off Glenburn Road north of Fall River Mills (canoes or cartop boats only; no gas engines), and Fall River/Glenburn access (limited to cartop boats).

Lassen Country

Until May 30, 1914, Mount Lassen was simply a landmark for early emigrant parties on their way across the mountains into the Sacramento Valley. Then began the year-long eruptions of smoke, stones, steam, gases, and ashes that culminated in the spectacular events of May 19, 1915.

On that day a red, glowing bulge of lava spilled over the sides of the crater, melting the snow on the mountain's northeastern flank and sending 20-ton boulders and devastating floods of warm mud 18 miles down into the valleys of Lost and Hat creeks.

Three days later, Lassen literally blew its top, blasting hot gases and ash that scythed down forests and sent up a mushroom cloud darkening skies as far east as central Nevada. Though the mountain is quiet today, visitors to Lassen Volcanic National Park see striking reminders of its volcanic activity, such as bubbling mud pots and hissing fumaroles. Even place names ring with geologic drama: Devils Kitchen, the Devastated Area, Bumpass Hell. You'll find six lakes to fish (non–power boats are allowed on the largest) and 150 miles of backcountry trails to hike, including a 17-mile segment of the Pacific Crest National Scenic Trail.

As the state's national parks go, 106,000-acre Lassen is not overcrowded, seeing about 500,000 annual visitors (compared to Yosemite's nearly 3½ million). Even on a summer weekend you should be able to find a campsite, and if you visit in autumn you may get downright lonesome.

Getting to the park. Lassen is about 180 miles north of Sacramento. Most people approach it from Redding via State 44, or from Red Bluff on State 36. The park headquarters is in Mineral, 40 miles east of Red Bluff; its hours are 8 A.M. to 4:30 P.M. daily in summer, weekdays the rest of the year. You can get information there or at the park's entrances on State 89.

Camping. Seven campgrounds dot the park (see page 120); only Juniper Lake is free. All are filled on a first-come basis, and those at Summit and Manzanita lakes are the most popular. You'll need a wilderness permit (free at any ranger station) for backcountry camping.

Accommodations. The sole lodging in Lassen Park is rustic, comfortable, hard-to-get-into Drakesbad Guest Ranch in Warner Valley (see page 88). Outside the park, you'll find a number of unpretentious resorts along State 36 between Mineral and Chester and a smaller number along State 89 to the north. For a listing of all area accommodations, request a copy of the Lassen Park Guide from the park (address on page 82).

A park drive

A good introduction to Lassen, State 89 ribbons for 30 miles among many of the park's most interesting features. It crosses a shoulder of the volcano at 8,512 feet. Pick up a Road Guide (small charge) at one of the entrance stations. After the first snowstorm, the road is closed until late spring, except for the section leading to the park's ski area (see page 124).

Bumpass Hell. Biggest and showiest of the thermal areas, Bumpass Hell is 6 miles north of the southern entrance. From the parking lot, a 1½-mile trail leads to the rotten-egg wonderland of boiling sulfur springs, hot mud pools, and other mineralized landscape phenomena.

Lassen Peak Trail. Almost 8 miles from the entrance you'll find the trailhead to the top of the mountain. The hike is not difficult; it takes about 2 hours to ascend the 2,000 feet from the highway. A hat, sunscreen, and a windbreaker might come in handy.

If your summit arrival coincides with a ranger talk, you'll get an introduction to volcanoes; check information stations for talk schedules. Otherwise, your reward is a good view of Mount Shasta, the Coast Range north to the Trinity Alps, and the distant Sierra Nevada.

Devastated Area. About 3 miles northwest of Summit Lake, you'll see evidence of the swath of destruction carved by Lassen's eruptions.

Chaos Crags. The splintered rocks off to the west beyond the Devastated Area are plug volcanoes, similar to Lassen but only 1,000 to 1,200 years old. The massive boulder field in front was probably the result of an avalanche of rock that sped across the slope at speeds of up to 100 miles per hour.

Lassen's eastern side

Spectacular as State 89 is, it reveals only a small portion of the park. If you have the time, good scenery is also to be found elsewhere.

Butte Lake. The largest of Lassen's cinder cones rises near Butte Lake (stocked with rainbow trout) in the park's northeastern corner. To get there from the park, follow State 44 east 24 miles to Forest Road 32N21; then follow signs 6½ miles to Butte Lake Campground.

A trail ascends the 700-foot cone, which last erupted in 1851. The trek is arduous; you sink back one step for every two you take. But the summit view is eerily beautiful.

Warner Valley. Well known for its Drakesbad Guest Ranch, this glacier-scalloped valley is also a lovely place to camp. A 2⅓-mile trail to Boiling Springs Lake starts at the campground below, crosses Hot Springs Creek, and runs through white firs and lodgepole pines to the lake. A 2-mile trail leads to the bubbling mud pots at Devils Kitchen.

To get there from Chester, on State 36, take Feather River Drive north and follow the signs for 17 miles.

Juniper Lake. Largest and deepest of Lassen's lakes, Juniper is tucked into the park's southeastern corner. A good 2-mile trail takes you up to 8,048-foot Mount Harkness, a shield volcano with views of Lassen and Chaos Crags. From Chester, take Feather River Drive about 13 miles north to the campground.

A wooden trail snaking through Bumpass Hell, largest and showiest of Lassen Volcanic National Park's thermal areas, gives visitors a good look at boiling springs and gurgling pools.

Lassen's backcountry. Fully three-quarters of the park is wilderness, inviting day hikers and backpackers. One favorite midsummer hike starts at Summit Lake Campground (on State 89, midway through the park) and pokes almost 2 miles east to Echo Lake, then an additional 2 miles to Upper and Lower Twin Lakes.

Around the park

Two large lakes and a collection of smaller waters lie within close range of Lassen. Popular with swimmers, water-skiers, boaters, and anglers, Almanor and Eagle are just a few miles from the park; Lakes Basin Recreational Area is almost on the border of Plumas and Sierra counties. Hikers enjoy the Bizz Johnson Trail, a 30-mile entrée to the country between Westwood and Susanville; access is from State 36.

Lake Almanor. In Plumas County, 80 miles east of Red Bluff on State 36, 52 square miles of azure water mirror snow-capped Mount Lassen. The forest-rimmed lake, created by a dam on the Feather River, is also easily reached from U.S. 395 and State 70. Small resorts along the shore offer boat rentals, docking, and launching areas.

Fishing is excellent for trophy rainbow and brown trout, kokanee salmon, bass, catfish, and perch. Gould Swamp is the "hot spot" in spring; summer night fishing near the shore is productive. Other recreational choices include a nine-hole golf course, sailboat races, hunting, and rock collecting. Several cross-country ski areas operate in winter.

Eagle Lake. This Lassen County lake, one of the state's largest, is also one of its cleanest and least crowded. Here are plenty of spacious, tree-sheltered campgrounds and 27,000 acres of clear blue water for excellent sailing. At its southern end, Gallatin Beach has a store, marina, boat rentals, ramp, sandy beach, and shady picnic area.

The lake serves as a feeding ground for a rare breeding colony of osprey. Fishing is good for the large Eagle trophy trout, a natural hybrid that is the only game fish adapted to the unusually alkaline water. The limit is three, and 7-pound catches are possible.

To get to the lake from Lassen, head east on either State 44 or State 36; the highways join west of Susanville, the closest town. County A1 reaches Gallatin Beach and the campgrounds; State 139 runs along the eastern shore.

Lakes Basin Recreational Area. About halfway between Lassen Park and Lake Tahoe, a collection of small lakes is located conveniently close to State 89. Grassy Lake (closest to the highway) is often overfished; nearby Big Bear and Little Bear lakes hold rainbow trout, and Cub and Silver lakes harbor brook trout. At Long Lake, the largest of the group, you can rent boats.

Distances between lakes are short; you can hike, fish, and return to your car the same day. There's trailside camping at Silver Lake, an easy walk to less fished lakes. To get to the lakes from State 89, turn off at Graeagle (a golfer's getaway) and follow Gold Lake Road south.

Wildlife Watching

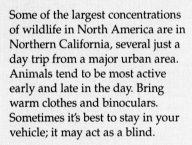

Some of the largest concentrations of wildlife in North America are in Northern California, several just a day trip from a major urban area. Animals tend to be most active early and late in the day. Bring warm clothes and binoculars. Sometimes it's best to stay in your vehicle; it may act as a blind.

Bald eagles. Up to 800 bald eagles come to the Klamath Basin refuges near the Oregon border each year. The visitor center at Tule Lake National Wildlife Refuge (see facing page) issues self-guided tour maps and information.

Elephant seals. The only mainland rookery of these huge, lumbering pinnipeds (bulls weigh up to 7,700 pounds) is at Año Nuevo State Reserve off State 1, 55 miles south of San Francisco. Reservations are required to join 2½-hour, 3-mile guided walks over the dunes daily from December through March; call MISTIX at (800) 444-7275. There's a small fee to visit.

Pronghorn antelopes. Pronghorns are second only to cheetahs in speed, having been clocked at 61 miles per hour. Fortunately for onlookers, they're curious, so don't bother trying to hide. For best viewing, follow U.S. 395 south from Susanville to Honey Lake or north to Alturas.

Sandhill cranes. The Merced National Wildlife Refuge in the Central Valley hosts some 12,000 of these stately, shy, and skittish creatures each winter. Drive 8 miles south of Merced on State 59 and 6 miles west on Sandy Mush Road.

Snow geese. You'll probably hear these vociferous white waterfowl before you see them. The Sacramento National Wildlife Refuge gets up to 300,000 (peak population in January). From Interstate 5, take the Norman Road exit (south of Willows) and follow the signs.

Tule elk. A good herd of these small elk is found in the San Luis Wildlife Refuge. Leave Interstate 5 at Los Banos and head north on State 165. In August and September, bulls round up a harem and defy challengers.

The Northeastern Corner

Centuries ago, flaming volcanoes in northeastern California spread rivers of liquid rock over the land below. On cooling, they formed one of the state's most fascinating landscapes—a rugged terrain of yawning chasms, cinder cones, and craters. Its official name is Lava Beds National Monument.

Adjoining the monument to the north are Tule Lake and Lower Klamath national wildlife refuges, havens for millions of migratory birds. Some 200 species have been sighted there, among them the largest collection of bald eagles in the continental United States. They're usually in residence between November and March.

If the Warner Mountains were near a large city, they would be famed for their scenery and aswarm with visitors. But because they are in the state's lightly traveled northeastern corner, they still promise adventures and discoveries.

Wildlife refuges

The Tule Lake and Lower Klamath wildlife refuges along the California-Oregon border make this area a stop-off for the largest concentration of waterfowl on the North American continent. Some 2 million birds drop by the Tule Lake wetlands each year.

Bird-watching and photography are two reasons for a visit; seasonal hunting is also permitted in some areas. Best viewing is in spring and autumn; peak numbers of waterfowl arrive in early November.

For a map, stop by the visitor center on Hill Road, west of Tulelake. The best route to the refuges from Interstate 5 is via State 97 north from Weed to 161 (State Line Road), along the top of the Lower Klamath Lake.

Lava Beds

"Nobody will ever want these rocks. Give me a home here," requested Modoc Indian Chief Captain Jack. Though he was wrong (the area was given monument status in the 1800s), he and his renegade band successfully defended their stronghold against federal and volunteer troops for 5 months in 1872 and 1873. Plaques document major battlegrounds and hideouts of the Modoc War.

Just off State 139, almost at the Oregon border, the 72 square mile national monument contains 1,500-year-old lava flows, high cinder buttes, pictographs and petroglyphs, and what may be the world's most outstanding exhibit of lava tubes. The largest group is on Cave Loop Road near park headquarters in the southeastern section. Mushpot Cave, an extension of the visitor center, is the only lighted lava tube. Check at the center about others; rangers lead walks and lend flashlights for exploration. Rattlesnakes are active in warm weather.

A 40-unit campground (no hookups) adjoins the southeastern entrance. Water is available in summer; check with the visitor center the rest of the year. Closest rooms, food, and gasoline are in Tulelake, the horseradish capital, 30 miles to the east.

The most direct route is to take State 299 east toward Canby and go north 26 miles on State 139. Coming from the Tule Lake National Wildlife Refuge, go south on State 139 for 4 miles to Great Northern Road and follow the signs to the entrance near Tulelake.

Medicine Lake

Medicine Lake is an easy detour from Lava Beds National Monument. You follow a paved road around Glass Mountain, a 7,622-foot pile of black obsidian, the rock once prized by Indians for tools and weapon points. For directions and road conditions, call the monument at (916) 667-2282.

To get to the lake from Tulelake, head south on State 139 and follow the signs west on County 97. This remote lake is big (600 acres), high (6,700 feet), starkly beautiful, and so clear that you can usually see 30 feet down.

You're likely to have the beach on the southeastern shore practically to yourself, your pick of campsites at the three Forest Service campgrounds, and plenty of elbow room when swimming or angling for trout.

Warner Mountains

The topography of the Warner Mountains may bring to mind parts of the Rockies, with their abrupt rocky summit ridges and long western slopes covered in a patchwork of pine, aspen, fir, juniper, sage, and grasses. You won't find resorts or lodges in this high country, but you can take day trips or arrange for packers from Alturas, the closest town, at the junction of State 299 and U.S. 395.

Along the town's Main Street you'll find a free Modoc County Museum (Indian and pioneer relics; open daily May to November) and the refurbished, last-century Niles Hotel and Saloon. The Brass Rail on U.S. 395 is a good bet for inexpensive family-style Basque dinners.

Getting there. State 299, the only paved road across the Warners, descends into Surprise Valley, a ranching area north of Cedarville. A gravel road across Fandango Pass to the north lets you make a loop trip back to U.S. 395.

Cedarville's most historic building is the Bonner Trading Post, built in 1865 for immigrants and settlers. Fort Bidwell, at the valley's northern tip (bed-and-breakfast inn, little theater), was an army outpost from 1866 to 1892 and a school for Paiute Indians until 1930.

South Warner Wilderness. The highest part of the mountains is a 70,000-acre wild area where the only signs of civilization are grazing sheep and cattle. For information, contact the Forest Service in Alturas (441 North Main Street) or phone (916) 233-5811.

The 24-mile Summit Trail hugs the top of the range and skirts the three highest peaks: Squaw, Warner, and Eagle, all climbworthy. Side trails lead to fine trout fishing in Pine, Mill, and East creeks and South Emerson and Patterson lakes.

Sierra Nevada

The great naturalist John Muir described it as a "range of light": the Sierra Nevada, largest single mountain range in the country. Rising gradually from the floor of California's Central Valley, these snowcapped mountains ascend to jagged crests more than 14,000 feet high before plunging almost vertically to the east. They stretch along nearly two-thirds of the state's eastern border, encompassing mile after mile of alpine lakes, thundering waterfalls, and towering forests.

It's the wealth of outdoor recreation found in these lofty elevations that most attracts visitors. Hiking trails climb mountain slopes, cross lush meadows, and drop into river-carved canyons. Anglers try their luck in crystalline lakes and streams, and stunningly blue Lake Tahoe provides miles of boating and waterskiing opportunities. In winter, skiers flock to the Sierra's famous slopes.

Dramatic Yosemite Valley, sculpted by glaciers, attracts visitors with awe-inspiring scenery year-round, but the national park is at its most dramatic in spring. Then waterfalls cascade over the valley walls to splash on rocks more than 1,000 feet below, creating some of the Sierra's most spectacular vistas.

A golden era

Snuggled into the Sierra foothills between Tahoe and Yosemite lie remnants of gold rush days—historic towns and rushing streams where visitors still pan for "color." Some of the old mines have

"Grandest of all the special temples of nature" was John Muir's accolade to Yosemite National Park. From El Capitan's dome in the background, Yosemite Valley's Merced River would resemble a silver thread.

been reopened, but most of the region's wealth today comes from the antique stores, gift shops, restaurants, and inns that crowd old towns along State 49.

Hamlets off this main highway are also worth a visit. Many are covered by a facade of modernity; others verge on ghost town status. A few have been preserved as state historic parks.

Planning your trip

The fastest and most direct way to approach the northern Sierra from the San Francisco area is via Interstate 80, which cuts east through the foothills and Tahoe National Forest to cross the mountains at Donner Pass, named for an ill-fated pioneer party.

Other all-year highways reach Lake Tahoe at its southern rim: U.S. 50 links Sacramento and Carson City, Nevada, and State 88 joins State 89 after crossing 8,573-foot Kit Carson Pass.

To the south, State 4, State 108, and State 120 (through Yosemite National Park) are closed in winter due to snow. All-year routes to Yosemite are State 140 and State 41. State 49 is a year-round gold country highway.

When to go. All roads in and around the Sierra Nevada are open from late spring to early autumn. Summer daytime temperatures in the higher elevations usually range upward from the 70s, with nights cooling to the 50s and 60s. Summer rain is unusual.

In winter, expect crisp days and cold nights. Though snowfalls have been much below normal in recent years, a storm can quickly drop several feet of snow and force temporary highway closures. Always carry chains on winter drives.

The Sierra foothills are at their most colorful in spring and autumn. Summer temperatures can climb to 100°, and winter rains make sightseeing a chilly business.

Where to stay. An array of lodging from luxurious alpine resorts to modest cottages and roadside motels awaits Sierra travelers. Gold rush communities abound with quaint bed-and-breakfast inns and century-old hotels. Campers will find plenty of tent sites in state and national parks, but prime locations like Lake Tahoe and Yosemite Valley require reservations well in advance for summer (see pages 120–122).

Contacts

These agencies offer information on attractions and accommodations. See additional contacts throughout this chapter.

Lake Tahoe Visitors Authority
1156 Ski Run Blvd.
(P.O. Box 16299)
South Lake Tahoe, CA 95706
(800) 288-2463 *(trip planning, lodging)*
(900) 776-5050 *(road, ski, weather conditions; $1 per minute)*

Tahoe North Visitors & Convention Bureau
950 N. Lake Blvd., Suite 3
(P.O. Box 5578)
Tahoe City, CA 95730
(800) 824-6348

Yosemite National Park
Yosemite, CA 95389
(209) 372-0265 *(information weekdays)*
(209) 372-0264 *(24-hour recorded information)*

The Northern Sierra

Thousands of acres of forested land north of Lake Tahoe offer secluded spots for trout fishing, swimming, camping, hiking, and horseback riding. Much of Plumas National Forest is in Feather River country; Tahoe National Forest extends south and east to the Nevada border.

For a map of roads, trails, campsites, and lakes, contact Plumas National Forest, P.O. Box 1500, Quincy, CA 95971, or Tahoe National Forest, Highway 49, Nevada City, CA 95959 ($2 charge).

Feather River country

Rich in scenery and history, the Feather River region presents a varied topography—rocky canyons, fern-filled ravines, high mountains, leaf-covered foothills, chaparral-swathed slopes, and second-growth forests of pine and fir. Through all this flows the river named in 1820 by Spanish explorer Don Luis Arguello, who happened to reach its lower end when band-tailed pigeons were migrating and scattering feathers on the water.

State 70 follows the North Fork of the Feather, affording fine views of the canyon. Cabins and campgrounds line much of the highway. Stub roads lead to old mining settlements, pocket valleys cultivated since 1850, and trout-filled lakes. Trails take off where roads end. You'll find a backpack handy for spur-of-the-moment hikes.

The Middle Fork (the most rugged) provides some of the state's finest trout fishing. Site of early placer mining, the South Fork has swimming holes and streamside trails. Along its stretches lie seven reservoirs; the highest (5,000 feet) is 500-acre Little Grass Valley Lake.

Oroville. Gateway to the Feather River country, Oroville (population 10,000) lies 70 miles north of Sacramento on State 70. It began life as Ophir City, a boisterous tent town of gold rush days. In the 1870s its Chinatown was California's largest.

One visible reminder of that era is the Chinese Temple at Elma and Broderick streets. Built in 1863, it's now a museum of Oriental artifacts. A self-guiding tour (small fee) reveals chapels, a garden, and collections of puppets, costumes, and tapestries. Hours and days vary, but the museum is open from mid-January through November.

Another landmark is the Judge C. F. Lott Memorial Home in Sank Park (Montgomery Street between 3rd and 4th avenues). Completed in 1856, the white frame dwelling is furnished with period pieces. It's open Friday through Tuesday from 11 A.M. to 4:30 P.M. year-round, Wednesday and Thursday afternoons in summer (small fee).

Cherokee. Ten miles north of Oroville on Cherokee Road you'll see the shells and foundations of buildings that once made up the tiny gold-mining town of Cherokee. The first diamonds discovered in the United States were picked out of a sluice box here in 1866, but no extensive diamond mining was ever done.

Lake Oroville. With a surface area of about 15,800 acres and about 167 miles of shoreline, this lake 5 miles northeast of Oroville was created by the towering Oroville Dam built on the Feather River in 1968. The adjoining power-house can generate enough electricity to supply a city of a million people. Films on the project are shown at the visitor center.

Now a state recreation area, the lake is popular with sailors, boaters (houseboat and power boat rentals), waterskiers, swimmers, and anglers. Both drive-in and boat-in campsites can be reserved through MISTIX.

Feather Falls. North and east of Lake Oroville is Feather Falls Scenic Area, a 14,890-acre preserve of forested canyons, soaring granite domes, and plunging waterfalls. The region got its name from the 640-foot, plumelike cascade of the Feather River.

In the spring and early summer you get a good view of the falls by boating to the end of the Middle Fork arm of Lake Oroville and then climbing a hazardous ½-mile trail. For an eagle's-eye overlook, follow a 3½-mile trail from a road turning off at the village of Feather Falls, south of the falls on Lumpkin Road.

Though the Milsap Bar Road crosses the Middle Fork at the upper end of Bald Rock Canyon, not even a foot trail descends to its inner depths. To reach the Milsap Bar Bridge from Lake Oroville, follow the Oroville-Quincy Highway (County 162) north to the Brush Creek Ranger Station (about 18 miles from the Forbestown Road junction at the south end of the lake). Then head east on Milsap Bar Road about 7 miles.

Bucks Lake. At an altitude of 5,000 feet, this 20,000-acre lake near the old gold-mining town of Quincy glitters peacefully amid forested valleys and rocky mountaintops. Boating, swimming, waterskiing, and fishing are its prime attractions. Trails lead to other lakes; the Pacific Crest National Scenic Trail crosses Bucks Lake Road about 3 miles east.

Two south shore resorts (open May through October) offer cabins, restaurants, stores, gas pumps, launch ramps, and boat rentals. Sites at five U.S. Forest Service campgrounds are available on a first-come basis. Pick up campground maps (small charge) at Plumas National Forest offices, 159 Lawrence Street, Quincy (open weekdays).

To reach the lake from Oroville, follow State 70 for 80 scenic but winding miles to Quincy and then head west on County 162 for 17 miles. The Oroville-Quincy Highway (County 162) is scenic and shorter (50 miles), but the last 17 miles are unpaved.

A scenic trio

On to the east, three parcels of Sierra scenery offer more recreational opportunities and some glimpses of California history.

Plumas-Eureka State Park. On the slopes of Eureka Peak in Plumas

County, the nearly 5,000-acre Plumas-Eureka State Park surrounds the old mining town of Johnsville, 6 miles west of the intersection of State 70 and State 89. Hiking trails lead around Eureka Peak and south to the Sierra Buttes and more than 30 lakes in the Lakes Basin Recreation Area. The area is known for brook and rainbow trout fishing.

Summer campers will find 67 sites along Jamison Creek (reserve through MISTIX). The area's gold-mining past can be explored at a mining museum (open daily in summer); the nearby stamp mill is being restored. Though the campground closes in October, the park is open year-round. Heavy snowfall attracts cross-country and downhill skiers to Eureka Bowl.

Donner Lake. Along Interstate 80 about 2 miles west of Truckee lies Donner Lake, a favorite trout fishing and sailing spot. The state park museum tells the story of the Donner Party, trapped here for the winter of 1846–47. Almost half of the 89 pioneers perished; a monument to them rests on a stone base 22 feet high, the depth of the snow that fateful winter. There's a small fee to visit the museum, open year-round.

Desolation Wilderness. Southwest of Lake Tahoe, Desolation Wilderness is a favorite of Sierra high country devotees. "Desolation" describes some of the area's wild and lonely terrain, its huge boulders and glacier-polished slopes nearly devoid of trees. Peaks ranging from 6,500 to 10,000 feet cradle more than 70 named lakes.

Within these 63,469 acres, you can hike about 100 miles of trails from 11 major trailheads. The much-used Pacific Crest trail connects many lakes, tranquil oases for fishing. Pack trips are extremely popular.

Despite its name, Desolation is the most crowded wilderness in the United States. It's so popular that wilderness permits are required year-round, and a quota system is in effect from mid-June to Labor Day. Free wilderness permits, required for both day and overnight use, are available in person or by mail from the U.S. Forest Service, 870 Emerald Bay Road, Suite 1, South Lake Tahoe, CA 96150. For reservations, call (916) 573-2600.

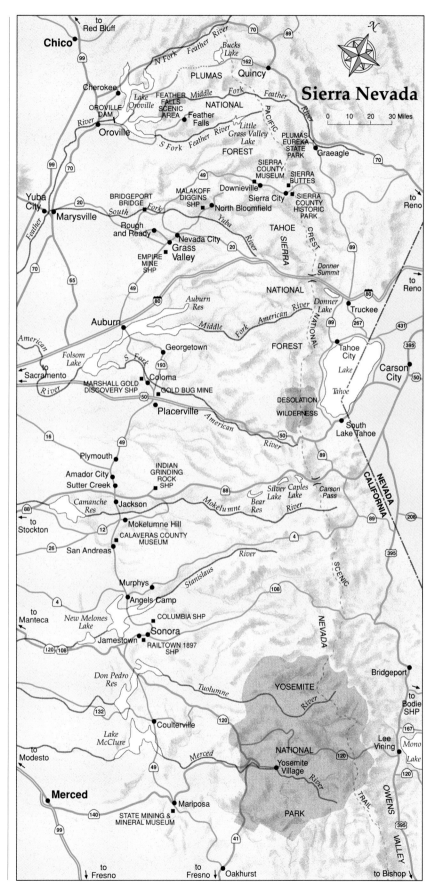

*Lake Tahoe's alpine setting and array of entertainment ensure year-round visitors.
The view is across the lake from Nevada's Sand Harbor to the snow-tipped mountains
on the California side.*

Lake Tahoe

Between the two main emigrant routes of California's early settlers—now Interstate 80 and U.S. 50—lies large and lovely Lake Tahoe. Rimmed by snow-capped Sierra Nevada peaks, this clear and unbelievably blue lake is shared by California and Nevada.

North America's largest alpine lake, Tahoe is 22 miles long, 8 to 12 miles wide, and 1,645 feet at its deepest point. It contains enough water to cover the entire state of California to a depth of 14 inches.

The lake basin was a gathering spot for the native Washoe Indians; later its heavily timbered slopes became a prime source of lumber. Tahoe blossomed as a resort area as early as the 1870s. Fifty years later skiing was introduced, and roads to the lake were kept open all winter. But it wasn't until the late 1950s that the building boom began. Then, ski lodges and gambling casinos (Nevada side) sprang up, turning Tahoe into an all-year attraction.

Planning a visit

Tahoe boasts an average 247 sunny days a year and an annual snowfall of 25 to 40 feet. Snow can fall anytime from October to June. You can expect summer days to be warm, but Tahoe's 6,227-foot elevation makes for cool nights.

Getting there. Planes, trains, buses, and major highways make it easy to reach Lake Tahoe. Two major airports serve the area: Cannon International in Reno (about 1 hour away) and the smaller Lake Tahoe Airport at the southern end of the lake. Both provide shuttles, taxis, limos, and rental cars. Tahoe-Truckee Airport north of the lake welcomes small planes.

Amtrak trains between the San Francisco area and Chicago stop north of the lake at quaint Truckee, a former lumber and railroad town turned gentrified ski center; it's about a 6-hour rail trip from the Bay Area. Greyhound buses reach both ends of the lake.

By car, it takes about 5 hours in good traffic from the Bay Area via Interstate 80 to reach the north shore, slightly longer to get to the south shore on U.S. 50. (On either route, traffic is at its worst on summer weekends and on ski weekends, when weather conditions may add to the congestion.) If you're not in a hurry, a combination of State 88 and State 89 offers a scenic alternative. From Southern California, the fastest route north to Tahoe is U.S. 395 to U.S. 50.

Lodging. Cozy cabins, condos, country-style inns, budget motels, modern lodges, and glamorous resorts—Tahoe has them all. Once you've decided on a north or south shore base, a single toll-free call to the appropriate visitor center (see page 95) lets you make reservations at many lake properties.

Camping. More than 20 public and private campgrounds around Tahoe offer a choice of sites. With a few exceptions (including Mount Rose, Zephyr Cove, and Nevada Beach), most are in California. For information on state campgrounds, see page 122; for U.S. Forest Service campgrounds, call (916) 573-2600.

The Tahoe Douglas Chamber of Commerce (Highway 50 at Round Hill Shopping Center a couple of miles north of the state border), has information on Nevada campsites; call (702) 588-4591.

Activities at the lake

The snowy slopes around the lake are the focus of winter fun—the Tahoe Basin is one of the most compactly developed ski regions in the world. Summer pastimes revolve around the lake itself, but they aren't limited to boating, swimming, and waterskiing. You can cruise across the lake on a stern-wheeler, or get a bird's-eye view from an aerial tram or even a hot-air balloon (check the Yellow Pages). Golfers head for one of the area's dozen resort courses (see page 123). And casinos just across the Nevada border, south and north, offer year-round, around-the-clock gambling as well as big-name entertainment, splashy revues, and a variety of lounge acts.

Boating. Lake Tahoe is a mecca for boaters and water-skiers. There's plenty of room for everyone, and the coves and harbors along the lakeshore are appealing. If you bring your own boat, you'll find plenty of launching ramps, but during the busy summer season, you may have trouble securing a mooring. If a storm appears imminent, don't venture far from shore; the water can become very rough.

Several companies offer raft trips on the Truckee River north of Tahoe City. Check the Yellow Pages for listings.

Cruising. Two stern-wheelers offer sightseeing cruises on the lake. The 500-passenger *Tahoe Queen* operates Emerald Bay and dinner cruises year-round from South Lake Tahoe. The 360-passenger *M.S. Dixie*, based at Zephyr Cove (Nevada), operates Emerald Bay, Glenbrook Bay, brunch, and cocktail cruises April through October. North Tahoe Cruises also offers boat tours out of Tahoe City. (See page 124.)

Swimming. Polar bears would love this lake; the icy waters only get up to 68° in midsummer. The hardy will find plenty of public beaches around the lake. At the south end, the U.S. Forest Service oversees three stretches of sand off State 89: Pope, Kiva, and Baldwin. You can also swim at Emerald Bay, D. L. Bliss, and Sugar Pine Point state parks just to the north off State 89, and at South Lake Tahoe Recreation Area off U.S. 50.

The north shore offers public beaches at Tahoe City and Kings Beach. On the Nevada side, try Sand Harbor Beach State Recreation Area (north shore) and Nevada Beach Campground (east shore). Boat harbors such as Zephyr Cove (east shore) also have beaches.

Fishing. Lake Tahoe never freezes, so you can fish all year. Kokanee salmon and rainbow and brown trout abound in the lake and nearby streams. A license from either California or Nevada is valid all over the lake; sporting goods stores offer 1-day licenses.

You can fish from one hour before sunrise to two hours after sunset. Chumming is illegal, and there's a five-fish limit (no more than two mackinaw). Half-day fishing charters are available at both the south and north ends of the lake; check the Yellow Pages under "Fishing Parties."

Cycling. Bikers may choose from more than 12 miles of safe, paved biking trails with great lake views. The longest runs more than 5 miles from Tahoe City south to Homewood on the west shore. Near Camp Richardson at the southern end, a delightful 3½-mile trail meanders through forest and along streams close to the beaches. Ask for maps at bicycle rental shops.

Hiking and riding. More than 90 miles of a planned 150-mile circle of hiking and equestrian trails have been com-pleted. Present access points are Tahoe City, State 50 at Spooner Summit (Nevada side), and State 89 at Luther Pass (south of the lake). A maximum 10 percent grade makes the trails good for beginners as well as advanced walkers. For information on camping (allowed along the trail), call the U.S. Forest Service at (916) 573-2600.

In summer, horses can be rented for trail rides from Cascade, Camp Richardson, Stateline, Sunset Corral, and Zephyr Cove stables on the south shore. North shore stables include Alpine Meadows, Cold Stream, Hilltop, Northstar, Ponderosa Ranch, Squaw Valley, and Tahoe Donner.

Skiing Tahoe. Downhill enthusiasts enjoy a variety of terrain in a cluster of fine ski areas, from the country's largest (Heavenly Valley) to the site of the 1960 Olympics (Squaw Valley). For the Nordic buff, the area boasts more than 30 ski-touring centers, some of which are located at the major downhill areas. Most offer rentals, instruction, and group tours.

For maps and general information, contact Lake Tahoe Visitors Authority or Tahoe North Visitors & Convention Bureau (see page 95). For information on specific resorts, see pages 123–124.

Aerial trams. For the best area view from the south shore, ride the Heavenly Valley Aerial Tram at South Lake Tahoe. It climbs to a restaurant about 2,000 feet above the lake. Take Ski Run Boulevard southeast from U.S. 50 to get to the tram, open 10 A.M. to 10 P.M. daily in summer, 9 A.M. to 5 P.M. at other times ($9.50 adults).

Across the lake, the Squaw Valley Cable Car operates from 9 A.M. to 10 P.M. in winter, 9 A.M. to 5 P.M. the rest of the year ($10 adults, $5 ages 12 and under). The tram takes you to the ski area's High Camp at 8,200 feet (restaurants, ice rink). Squaw Valley is off State 89 north of Tahoe City.

Circling the lake

A 72-mile road encircles the lake close to shore, offering beautiful views on all sides. Occasional winter snows may close a section of State 89 on the west shore around Emerald Bay.

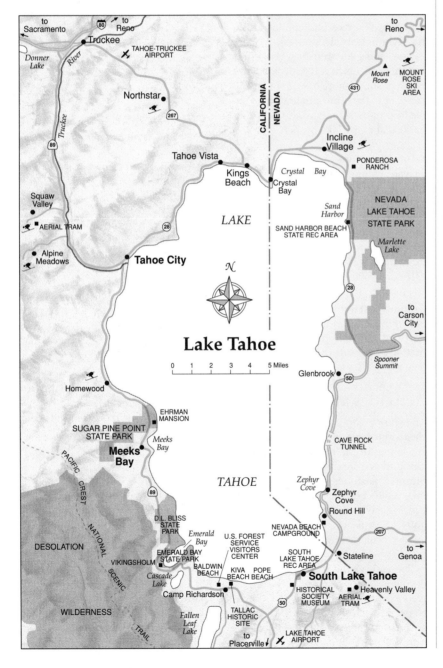

South shore. Lake Tahoe's lively south shore is the most heavily populated part of the lake. Resorts, motels, condominiums, restaurants, and shopping centers line U.S. 50 from the sprawling city of South Lake Tahoe past the border. Nevada's Stateline area is the gaming center, with such high-rise casino hotels as Caesar's, Harrah's, Harvey's (first on the lake), and Horizon.

A stop at the free Historical Society Museum (open 10 A.M. to 5 P.M. daily in summer), 3058 State 50 in South Lake Tahoe, provides a good introduction to the area's colorful past. You can also pick up a map to a self-guided auto tour of 20 historical landmarks.

From its split with U.S. 50 at the "Y" (location of discount outlets such as Mikasa and London Fog), State 89 winds north into national forest lands and provides access to two smaller lakes, Fallen Leaf and Cascade.

You can stroll around former summer estates and enjoy art shows and museums (summer only) at Tallac Historic Site, a 74-acre area on State 89 between Camp Richardson and Kiva Beach. The area is open spring through autumn. For information on hours and fees, call (916) 542-4166.

Just to the west, the U.S. Forest Service Visitor Center on Taylor Creek (open 8 A.M. to 6 P.M. daily in summer) has a nature trail and a stream profile chamber where you can observe the run of kokanee salmon in October.

West shore. Emerald Bay, at the southwest tip of the lake, is Tahoe's jewel. Completely surrounded by state parklands, the deep bay boasts the lake's only island, Fannette. The stone teahouse that you can see atop the island was built by the woman who erected Vikingsholm, a 38-room mansion at the head of the bay.

Tours of this onetime summer residence, patterned after an 800 A.D. Norse fortress, take place 10 A.M. to 4 P.M. June through September (small admission fee). From the lookout where you park your car, it's a 1-mile hike to the house; the return is uphill.

From the same parking area, you can take a short trail up to Eagle Falls, a good spot for photos. Picnic facilities lie nearby.

Northward on State 89, Meeks Bay has a beautiful beach and campground, and Sugar Pine Point State Park affords excellent views of the lake. In summer, tours of Sugar Pine's Ehrman Mansion are offered for a fee from 11 A.M. to 4 P.M. Parts of *Godfather II* were filmed here.

North shore. Tahoe City, at the junction of State highways 89 and 28, is the center for north shore skiing. Squaw Valley (aerial tram, new hotel) and Alpine Meadows ski areas are worth a detour in summer, as well, for the great scenery.

Gigantic trout can be viewed from Fanny Bridge (you'll see why it got its name), at Tahoe City. And you can bone up on early Tahoe history at the free Gatekeeper's Log Cabin Museum at 139 W. Lake Boulevard, open daily 11 A.M. to 5 P.M. from mid-May to mid-October.

Crystal Bay, on State 28 just into Nevada, is the hub of the north shore gaming. Several of the old casinos have been refurbished, including the Cal-Neva Club (once owned by Frank Sinatra).

The upscale Incline Village complex, 3 miles east, has a nearby ski area (Mount Rose), two 18-hole golf courses, tennis courts, riding trails, and the Hyatt resort and casino. A bit farther east on State 28, location scenes for TV's *Bonanza* series were filmed at the Ponderosa Ranch, open 9:30 A.M. to 5 P.M. May through October (ranchhouse tour, pony rides, gold panning). Admission is $7.50 adults, $5.50 ages 5 through 11.

East shore. South of Incline Village, State 28 passes one of the lake's most beautiful beaches, Sand Harbor at Nevada Lake Tahoe State Park (a day-use facility). Midway down the shore it intersects with State 50, which enters the Tahoe basin near historic Glenbrook Lodge, one of the first on the lake.

South at Cave Rock, the road goes through 25 yards of solid stone. The Washoe Indians regarded this rocky outcropping as holy; they placed their dead to rest in the waters below.

Zephyr Cove, a few miles farther, has another old-time lodge, cabins, a campground, a stable, and a beach. Before you reach the California state line, you'll pass the Round Hill shopping area; Nevada Beach Campground lies along the shore here.

Foothill Wineries

Forget the crowds in the Napa and Sonoma valleys. The serene Sierra foothills are home to several dozen small wineries eager for visitors. Most lie on back roads east of State 49 between Placerville and Murphys. Amador County's Shenandoah Valley, for example, boasts a cluster of 12 wineries ideally set up for an 18-mile, figure-eight tour.

Winemaking was a major industry here beginning around the time of the gold rush. But mine closings, a population exodus, Prohibition, and phylloxera did in all but a few cellars. Today the area is experiencing a renaissance, particularly in robust Zinfandels, as well as Sauvignon Blanc, Muscat, and Barbera.

You can explore the valley by car or bicycle; traffic is light. Weekends are the best time to assure open doors. Start your tour at the general store on State 49 in Plymouth (20 miles south of Placerville, or 32 miles east of Sacramento) and follow the signs. The wineries line Shenandoah Road and Shenandoah School, Bell, and Steiner side roads.

Sobon Estates (formerly the venerable D'Agostino Winery) is the best place to glean local wine history; it's 8 miles northeast of Plymouth on Shenandoah Road. Several wineries have picnic areas. For details on nearby food and lodging, call the Amador Chamber of Commerce at (209) 223-0350.

Gold Country

James Marshall changed the course of California history in January 1848 when he discovered gold in the millrace of Sutter's sawmill in Coloma. Within a year, California was known worldwide, and fortune seekers started the migration that would open the West.

Remnants of those times still exist in the gold rush country of the Sierra foothills. State 49 twists and turns for almost 300 miles through these rolling grass- and fir-clad hills, its elevation around 2,000 feet except where it dips into deep river canyons or climbs the mountains above Downieville.

Though the road could be driven in a day or two, a week is not too long for leisurely browsing. Many charming inns offer choices of lodging. Camping in summer can be uncomfortably hot except in higher, northern reaches.

Northern mines

Deep quartz mining was first developed in the region between Grass Valley and Sierra City. The area is also the birthplace of hydraulic mining, a highly destructive process in which entire mountain ridges were washed away.

Unlike the rest of the gold country, this region is best in summer. Your richest wanderings will be on side roads, often impassable with winter snows and spring runoff. Grass Valley and Nevada City make good bases for exploring. Make sure you have enough fuel and supplies for your outings; services are sparse.

Around Grass Valley. A disastrous 1855 fire destroyed the early community of Grass Valley, leaving little to recall the town's mining camp days except its narrow streets, scattered headframes, and the Empire Mine (see page 105), once the state's largest and richest gold mine.

Even the most sophisticated traveler is impressed by the vast display of mining equipment at the free Northstar Powerhouse Mining Museum (foot of S. Mill Street west of State 49). It's open 10 A.M. to 5 P.M. daily May through mid-

October; call (916) 273-4255 for other seasonal hours.

Several blocks up the street is a replica of the house occupied for some years by exotic dancer Lola Montez and her pet bear. Furnished with many of her belongings, the house is now occupied by the Grass Valley–Nevada County Chamber of Commerce: 248 Mill Street, phone (916) 273-4667.

Among the displays at the Grass Valley Museum in the century-old Mount St. Mary's Convent and Orphanage building (Church and Chapel streets) are a period schoolroom and an early-day doctor's office. The free museum is open noon to 3 P.M. Wednesday and weekends from June through October.

West of town. Detour 4 miles to see tiny Rough and Ready, which seceded from the Union in 1850 and did not legally return until 1948. (From Grass Valley, take West Main Street, which becomes Rough and Ready Highway). The I.O.O.F. Hall and the Fippin Blacksmith Shop, where Lotta Crabtree sang and danced, are among the town's oldest survivors. The Old Toll House now extracts revenues from the sale of antiques.

Several miles northwest is the longest remaining single-span covered bridge in the West. The 1862 Bridgeport Bridge (now closed to traffic) stretches 230 feet across the South Fork of the Yuba River and will soon be part of a new state park.

Nevada City. This appealing town has a well-deserved reputation for beautiful homes, intriguing shops, and carefully preserved antiquity. From here, you can head north 16 miles to the old mining town of North Bloomfield and Malakoff Diggins State Historic Park, an impressive example of hydraulic mining.

Prim Victorian houses with old-fashioned gardens (a few are inns) perch atop Nevada City's hills, sugar maples blaze with fall color, and a neat brick downtown is crammed with in-

triguing shops and museums. Pick up a walking tour map from the chamber of commerce, 132 Main Street.

Downieville and beyond. The mountain settlement of Downieville is still one of the most entrancing of the remaining gold towns. Its old stone, brick, and frame buildings, many built in the 1860s or earlier, face onto quiet, crooked streets and cling to mountainsides above the Yuba River. The Sierra County Museum (open daily in summer) is housed in an old Chinese store and gambling place along the highway.

The jagged Sierra Buttes overshadow the half-ghost town of Sierra City, 13 miles east. Between 1850 and 1852, miners tunneled through these dramatic granite peaks searching for gold. Sierra County Historical Park, an indoor-outdoor museum about a mile to the east, contains the Kentucky Mine's stamp mill, mining equipment, and Indian relics. You can take a guided tour (fee) Wednesday through Sunday from Memorial Day through September, weekends only in October.

Central Mother Lode

Much of California's gold country was called the Mother Lode, but the section between Auburn and Sonora contained the primary gold vein that gave the area its name. Thanks to tourism, this region retains many relatively intact mining towns, a concentration of inns, restaurants, and shops, and plenty of places to pan for gold, fish, boat, swim, or ski.

Auburn. The bustling town at the junction of State 49 and Interstate 80 has long since outgrown its historic heart, now marked "Old Town." For a look at some of its original brick and stone structures, walk along Lincoln Way and Court and Commercial streets just southwest of the highway junction. The gigantic gold-panner statue visible from the freeway honors Claude Chana's first strike.

The Gold Country Museum (1273 High Street in the fairgrounds south of

Quaint Nevada City's downtown streets are lined with vintage structures from 49er days; many house museums of the past.

Old Town) focuses on mining history. Exhibits include a walk-through shaft, working stamp mill model, gold dredge, and assay office. The museum is open 10 A.M. to 4 P.M. Tuesday through Sunday. The small admission charge includes nearby Bernhard Museum, built in 1851 as a hotel and later the home of a pioneer vintner.

Coloma. One of the most important historical stops in the Mother Lode, Coloma today is barely an echo of the boom town that flourished here in the early 1850s. Only a handful of original buildings still stand, most as part of a 265-acre state park (per-car fee).

Stop at the park's visitor center for a walking guide and a look at a small museum (good film). But most of the best exhibits and demonstrations (mostly in summer) are outdoors.

James Marshall discovered gold at Sutter's Mill, where a replica stands. You can try your luck with a pan across the river. On the hill behind town stands a statue of Marshall—who died a penniless recluse. On the way back, peer into his cabin and the nearby restored 1858 Catholic church.

Georgetown detour. A 13-mile detour leads east on State 193 to Georgetown, its 19th-century buildings still intact because a wide main street protected them against fires. Among them are the Balzar House (a former hotel and dance hall), the American Hotel (now the American River Inn), the Georgetown Hotel, and the Wells Fargo Building.

Placerville. Though it was one of the great camps of the Gold Country, Placerville retains only a few mementos of its lusty past. The city center on Main Street is squeezed into a long, narrow strip at the bottom of a ravine south of U.S. 50. Founded in 1848 as Dry Diggins, the town picked up the name of Hangtown next year after some grisly lynchings. The Old City Hall (built in 1857) and its next-door neighbor still serve as city offices.

The free county museum in the fairgrounds north of U.S. 50 includes replicas of an early-day store and country kitchen. It's open 10 A.M. to 4 P.M. Wednesday through Saturday, 1 to 4 P.M. Sunday in summer. In Bedford Park, a mile north of downtown, you can visit the Gold Bug Mine (page 105).

Sutter Creek. About 30 miles south of Placerville on State 49, this picturesque village has a main street lined with attractive old buildings, some sporting overhanging balconies. To learn their history, pick up a free city guide at the Bubble Gum Book Store.

The Sutter Creek Inn up the street (one of two side-by-side inns) was the 1859 home of one of the state's first senators. The Downs House, a block west on Spanish Street, was built in 1873 for a mine foreman.

Tiny Amador City, 2 miles north, is another sightseers' mecca. The brick Imperial Hotel has reopened as an inn and restaurant. The Mine House inn was once headquarters for the Keystone Mine.

Jackson. Though modern facades have transformed many of the old buildings along Main Street, this city has preserved some of its rich heritage. Lively National Hotel at the foot of the street claims to be the state's oldest continually operating hotel. A visitor center (junction of State 49 and State 88) has free guides to area cities.

Visit the county museum on Church Street (open 10 A.M. to 4 P.M. Wednesday through Sunday; donations requested) to learn about Jackson's mining role. Don't let the size of wee St. Sava's Serbian Orthodox Church on North Main fool you; it's the mother church for the western hemisphere.

The Kennedy and Argonaut mines at the north edge of town have been closed for decades, but headframes, some buildings, and huge tailing wheels built to carry waste to a settling pond over the hills still stand. To get a close look at the wheels, follow Jackson Gate Road northeast of downtown to Tailing Wheels Park. Along the road lie several of the city's best Italian restaurants, an antique store housed in the county's oldest building, and two bed-and-breakfasts.

State 88 (open all year) heads east over Carson Pass past several good summer trout lakes (Bear Reservoir, Silver Lake, and Caples Lake) and a couple of winter ski areas (the largest is Kirkwood).

About 12 miles east of Jackson off State 88, a side road leads north to the mining camp of Volcano, Indian Grinding Rock State Historic Park (huge outcropping used by Miwok Indians as a mortar, reconstructed village, and museum), and Daffodil Hill, where you'll see an explosion of spring color in a free hillside garden.

San Andreas to Angels Camp. Follow a sign marked "Historic" to get behind San Andreas' modern mask. The Calaveras County Museum (a three-building complex that includes the I.O.O.F. Hall, courthouse, and jail) a block east of Main Street is worth a stop. Black Bart was tried in the courthouse and awaited trial in the jail. The museum is open 10 A.M. to 4 P.M. daily (small fee). West of town, the intriguing Pioneer Cemetery dates back at least to 1851.

Thanks to Mark Twain, Angels Camp, 12 miles south, is probably best noted for its frog-jumping contest in May. You'll find a few remembrances of gold-mining days—the Angels Hotel, the ubiquitous I.O.O.F. Hall, and the indoor-outdoor mining museum at the north end of town.

Murphys detour. You'll feel as if the clock had stopped when you take State 4 east to Murphys (9 miles from State 49). Gingerbread Victorians peek from behind white picket fences, and tall locust trees border the main street.

The Murphys Hotel, opened in 1856, displays an illustrious register of temporary residents—U.S. Grant, Thomas Lipton, Horatio Alger, Charles Bolton (Black Bart), and more. Across the street, the Old Timers Museum displays gold rush memorabilia (open Friday through Sunday, small admission).

Southern mines

The placer and quartz veins in the southern gold country never rivaled those to the north. Tourists on their way to Yosemite arrived almost as soon as the prospectors.

Sonora. Sonora, at the junction of State highways 49 and 108, is as bustling today as a century ago, but considerably less rowdy. Layers of modernity cover the aged buildings lining Washington Street, the main thoroughfare, but a drive along narrow, hilly streets reveals many relics of the past.

Pick up a walking tour guide of Victorian homes at the century-old jail and museum at 158 W. Bradford Road or at the Tuolumne County Visitors Bureau offices, 55 W. Stockton Road. Graceful St. James Episcopal Church on Washington Street, built in 1860, is one of the gold country's most beautiful frame structures.

Columbia State Historic Park. Four miles north of Sonora via State 49 and Parrotts Ferry Road is Columbia, once called the "Gem of the Southern Mines" for its gold output. This living museum is an ideal place to learn about mining and miners.

Though it attracts thousands of visitors on summer days and appears quite commercial, the town is historically authentic. Stop by the park headquarters for a brochure outlining a 1½-hour stroll through the traffic-free streets. Children enjoy panning for treasure, riding the jouncing horse-drawn stagecoach, sipping sarsaparilla at a saloon, or even getting a haircut at the state's oldest barbershop.

From June through September, a free bus carries visitors to an operating gold mine. Theatrical performances take place in summer at the Fallon House Theater, and both the City Hotel and Fallon House are back in business as hostelries and restaurants.

Jamestown. Fire has been the enemy of this little town 3 miles south of Sonora, but a few proud structures remain, including some of the region's oldest operating inns. A profusion of antique stores, several places to pan for gold, and a couple of good restaurants add to its appeal.

At Railtown 1897 State Historic Park, you'll find the steam locomotives, vintage rolling stock, and 26-acre roundhouse and shop complex of the Sierra Railway. Nearly 200 feature movies, television shows, and commercials have been filmed along the narrow gauge line, which once connected mines with Central Valley shipping centers.

The park is open daily May through September, weekends and holidays the rest of the year, from 10 A.M. to 5:30 P.M. (small admission charge). Rail excursions over some of the original line run spring and through September (see page 126).

Coulterville. About halfway between Sonora and Mariposa, this photogenic little community is enriched by the presence of the Jeffrey Hotel (once a stagecoach stop, now an inn), built in 1851 of rock and adobe with walls 3 feet thick. The adjoining Magnolia Saloon displays firearms, minerals, coins, and other memorabilia.

Across the street are the remains of the Coulter Hotel and the Wells Fargo building (a museum), once operated by Buffalo Bill's brothers. In the small plaza are the local "hangin' tree" and the Whistling Billy, a small steam engine once used to haul ore from the Mary Harrison Mine north of town. The Sun Sun Wo adobe at the east end of Main Street is all that remains of a once-sizable Chinese population.

Mariposa. Halfway between Merced and Yosemite National Park, Mariposa has one of the choicest bit of architecture of the gold rush era. The two-story courthouse at the north end of town has been in use continuously since it was erected in 1854.

Don't miss the California State Mining and Mineral Museum in the fairgrounds on State 49 about 1½ miles south of its junction with State 140. One wing contains 20,000 gems and minerals. Artifacts and photographs in another wing tell the story of mining. A scale model of a stamp mill whirls into action with the push of a button. Dioramas in a tunnel cut into a hill behind the museum depict miners drilling and blasting. Hours are 10 A.M. to 6 P.M. daily (to 4 P.M. on Sunday). A moderate admission is charged.

Oakhurst. At the southern terminus of State 49, Oakhurst (called Fresno Flats in its heyday) shows little evidence of its hectic mining past, but the historical park at 427 High School Road displays remnants of it. The French-style chateau on the hill at 48688 Victoria Lane is Erna's Elderberry House, a mecca for diners.

Inside the Mines

Piles of tailings, jutting headframes, rusty monitors, and an occasional stamp mill—these reminders of the industry that changed California's destiny crop up throughout the gold country. But it's also possible to get a peek inside the mines that once burrowed into these hills.

At the Empire Mine State Historic Park in Grass Valley (1 mile east of State 49 on Empire Street), tours of one of the state's deepest and most productive sites include a brief entry into the mine itself. Visitors also see offices, shops, and the owner's residence. The 784-acre park (small admission) is open 10 A.M. to 5 P.M. daily except in winter. For details, call (916) 273-8522.

At Placerville's Gold Bug Mine, you can walk into a tunnel and examine an old stamp mill. The mine is open 10 A.M. to 4 P.M. daily in summer, weekends only in spring and autumn (small fee). Take Bedford Avenue to Gold Bug Park 1 mile north of U.S. 50. For information, call (916) 622-0832.

A summer visit to Columbia State Historic Park can include a tour to a nearby working gold mine. Free buses transport visitors from Main Street. For information, call (209) 532-4301.

At the California State Mining and Mineral Museum in Mariposa, you can walk through a 150-foot-long mine tunnel.

In Yosemite National Park's high country, LeConte Falls on the Tuolumne River tumbles over glaciated cliffs on its rush down the canyon.

Yosemite National Park

By any standards one of the nation's most spectacular parks, Yosemite is loved to death. More than 3 million people visit the century-old park annually, 70 percent of them arriving during the summer and most never venturing outside the 7 square miles of Yosemite Valley.

Though its monumental granite walls and high-diving waterfalls make the valley a logical place to begin a visit, there remain almost 1,200 square miles of less crowded splendor to explore: glaciers, giant sequoias, alpine meadows, trout-filled streams and lakes, and 13,000-foot Sierra Nevada peaks.

The Awhaneechee Indians were the park's first residents, camping, fishing, hunting, and collecting acorns here in summer. Trappers and prospectors glimpsed the valley, but no one else entered it until the U.S. Cavalry came on the scene in 1851. Word of its beauty spread quickly, and four years later the first party of tourists arrived to see the great U-shaped valley created by glaciers some two million years ago.

Park preservation

Yosemite is more than just another pretty place—it's the nation's first federally mandated park and the model upon which our national park system was based. In 1864, when President Lincoln signed legislation deeding Yosemite to California as a public trust (not a national park), the grant contained two separate wonders: Yosemite Valley and the Mariposa Grove of giant sequoias (now part of the park).

Hetch Hetchy Valley (later flooded by a dam on the Tuolumne River to give San Francisco drinking water) and the high country along the Sierra crest were added in 1890, when Yosemite National Park was created. Much of the credit for the establishment of the national park goes to pioneer environmentalist John Muir, who lobbied for its creation.

Yosemite is also a case study of what happens to an area that becomes too popular. Weekend traffic clogs valley roads and overflows parking lots, fragile areas are trampled by careless hikers and campers, and more than 1,000 structures clutter the valley floor.

Though a master plan to return the valley to a more natural state was never fully implemented, in part because of a lack of funds, some progress has been made. Computerized reservations for valley lodging and campsites simplify the search for a place to sleep, and free shuttle buses and paved bicycle paths link all of the valley's camping, lodging, and visitor centers, making it possible to get along just fine without a car. But the question of whether or not visitor areas should be limited in order to protect the environment remains a controversial one.

Park highlights

Yosemite is the Sierra Nevada's crown jewel. Within its limits lie ecosystems as diverse as foothill woodlands and alpine tundra, a grand backdrop for a bonanza of recreational possibilities.

Yosemite Valley. Barely 7 miles long and only a mile at its widest point, the valley is actually more like a canyon. Granite ramparts draped with thundering falls in the spring and etched in sharp relief by snow in winter soar more than 3,000 feet above the meadow, and great domes and pinnacles fringe canyon rims. The Merced River threads its way along the valley floor through groves of pines and oaks, thickets of shrubbery, and patches of flowers and ferns.

Visitor facilities are all in the valley's eastern end: lodging and convenience stores at Curry Village, Yosemite Lodge, and the historic Ahwahnee Hotel; a grocery and other services at Yosemite Village, where you'll also find the park headquarters and visitor center. A quarter-mile trail from the village leads to the base of 2,425-foot Yosemite Falls, the continent's highest waterfall.

You'll find a variety of activities available, from free nature walks and art classes to bicycle and raft rentals, horseback rides, and rock-climbing lessons. Details are printed in the free "Yosemite Guide," available at entry stations, most service facilities, and the Valley Visitor Center at busy Yosemite Village.

The visitor center also provides a basic overview of the park's natural history (as does the small nature center at Happy Isles to the east). The Indian Cultural Museum next door contains an exquisite collection of basketry. In the reconstructed village behind, you'll see tool making, basket weaving, beadwork, and Indian games demonstrated daily in summer.

Glacier Point. To appreciate its glacier-scoured geology fully, you have to leave the valley. At Glacier Point Overlook on the south rim you can see the entire valley, from Yosemite Falls to the sheared granite wall of Half Dome. Beyond rise the snow-clad peaks of the high country.

Glacier Point is a circuitous 30-mile drive from the valley. Take Wawona Road south to Chinquapin, and turn left onto Glacier Point Road (closed in winter about a mile beyond Badger Pass Ski Area). Stop at the Wawona Tunnel pullout for a classic view from Bridalveil Fall to Half Dome and beyond.

Bus service from the valley offers an option for those who'd like a one-way hike from the rim to the valley. Early morning is the best time to start out on the 9-mile Panorama Trail, longest and grandest of the routes to the valley. Take a picnic and water: spectacular overlooks can stretch this into a leisurely day-long outing.

Wawona & the Big Trees. The magnificent Mariposa Grove of giant sequoias lies near the park's south entrance (State 41), 36 miles from the valley. In this grand forest, more than 200 trees measure at least 10 feet in diameter. Largest—30 feet around and 210 feet tall—and probably the oldest is Grizzly Giant. A walk among the trees offers grand vertical views.

...Yosemite

Guided tours (fee) run from the valley to the grove in summer, with a stop at Wawona's lovely 1800s hotel and the Pioneer Yosemite History Center. If you drive on your own, park in the lot at the edge of the grove. One-hour tram tours carry visitors through the grove every 15 minutes from May to October (moderate fee). Or you can follow a 2½-mile trail to the upper grove.

Along the Tioga Road. If you leave Yosemite without a visit to the wild and uncrowded backcountry, you'll miss some of the park's finest scenery and best experiences. This land of majestic peaks, rocky chasms, wildflower-trimmed meadows, brilliant blue lakes, and innumerable rivers is accessible mainly by Tioga Road (State 120), usually open late May through October.

Just driving through, you learn a good deal about the natural history of these mountains from roadside exhibits. You'll discover even more if you do some exploring on foot.

Rustic cabins and lodges, tent camps, and more secluded campsites provide a choice of overnight accommodations. To prevent overcrowding, wilderness permits are now required for any overnight stay in the backcountry. They are available free at the Valley Visitor Center, Wawona, Big Oak Flat Information Station, or Tuolumne Meadows. It's a good idea to get your permit a day ahead, as trailheads fill up most summer weekends. Or you can reserve by mail from February through May; send a brief itinerary to Wilderness Permits, Box 577, Yosemite National Park, CA 95389.

Pick up backcountry maps and trail guides at park visitor centers and stores.

High Sierra loop. Five walk-in camps lie within a short day's hike of one another around Tuolumne Meadows. The woodstove-heated tent villages and cabins have comfortable beds and linens, showers and toilet facilities, hearty breakfasts and dinners, and, if you request them, box lunches for the trail. All you need to carry is a day pack with extra clothes, toiletries, and personal gear. The camp cost is $66 per night including meals; trail lunches are an extra charge.

If you prefer to sleep under the stars, you can reserve dinner or breakfast at the camps, which will also store food overnight for you so it won't attract bears (otherwise, be sure to use the cables or hooked poles provided for hanging your food).

Reservations, in great demand, are taken in early December for the next summer, but cancellations have been known to occur; call (209) 454-2002. Or you can try to reserve space on guided hikes or saddle trips.

You need to be in reasonably good shape to make these hikes. With trail elevations as high as 10,300 feet, hiking can be strenuous, requiring steady walks of as long as seven hours between camps.

Visitor strategy

Planning your Yosemite visit is essential, particularly if you're staying in the valley. Though it never hurts to call for last-minute cancellations, campsites and lodging are usually booked months in advance in summer. The quality of your experience will be better if you can avoid this peak period, especially around Memorial Day, Fourth of July, and Labor Day holidays.

Pick a season. For visitors who want to escape the crowds by visiting the high country, summer is still the time to go. While the valley is open year-round, most of Yosemite's 1,189 square miles are accessible only spring through autumn.

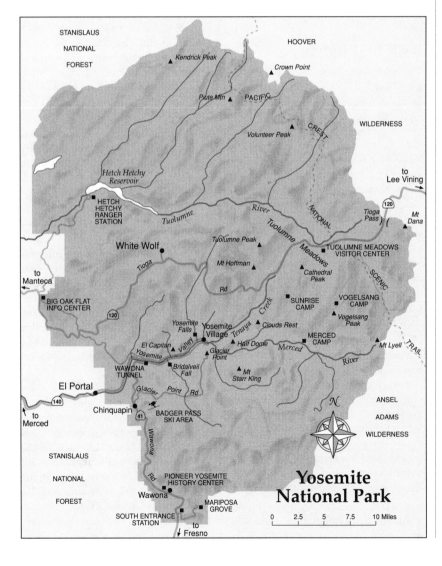

Yosemite National Park

Off-season visits (before Memorial Day and after September) can be spectacular. In autumn, the valley quiets down somewhat, campgrounds empty, nights get nippy, and leaves turn from green to crimson and gold. One reward of a Yosemite spring vacation is a chance to view the waterfalls at their best, roaring over cliffs to splash through misty rainbows on the valley floor.

For many people, winter's solitude restores the grandeur of the valley, returning its sense of wildness. Frosty weather makes hiking difficult but signals the beginning of snow fun. You can skate, sled, and ski tour against a backdrop of snow-etched canyon walls.

The park's ski season at Badger Pass (see page 124) usually lasts from Thanksgiving to mid April. A free bus shuttles visitors from the valley, about 20 minutes away. More than 350 miles of cross-country trails are also open.

Getting there. Yosemite Valley is a 4-hour drive from the San Francisco area. The park can also be reached by Amtrak and Greyhound to Merced. Two companies offer daily bus service between Merced and Yosemite year-round; for details call Yosemite Gray Line, (209) 383-1563, or Via Yosemite, (209) 722-0366. Yosemite Gray Line also offers service to the park from Fresno (location of the closest major airport). Rental cars are also available at the Fresno airport.

Three highways penetrate the park; you can pick up any of them from State 99, which runs north-south through the Central Valley. Curvy State 120, the Tioga Road (closed in winter), runs from Manteca on the west all the way to Lee Vining on the east side of the park. It's 81 miles from Merced to Yosemite Valley on State 140, the lowest and least winding of the main roads. From Fresno to the southern entrance via State 41 is an 89-mile drive.

Major roads from the west are kept open year-round; State 140 has first priority for snow removal. Always carry chains in winter. For current road conditions, call (209) 372-4605.

Getting around. Whenever and wherever possible, leave your car and use public transportation. Frequent free shuttle buses will whisk you through the valley from campgrounds and lodgings to major facilities and many trailheads.

Cycling is another easy way to get around. A good 9 miles of paved paths loop through the eastern end of the valley. You can rent single-speed bikes at Yosemite Lodge or Curry Village.

In summer, 2-hour narrated tram tours (fee) leave Yosemite Lodge every half-hour daily; there's an evening run on full moon nights. Buses are also available to Glacier Point, Mariposa Grove, and Tuolumne Meadows. Though they are seldom full, it's wise to reserve space by calling (209) 372-1240.

Lodging. Valley accommodations range widely in choice and price. Curry Village has rustic tent cabins (about $30 for two people), modern Yosemite Lodge and nearby cabins are mid-priced, and majestic stone-and-timber Ahwahnee offers luxury (around $185). All locations have restaurants; try the Ahwahnee's Sunday brunch even if you're staying elsewhere.

Lodging is also available at Wawona (pool, tennis court, 9-hole golf course, stables) and, in the high country off Tioga Road, at Tuolumne Meadows (tent cabins, central dining hall) and White Wolf (tent cabins, dining room). The Wawona Hotel, a national historic landmark near the Mariposa Grove, is open from mid-spring to early autumn. Tuolumne Meadows and White Wolf open when the weather permits.

Yosemite reservations may be made up to a year in advance; call (209) 252-4848. A deposit of one night's stay is required. To try for a cancellation, check the front desk of the hotel of your choice.

Another alternative is to establish a base outside the park. You can often find last-minute motel space in El Portal, Mariposa, Oakhurst, and other towns within an hour of the valley. Marriott's new Tenaya Lodge is an upscale choice in Fish Camp south of the park on State 41 (shuttle service provided).

Camping. Valley campgrounds are open from Memorial Day through the end of September. At least two in the valley and one at Wawona stay open year-round. Campgrounds in the high country remain open as long as weather permits.

During the camping season, campgrounds in Yosemite Valley, Hodgdon Meadow, Crane Flat, and Tuolumne Meadows are on a reservation basis through Ticketron. Sites can be reserved up to eight weeks ahead. To get applications for reservations at High Sierra camps for the following summer, call (209) 252-4848 in early November. They must be returned by the first Monday in December. For additional information, see page 120.

East of the Sierra

An ancient lake and a mining ghost town are two reasons to head east of Yosemite National Park.

Spectacular tufa formations surround Mono Lake (off U.S. 395 at Lee Vining), a 60-square-mile body of salty alkaline water that is a resting spot for millions of migratory birds. There's a visitor center on the south shore.

To the north is one of the West's best preserved mining ghost towns.

Bodie State Historic Park includes 170 weathered buildings from the town's gold-mining heyday of the 1870s. Rangers give free history talks at 3 P.M. daily except Monday and Thursday. To get to Bodie, take State 270 east from U.S. 395; the last 3 miles are unpaved.

In summer, you can reach U.S. 395 from Yosemite via the Tioga Road. Snow closes this and other roads from the west in winter.

Central Valley

*T*he flat Central Valley provides strong contrast to its east-west boundaries: the towering peaks of the Sierra Nevada and the hills of the Coast Range. At its southern edge rise the Tehachapi Mountains, while the foothills of the southern Cascades and the northern Coast Range rim it on the north.

It's a big valley, extending 465 miles from north to south and varying from 30 to 60 miles in width. Actually, it's two valleys, the Sacramento and the San Joaquin. Both have namesake rivers meandering through much of their lengths.

Though the San Joaquin Valley extends south beyond Bakersfield, our coverage in this book ends at Fresno.

Contacts

These agencies offer information on attractions and accommodations. See additional contacts throughout this chapter.

Sacramento Convention & Visitors Bureau
1421 K St.
Sacramento, CA 95814
(916) 449-6711

Sacramento Visitor Information Center
1104 Front St.
Sacramento, CA 95814
(916) 442-7644

Fresno Convention & Visitors Bureau
808 M St.
Fresno, CA 93721
(800) 543-8488

For a description of the southern part of the valley, see our companion book, the *Southern California Travel Guide*.

A traveler's view

Thanks to irrigation, the 18,000-square-mile Central Valley is the richest agricultural region in the world. Orchards, vineyards, and such staple crops as onions, sweet potatoes, grain, and cotton form the area's economic base.

Recreation is plentiful throughout the valley, whose lakes and rivers afford many opportunities for rafting, waterskiing, fishing, and picnicking. The Delta, a vast inland sea, provides more than 1,000 miles of interconnecting waterways ideal for houseboating.

Sacramento, the valley's largest city and the state capital, brims with pioneer history and gold rush allure. It's also home to the West's first art museum and the state's first theater. The railroad museum in Old Sacramento is the largest of its kind in the world.

Nearby Stockton, on a wide stretch of the Delta, is the area's major port, hosting oceangoing freighters. Farther south lie Modesto, Merced, and Fresno, agricultural communities that also act as gateways to the gold country and high Sierra regions.

Planning a trip

The Central Valley sizzles in midsummer, but residents and visitors cool off in the many lakes, rivers, and mountain retreats nearby. The rest of the year is pleasant except for occasional dense, low-lying fogs in winter.

Where to stay. Sacramento makes a good base for exploring the valley. Most of the major highways through central California pass through or around the city. And it's served by a number of major carriers and commuter airlines, as well as Amtrak and Greyhound.

The rapidly growing city (current population hovers around 370,000) offers a variety of accommodations, including the restored *Delta King* riverboat, the upscale Sterling Hotel (a refurbished 19th-century mansion), and several downtown bed-and-breakfast inns.

All large valley cities have some air, rail, and bus service (Fresno's regional airport is particularly busy). Rental cars are available in major cities.

Getting around. You'll need a car to explore this far-flung area. Interstate 5, on the valley's western side, is the most heavily traveled route between Southern and Northern California. A swift but somewhat monotonous freeway, it bypasses the towns that grew up along State 99, the slower highway to its east.

A number of east-west feeder roads connect the two routes, passing through small farming communities, and the two highways join at Red Bluff, just north of the valley.

Sacramento lies about halfway between San Francisco and Lake Tahoe on Interstate 80, the region's major east-west artery. From Sacramento, U.S. 50 also reaches east into the Sierra toward Lake Tahoe and Nevada beyond. Interstate 580 from the Bay Area slices through the valley, connecting with Interstate 5 near Stockton.

An impressive landmark in downtown Sacramento since 1874, the golden-domed State Capitol contains art and history displays. Free tours take place daily.

Sacramento

Sacramento's history began with the splash of Captain John A. Sutter's anchor in the American River in 1839. Sutter, a Swiss immigrant, had navigated up the Sacramento River from San Francisco en route to a 50,000-acre parcel of land granted him by the Mexican government. On a knoll not far from the anchorage, he built a fort to protect his 76-square-mile holding, established an embarcadero, and called the area New Helvetia.

When gold was discovered at Sutter's sawmill in Coloma, Sacramento quickly became a lusty boomtown, connected to other communities like Marysville and Red Bluff by river steamer and sailing schooner. When the gold ceased to pan out, agriculture developed, and the city emerged as a supply center.

Outdoor family fun

Although it's adorned with wide, tree-lined boulevards and elegant Victorian houses and boasts a variety of recreational activities and attractions, Sacramento is often overlooked by visitors. Yet it's a rewarding stop.

Cruises. Riverboats ply the Sacramento on 1½-hour narrated cruises from spring through autumn. Short cruises depart from the L Street Landing in Old Sacramento, the redeveloped historic district. Longer trips through the Delta between Sacramento and San Francisco leave from the port (west side of the river, south of Interstate 80) on weekends from May to October (see page 124).

American River Parkway. A 23-mile-long strip of green connects several parks (picnic sites, hiking and riding trails, boat-launching facilities, and an 18-hole golf course) along the banks of the American River between Nimbus Dam to the northeast and the stream's junction with the Sacramento River. A paved bicycle trail runs 30-plus miles from Discovery Park to Folsom Lake.

William Land Park. Bounded by Freeport and Riverside boulevards, 13th Avenue, and Sutterville Road, this large park in south Sacramento offers several child-pleasers: the Sacramento Zoo (open daily; small fee) and Fairytale Village (open daily February through November, variable winter schedule; small fee). The park also has pools, gardens, a public golf course, baseball diamonds, picnic grounds, and a grove of flowering cherries. In summer, Shakespeare finds evening audiences in the park's outdoor amphitheater.

Gibson Ranch County Park. Northeast of the downtown area, a 326-acre 1870s ranch delights youngsters, who can feed farm animals, watch milking demonstrations, see early-day farm equipment, and fish in a lake alive with ducks, mudhens, geese, and muskrats. To get there, take Watt Avenue north to Elverta Road, turn left and follow it to the entrance. The free park is open daily from 7 A.M. to dusk.

Sacramento Science Center. The dry title belies the interesting displays at this combination natural history and physical science complex, located northeast of downtown at 3615 Auburn Boulevard. A live animal hall of more than 45 species of mammals, birds, and reptiles hosts weekend shows at 2 and 4 P.M. Planetarium shows take place weekends at 11 A.M. and 3 P.M. A trail roams through the nature area outside (picnic tables available). A modest admission is charged; shows are extra.

Capital beginnings

It's not surprising that Sacramento became the state capital in 1854. Its prime location has always made it a vital link in the state's river, rail, and highway network. California's first railroad began here in 1856, and a few years later the city became the western terminus of the Pony Express line.

Capitol Park. An oasis on hot summer days, the 40 well-landscaped acres surrounding the capitol building include plantings from around the world. A 10-day Camellia Festival in March showcases the park's more than 800 varieties. You'll also notice several monuments and a wealth of squirrels.

Capitol tour. Office buildings line the Capitol Mall corridor as you near the domed capitol at 11th Street between L and N. A $68-million restoration has returned 19th-century grandeur to the massive structure.

Two different guided tours take place every hour between 9 A.M. and 4 P.M. weekdays, from 10 A.M. on weekends. A third tour is added in summer. Free tickets are issued a half-hour before each tour from the office in the basement. Or you can wander through seven historic rooms on your own after picking up a free brochure. A short film describes the building.

Old Governor's Mansion. This elegant 19th-century Victorian at 16th and H streets was home to 13 California governors. Now vacant, it's open only for guided tours, which take place daily on the hour from 10 A.M. to 4 P.M. Expect a small admission fee.

Old Sacramento

This four-block-long historic district along the east bank of the Sacramento River (between Capitol Mall and I Street) preserves the largest collection of gold rush–era buildings on the Pacific Coast. Visitors stroll plank sidewalks past 100 fully restored brick-and-frame structures, many housing turn-of-the-century museums. No ghost town, this 28-acre area teems with restaurants, gift shops, and offices.

Start your walking tour at the visitor center (1104 Front Street), open daily from 9 A.M. to 5 P.M. Maps there show landmarks and attractions.

You'll pass the 1849 Old Eagle Theater (Front and J streets), the period schoolhouse (Front and L), and the B. F. Hastings Building (2nd and J), where museums commemorate the Pony Express, Wells Fargo, and the California Supreme Court.

California State Railroad Museum. This impressive interpretive railroad museum (2nd and I streets), the largest in the world, is the area's premier attraction. More than 20 restored locomotives and cars and a wealth of historical railroad exhibits are on display. A film describes 19th-century railroads. The authentic reconstruction of the nearby 1876 Central Pacific Passenger Station recalls the sights and sounds of the era. On summer weekends, a steam train takes passengers on a 45-minute ride (see page 126).

Tickets good for a same-day visit to both locations (open 10 A.M. to 5 P.M.

daily) are $5 for adults, $2 for children 6 to 17. Train rides are extra.

Sacramento History Museum. The facade of the red brick building at Front and I streets housing memories of the city's colorful past is a true replica of the public building (city hall, jail, and waterworks) constructed on this site in 1854. Inside, it looks more like an ultramodern mall, with a sunken theater, an extensive gold collection, a canning line, and a re-created 1920s farm kitchen. The museum is open 10 A.M. to 4:30 P.M. Tuesday through Sunday; a modest admission fee is charged.

Delta King. You can overnight aboard the 285-foot stern-wheeler moored along the riverfront or visit its museum, theater, shops, restaurant, and lounges. A sister ship of the *Delta Queen* (now on the Mississippi River), it carried passengers between Sacramento and San Francisco in the 1920s and 1930s.

Other city attractions

Sutter's reconstructed fort, the West's oldest art museum, and showcases for almonds, Indian artifacts, and vintage cars make other interesting stops around town.

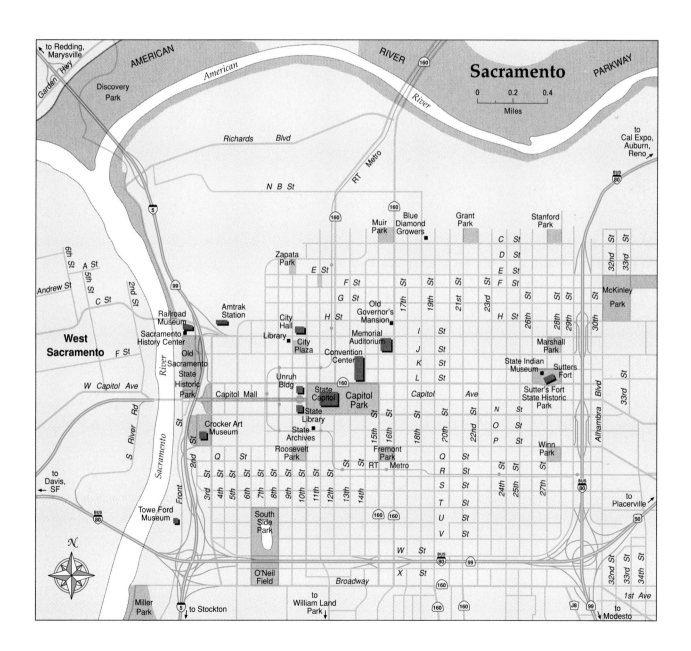

Evening strollers and cyclists pass Old Sacramento's riverfront park; the restored stern-wheeler Delta King, now a hotel, floats in front of the Tower Bridge. Tracks carry steam-powered excursion trains.

...Sacramento

Sutter's Fort State Historic Park. Headset narration allows visitors to tour Captain Sutter's first settlement at their own pace. The fort looks much as it did in 1846, with blacksmith shops, a prison, and living quarters. Located at 2701 L Street, it's open daily (except major holidays) from 10 A.M. to 5 P.M. The modest admission includes headsets.

State Indian Museum. At 2618 K Street (adjacent to Sutter's Fort), this recently revitalized museum interprets the tribal life of California's Native Americans, with displays of artifacts, jewelry, and clothing. The basket collection is particularly good. Hours and admission fees are the same as at the fort.

Crocker Art Museum. The elegant craftsmanship of this stately Victorian mansion built by Judge E. B. Crocker in 1873 to house his private art collection made a perfect setting for its grand displays. But a glass pavilion connecting it to the Crockers' actual home has added space. Of particular interest are its Asian art and contemporary California paintings. On the first floor, a Discovery Gallery caters to children's interests.

The museum, at 216 O Street, is open Tuesday through Sunday, 10 A.M. to 5 P.M. (to 9 P.M. on Thursday). Admission is modest.

Towe Ford Museum. Car buffs shouldn't miss this unique collection of antique Fords at 2200 Front Street. It's the world's most complete, with every year and model from 1903 to 1953 including Phaetons, roadsters, woodies, and other fondly remembered styles. On weekends, shuttle buses run between it and the Sacramento Visitor Information Center (see page 110). Open 10 A.M. to 6 P.M. daily, the museum charges admission of $5 for adults, $2.50 for teenagers, and $1 for children.

Blue Diamond Growers. Nuts are the theme at this almond factory (18th and C streets). Free guided tours (9 and 10 A.M., 1 and 2 P.M. weekdays) include a film (also shown Saturday).

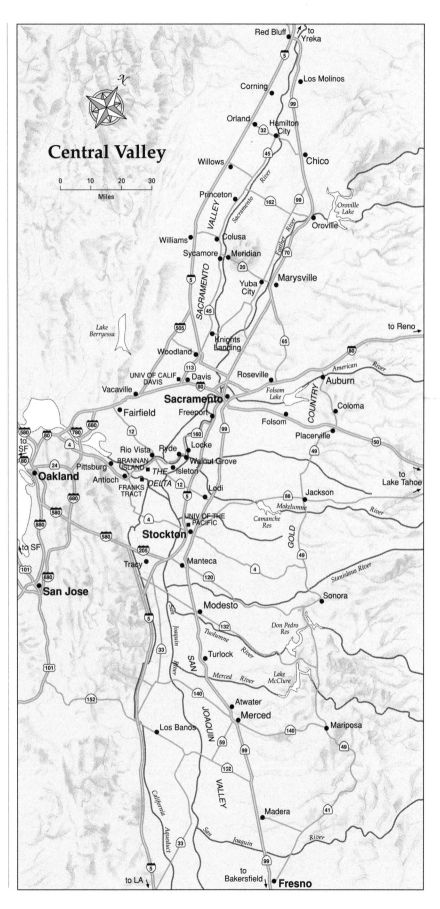

Central Valley

Along the Sacramento

The quiet towns and countryside along the banks of the Sacramento River north of the capital city seem little changed since their beginnings in the early 1900s. To explore by car, you'll have to stray slightly off busy interstates onto two-lane, lightly traveled back roads that follow the river's meanderings. If possible, plan your drive for spring or early summer: cottonwoods have leafed out, fruit orchards are in bloom, crops are planted, and summer's heat hasn't yet descended on the valley.

Boating. If you pick your time and place, there's plenty of elbow room on the river for fishing, boating, and waterskiing. Most towns and fishing resorts along the route have boat-launching facilities. Your best bet for gas to the north of Colusa is Los Molinos, about a mile east of the river.

How to get there. If you're heading east on Interstate 80, turn north on State 113 at Davis (home of a University of California campus). To reach State 113 from Sacramento, exit Interstate 5 at Woodland (full of turn-of-the century architectural gems) and follow the signs.

Along the route

At Knights Landing, a small community somewhat reminiscent of towns along Mark Twain's Mississippi, turn left onto 4th Street, a narrow levee road along the river's south bank, to reach State 45. As the road angles northwest across open farmland, note the rice "checks"—flooded paddies surrounded by low levees.

Past the town of Sycamore, detour east across the river on State 20 to visit the quiet streets of Meridian. A small grocery store near the river can provide the makings for a picnic lunch.

Colusa, 5 miles farther north on State 45, is a popular swimming and waterskiing center. A 67-acre recreation area on the west bank of the river has a launching ramp, picnic sites, a sandy beach, and unimproved campsites.

Three miles southwest of town lies one of the Sacramento Valley's four wildlife refuges, winter home for millions of migratory wildfowl. For a walking tour, pick up a map at the headquarters.

At Princeton (about 15 miles north of Colusa), you can board the last operating ferry on the Sacramento River for a 2-minute ride across the river. State 45 continues north 23 miles to Hamilton City. From here, you can turn west to reach Interstate 5 at Orland or head east to Chico, off State 99.

Chico

At the north end of the Central Valley lies the college town of Chico, founded in 1849 on a ranch purchased by John Bidwell, a Civil War–era general and former gold miner. If his antebellum-style house and its surrounding parkland (now a 2,400-acre state park) look familiar, you might have seen them in such movies as *Gone with the Wind*.

Guided tours of the mansion, located at 525 The Esplanade, take place from 10 A.M. to 5 P.M. daily (small admission). The large park (picnic sites, playing fields, wilderness areas) winds along Chico Creek 10 miles into the foothills.

Detours from Interstate 5

Two favorite outings lie near Sacramento within easy striking distance of Interstate 5: Vacaville, 30 miles west on Interstate 80, and Folsom, 15 miles east off U.S. 50.

Vacaville. Much of this city's visitor appeal centers an the Nut Tree, a dining spot–cum–amusement park and shopping center. Now a large complex of restaurants and stores complete with private airport, it all started with a single black walnut tree planted in 1860 to shade passersby on the Emigrant Trail.

An addition to the property is the large factory outlet center (open daily to 9 P.M.) on the south side of Interstate 80. And a block away (junction of Interstate 80 and 505), you can work your way through the giant mazes of the WOOZ ($6.50 adults, $5 ages 5 through 12); call (707) 446-3977 for seasonal hours.

Folsom. The gaslight and restored buildings along Sutter Street whisper of this town's gold-mining past. The chamber of commerce is in the old Southern Pacific depot at Sutter and Wool streets; old cars are on display outside. A blacksmith shop and miner's cabin stand nearby.

Johnny Cash helped familiarize people with Folsom State Prison, 2 miles north of town. A gift shop at the main gate sells items crafted by the prisoners, and a fascinating museum documents the history of incarceration in California.

The 75-mile shoreline of Folsom Lake is all part of a state recreation area popular with boaters, waterskiers, anglers, campers, and picnickers. Hikers and horseback riders have 65 miles of trails to roam.

The Delta

The Sacramento–San Joaquin Delta, an irregularly bounded area of almost 740,000 acres (50,000 of which are water), extends from Sacramento south to Tracy and from Stockton east as far as Pittsburg. With almost 1,000 miles of navigable sloughs bearing such astonishing names as Hog, Little Potato, Lost Whiskey, Little Conception, and Lookout, it's a boater's haven.

Once a densely forested everglade, the area was denuded to feed the furnaces of old riverboats. The muddy expanses that remained were later transformed into hundreds of levee-rimmed islands (many still called "tracts"), where enterprising farmers prosper with asparagus and fruit crops.

Fed by two of the West's largest rivers, the Sacramento and the San Joaquin, the Delta also accepts tribute from the Mokelumne, Stanislaus, Tuolumne, Merced, and Kings rivers before tumbling on into the San Francisco Bay.

Exploring the Delta

One of the most startling experiences for new visitors to the Delta is to look across a flat field of swaying grain and see the profile of a freighter moving silently along a levee top. Yet it's as characteristic of the region as the sudsy wake of a water-skier's craft or the bobbing of a fishing boat.

Interstates 5, 80, 580, and 680 encircle this vast waterway, yet you hardly know it's there. To gain access by car, you have to travel State highways 4, 12, or 160 and some of the county roads. A detailed map of the region can be obtained from area tackle shops; or send $2.75 to Delta Map, P.O. Box 9140, Stockton, CA 95208.

Boating. The best and most popular way to explore this watery world is by boat. Bring your own or rent anything from a houseboat to a fishing skiff. One- and two-day boat tours are also available from Sacramento, Stockton, and San Francisco (see page 124). Shorter summer cruises also depart from Brentwood and Isleton.

Houseboats can be rented all through the Delta. For a listing of agencies, contact the chambers of commerce for Antioch—(415) 757-1800—and Stockton—(209) 466-7066.

The basic navigational guide in the Delta region is Chart 5527SC (San Joaquin River). Chart 5528SC is a guide to the Sacramento River from Andrus Island to Sacramento, including the northern reaches of the Delta. For information and the price of the charts, write to the Distribution Division (C44), National Ocean Survey, Riverdale, MD 20840.

For free pamphlets on state boating regulations and water safety, write to Commanding Officer (B), 12th Coast Guard District Office, 630 Sansome Street, San Francisco, CA 94126.

Fishing. Autumn is the peak run of one of the Delta's most sought-after game fish, the striped bass. Salmon and steelhead also pass through here on their autumnal migration up the Sacramento River, but the area seldom presents ideal water conditions for trout fishing. Year-round residents include catfish, black bass, bluegill, and giant sturgeon. Bait and tackle shops can update you on fishing conditions and provide the names of good guides.

Cycling. Biking the Delta means two-wheeling along level, lightly traveled roads atop levees separating low-lying fields from higher waters. A spring ride lets you survey acres of blooming pear tree tops while avoiding summer's heat and high winds (though winds can be a problem year-round). Three convenient spots to park your car and begin your ride are at Brannan Island State Recreation Area (day-use fee), Sacramento County's Hogback Island Access ($3, weekends only), and the River Road in Walnut Grove. To see freighter traffic, cycle on Sherman and Andrus islands; Grand, Sutter, and Ryer islands have pear orchards.

Camping. Brannan Island State Recreation Area has about 150 campsites for tents and motor homes and a public boat launch; phone (916) 777-6464 for fees and reservations. Private campgrounds are scattered throughout the Delta; detail maps show locations.

Dining. To serve the recreational flotilla on the Delta, a number of restaurants are anchored along the water. Architecture ranges from steamboat revival to neoclassical, and cuisine runs from crayfish to chateaubrand. Most restaurants have their own dock space; some are open only in summer.

Brannan Island and west Stockton offer the greatest variety. Other landmark eateries include Grand Island Mansion (an opulent estate open for Sunday brunch only), Ryde Hotel (a Prohibition-era hotel and restaurant), and Giusti's (a rustic Italian restaurant at Snodgrass Slough).

Delta towns

Sightseeing along the Delta reaps rewards. You can buy fresh produce at roadside stands, pack a picnic to enjoy at Brannan Island park, or poke around riverfront communities like Walnut Grove, Freeport, Locke, and Ryde.

State 160 (the Delta Highway) winds 45 miles along the Sacramento River. It's a slow but scenic route between the Central Valley and the Bay Area.

Isleton. Many of the shops in this once-important riverboat port and canning center now stand vacant, though there are a few exceptions. Quong Wo Sing Company store has been owned by the same family for four generations. If you're visiting in early spring, turn onto Isleton Road from State 160 to see the sandhill cranes that winter here.

Locke. Built around 1915 by members of a Chinese association who worked on Delta levees, railroads, and farms, Locke today has fewer than 100 residents. A stroll along its wooden walkways past false-front buildings gives you an inkling of its much livelier past. The Dai Loy Gambling House Museum is a big draw, as is Al's Place, a saloon noted for its hamburgers and steaks.

San Joaquin Valley

South of Sacramento, the Central Valley follows the course of the San Joaquin River, which flows northward to meet the Sacramento. State 99 and Interstate 5 are its north-south corridors, Interstate 580 (south of Stockton) and State 152 the major routes westward toward the coast. Of all of the cities straddling State 99, Stockton and Fresno offer the most visitor attractions.

A longtime agricultural center, the valley is noted for its acres of orchards and vineyards and, farther south, cotton fields. The grapes grown around Lodi and Stockton are pressed into premium wines. Free tasting rooms in the Stockton area welcome visitors.

Stockton area

A boomtown in the 1850s, Stockton today is an important port city connected to the San Francisco Bay Area by a 76-mile deep-water channel. Docks along the western edge of town serve some 700 freighters a year. Several excursion boats offer regular river cruises. For information, contact the Stockton–San Joaquin Convention and Visitors Bureau, 46 W. Fremont Street, Stockton, CA 95202; phone (800) 888-8016.

City attractions. Down at the harbor, Stockton Waterfront Warehouse (445 W. Weber Avenue) offers waterside dining choices. At Pacific Avenue and Stadium Drive, the ivy-covered, Gothic-style buildings and green lawns of the venerable University of the Pacific give it the ideal campus look.

The free Haggin Museum in Victory Park (Pershing Avenue at Rose Street) documents county history. It's particularly noted for its fine collections of Hudson River School paintings and California Indian baskets.

An oasis for families with small children is Pixie Woods Wonderland in Louis Park (Monte Diablo and Occidental streets). Amidst a fantasyland setting are amusement rides and a petting zoo (admission). It's open 11 A.M. to 6 P.M. Wednesday through Friday and noon to 5 P.M. weekends from mid-June to early September. Hours are shorter in spring and autumn; it closes in winter.

Fresno

A 19th-century farming town, fast-growing Fresno is now the state's eighth-largest city and the valley's financial and agricultural center. Its downtown is parklike. To get your bearings, stop by the Fresno Convention and Visitors Bureau (808 M Street), open 8 A.M. to 5 P.M. weekdays.

Dining options. In the early 1900s Basque shepherds came from France and Spain to work on ranches around the valley. In the winter they lived in Fresno boarding hotels, two of which still stand. For a typical Basque family-style lunch, visit the Santa Fe (935 Santa Fe Street) or Yturri (2546 Kern Street) hotels near the railroad station. The Yturri also serves dinner.

Because Fresno has been a favorite of Armenian immigrants since the 1880s, you're as likely to find lavash as French bread in its markets. For fresh picnic fixings, stop by these two downtown bakeries: Hye Quality (2222 Santa Clara Street) and Valley (502 M Street). Or have lunch at George's Shish Kebab (Galleria, 2405 Capitol Street).

Restored homes. Two of the city's restored 19th-century houses are open for tours (small fee). Guided walks through the Meux Home (1007 R Street) take place noon to 3:30 P.M. Friday through Sunday. A bonus to visiting the Edwardian mansion of raisin baron Theodore Kearney (7160 West Kearney Boulevard, 7 miles west of downtown) is the chance to wander around its spacious grounds. Tours are offered from 1 to 4 P.M. Friday through Sunday.

Museums. The Fresno Metropolitan Museum of Arts, History, and Science (1555 Van Ness Avenue) houses a sizable collection of paintings, ranging from old masters to trompe l'oeil; there is also an array of Ansel Adams' photographs and historical exhibits. The museum (small fee) is open Wednesday through Sunday, 11 A.M. to 5 P.M.

The Fresno Art Museum (2233 N. 1st Street) offers rotating exhibits, foreign film programs, concerts, and a gift shop. There's a small charge to visit.

Roeding Park. A pioneer nurseryman planted verdant Roeding Park (Olive or Belmont exits off State 99) with hundreds of trees, making this 157-acre oasis a great spot to picnic. Here, too, are camellia and rose gardens, tennis courts, lakes, a children's Story Land (fee), and Fort Miller Block House, where free historical exhibits are open afternoons from May to October.

Chaffee Zoological Gardens, at the southeastern corner of the park, contains more than 700 animals, Asian birds, and reptiles. Of particular interest are the elephant compound, reptile house, and denizens of the tropical rain forest and Australian Outback. The zoo (fee) is open 10 A.M. to 5 P.M. daily.

Other valley stops

Micke Grove Park and Zoo (Lodi, 9 miles north of Stockton). The San Joaquin County Historical Museum, a zoo, a Japanese garden, and shady picnic sites are only some of the reasons to stop at this 120-acre county park (open daily, per-car admission).

McHenry Mansion and Museum (15th and I streets, Modesto). Though movie mogul George Lucas is the favorite son these days, the McHenrys were one of Modesto's pioneer families. Their 1863 restored home is open for free tours Tuesday through Thursday and Sunday afternoons.

Castle Air Museum (Castle Air Force Base, 6 miles north of Merced). Some three dozen lovingly restored military planes are displayed, from World War II to the present. They range in size from a drone too small to carry a pilot to the gigantic B-52. The free museum is open daily, 10 A.M. to 4 P.M. A restaurant and gift shop add to its appeal.

A young "conductor" poses proudly at the Western Railway Museum, a 25-acre, open-air collection of vintage rolling stock in the Delta region (see page 126).

An Activity Guide

Camping at National Parks

Advance planning will help you get the most out of a camping trip to one of California's national parks or monuments. For information and campsite fees (currently $3 to $12 per night), contact the individual parks listed below or the National Park Service, Western Regional Information Office, Fort Mason, Bldg. 201, Bay and Franklin Streets, San Francisco, CA 94123; phone (415) 556-0560.

Maximum RV length accepted varies from campground to campground—be sure to check ahead of time.

Lassen Volcanic National Park (see page 90). Information: (916) 595-4444. The park's seven campgrounds are open only from June to fall; heavy snows limit park access in winter. State 44 and State 89 lead to the park, located 47 miles east of Redding. Most campgrounds close in September, but two—Butte Lake and Manzanita Lake—remain open into October.

Three campgrounds are reached by the Lassen Park Road, a 30-mile paved scenic route winding through the western part of the park. Largest of the park campgrounds is *Manzanita Lake* (179 tent/RV sites, sanitary disposal station, disabled facilities, elevation 5,890 feet), at Manzanita Lake near the park's northwest entrance. About 4½ miles northeast is *Crags* (45 tent/RV sites, pit toilets, elevation 5,700 feet). Another large camping area is *Summit Lake, North and South* (48 tent and 46 tent/RV sites, disabled facilities, elevation 6,695 feet), about 12 miles southeast of Manzanita Lake on Lassen Park Road.

In the park's northeast corner is *Butte Lake Campground* (98 tent/RV sites, disabled facilities, elevation 6,100 feet), located 18 miles southeast of Old Station off State 44 (last 6½ miles unpaved). At the southwest entrance is *Southwest Campground* (21 tent sites, flush toilets, adjacent food service, elevation 6,700 feet). Two remote campgrounds near the southeast corner of the park are *Juniper Lake* (18 tent/RV sites, no piped water, pit toilets, elevation 6,790 feet), 13 miles northwest of Chester on the Chester–Juniper Lake Road; and *Warner Valley* (18 tent/RV sites, pit toilets, elevation 5,650 feet), 17 miles northwest of Chester on the Chester–Warner Valley Road.

Lava Beds National Monument (see page 93). Information: (916) 667-2282. Open year-round is *Indian Well Campground* (40 tent/RV sites, elevation 4,770 feet).

Pinnacles National Monument (see page 57). Information: (408) 389-4526. There are 23 year-round tent sites at *Chapparal Campground*, 11 miles northeast of Soledad on State 146.

Point Reyes National Seashore (see page 69). Information: (415) 663-1092. No vehicle campgrounds. Four hike-in campgrounds (charcoal braziers, pit toilets, no drinking water; reservations necessary) are open year-round by permit, available at the Bear Valley Visitor Center.

Redwood National Park (see page 81). Camping facilities within this federally administered area are located in three state parks. Campsite reservations can be made between 48 hours and 8 weeks prior to date of arrival through the MISTIX reservation system (see page 121).

Del Norte Coast Redwoods State Park. Information: (707) 464-9533. Located 9 miles south of Crescent City, this park is open April to October (8 tent and 107 tent/RV sites, disposal station, elevation 400 feet).

Jedediah Smith Redwoods State Park. Information: (707) 464-9533. Located 9 miles northeast of Crescent City off U.S. 199, the park is open all year (108 tent/RV sites, disposal station, disabled facilities, elevation 250 feet).

Prairie Creek Redwoods State Park. Information: (707) 488-2171. Located north of Orick off U.S. 101, the park has two campgrounds, both open year-round: *Elk Prairie* (74 tent/RV sites, disposal station, disabled facilities, elevation 150 feet), 6 miles north of Orick; and *Gold Bluffs Beach* (25 tent/RV sites, no piped water, elevation 0 feet), 8 miles north of Orick off U.S. 101 via Davidson Road.

Whiskeytown Unit of the Whiskeytown-Shasta-Trinity National Recreation Area (see pages 84–85). Information: (916) 241-6584. Open year-round are *Oak Bottom* (100 tent and 50 RV sites, reservations available, disposal station, elevation 1,250 feet), located 13 miles west of Redding off State 299; and undeveloped *Brandy Creek* (37 RV sites, elevation 1,250 feet), located 14 miles west of Redding off State 299 on Kennedy Memorial Drive.

For camping in Shasta-Trinity National Forest, phone (415) 705-2874.

Yosemite National Park (see page 107). Information: (209) 372-0264. Three all-year campgrounds and 11 seasonal areas offer more than 1,800 campsites. Five campgrounds are in Yosemite Valley; others are along Tioga Road and Big Oak Flat Road, off Glacier Point Road, and near Wawona. Reservations (recommended May through September) may be made for some campgrounds up to 8 weeks in advance at local Ticketron outlets or by calling (800) 452-1111 (small fee).

Maximum length of stay is 30 days, except from June 1 to September 15, when stays are limited to 7 days in Yosemite Valley and 14 days outside the valley.

In Yosemite Valley (elevation 4,000 feet), campgrounds border the Merced River near the east end of the valley, generally between Yosemite Village and Curry Village. One valley automobile campground is kept open all year (specific site varies); others open in April or May and close in October or November. Campgrounds include *Lower River* (138 tent/RV sites, disposal station), *Upper River* (124 tent sites), *Lower Pines* (172 tent/RV sites, disabled facilities), *North Pines* (85 tent/RV sites), and *Upper Pines* (238 tent/RV sites, disposal station). *Sunnyside* is an all-year walk-in campground (35 tent sites).

Two additional all-year campgrounds are *Wawona* (100 tent/RV sites, elevation 4,000 feet), located 1 mile northwest of Wawona on State 41, and *Hodgdon Meadow* (105 tent/RV sites, elevation

4,872 feet), 9 miles west of Crane Flat just off Big Oak Flat Road.

Open June to September is *Bridalveil Creek Campground* (110 tent/RV sites, elevation 7,200 feet), off the Glacier Point Road about 8 miles east of Chinquapin.

The Tioga Pass Road cuts through Yosemite's high country. Opening in May is *Crane Flat Campground* (166 tent/RV sites, elevation 6,190 feet); opening in June are *White Wolf* (87 tent/RV sites, elevation 8,000 feet) and *Tuolumne Meadows* (314 tent/RV sites, disposal station, elevation 8,600 feet). Three other Tioga Road campgrounds also open in June, but with simpler facilities (no piped water, pit toilets): *Tamarack Flat* (52 tent/RV sites, elevation 6,315 feet), *Yosemite Creek* (75 tent/RV sites, elevation 7,659 feet), and *Porcupine Flat* (52 sites, elevation 8,100 feet). All campgrounds along the Tioga Road close by mid-October.

Walk-in campgrounds for backpackers are located in Yosemite Valley at *Backpackers Campground* (25 sites), and along the Tioga Road at *Tenaya Lake* (50 sites) and *Tuolumne Meadows* (25 sites). Hikers who wish to stay at Yosemite's famed High Sierra camps should make reservations months in advance; for information, phone (209) 454-2002.

Camping at State Parks

Camping at state parks and beaches gives you easy access to swimming, fishing, nature hikes, and other fun. We list some of the most popular beach and inland sites. A detailed guide to state park facilities is available for $2—contact the Publications Section, California Department of Parks & Recreation, P.O. Box 942896, Sacramento 94296-0001; phone (916) 322-7000.

Campsite reservations can be made for most parks between 48 hours and 8 weeks prior to date of arrival through the MISTIX reservation system. To charge reservations to a Visa or MasterCard number, or to obtain an informational brochure, phone (800) 444-7275 (California only) or (619) 452-1950 (out of state) on weekdays from 8 A.M. to 5 P.M., or weekends from 8 A.M. to 3 P.M.

Camping fees generally range from $7 to $20 per campsite per night, plus a $3.95 nonrefundable reservation fee. RV hookups or premium beachfront campsites may be slightly higher.

Self-contained recreational vehicles can overnight at several state parks and beaches on a first-come, first-served basis. Regular fees apply for en route sites.

BAY AREA

Big Basin Redwoods State Park, 9 miles northwest of Boulder Creek off State 9 on State 236 (Santa Cruz County); 146 campsites, disposal station. Hiking and equestrian trails, museum. Contact: (408) 338-6132.

Half Moon Bay State Beach, ½ mile west of Half Moon Bay (San Mateo County); 50 campsites, disposal station, en route camping. Fishing, nature program. Contact: (415) 726-6238.

Henry Cowell Redwoods State Park, 5 miles north of Santa Cruz on Graham Hill Road (Santa Cruz County); 113 campsites. Hiking and equestrian trails. Contact: (408) 335-4598.

Mount Tamalpais State Park, 11 miles west of Mill Valley on Panoramic Highway (Marin County); 16 tent campsites, en route camping. Hiking trails, visitor center. Contact: (415) 388-2070.

Samuel P. Taylor State Park, 15 miles west of San Rafael on Sir Francis Drake Boulevard (Marin County); 60 campsites, disposal station, en route camping. Swimming, hiking and equestrian trails. Contact: (415) 488-9897.

CENTRAL COAST

Manresa State Beach, 10 miles south of Santa Cruz off State 1 (Santa Cruz County); 64 campsites. Swimming, fishing, hiking. Contact: (408) 761-1795.

New Brighton State Beach, east end of Capitola off State 1 (Santa Cruz County); 108 campsites, disposal station, en route camping. Swimming, fishing. Contact: (408) 475-4850.

Pfeiffer Big Sur State Park, 2 miles southeast of Big Sur off State 1 (Monterey County); 217 campsites, disposal station. Swimming, fishing, hiking trails. Contact: (408) 667-2315.

Seacliff State Beach, in Aptos off State 1 (Santa Cruz County); 26 sites with hookups. Swimming, fishing, visitor center, museum. Contact: (408) 688-3241.

Sunset State Beach, 16 miles south of Santa Cruz off State 1 (Santa Cruz County); 90 campsites. Swimming, fishing, hiking trails. Contact: (408) 724-1266.

GOLD COUNTRY & SIERRA

Calaveras Big Trees State Park, 4 miles northeast of Arnold on State 4 (Calaveras County); 129 sites, disposal station. Swimming, fishing, hiking and ski trails. Contact: (209) 795-2334.

Indian Grinding Rock State Historic Park, 11 miles northeast of Jackson off State 88 (Amador County); 21 campsites. Reconstructed Miwok village, visitor center, museum. Contact: (209) 296-7488.

Malakoff Diggins State Historic Park, 21 miles northeast of Nevada City on State 49 and Tyler Foote Crossing (Nevada County); 28 campsites. Swimming, fishing, hiking and equestrian trails, visitor center, museum. Contact: (916) 265-2740.

Plumas-Eureka State Park, 5 miles west of State 89 at Blairsden on County Road A14 (Plumas County); 67 campsites (summer), disposal station. Swimming, fishing, hiking and equestrian trails, museum. Contact: (916) 836-2380.

LAKES & RIVERS

Brannan Island State Recreation Area, 3½ miles south of Rio Vista off State 160 (Sacramento County); 100 campsites with water hookups, disposal station, dock. Swimming, fishing, visitor center. Contact: (916) 777-6671.

Clear Lake State Park, 3½ miles northeast of Kelseyville on Soda Bay Road (Lake County); 147 campsites, disposal station. Swimming, fishing, boating, hiking trails. Contact: (707) 279-4293.

Colusa–Sacramento River State Recreation Area, 9 miles east of Interstate 5 at the north end of Colusa (Colusa County); 22 campsites, disposal station, en route camping. Swimming, fishing, boating. Contact: (916) 458-4927.

Folsom Lake State Recreation Area, 5 miles northeast of Folsom (Placer, El Dorado, and Sacramento counties); 160 campsites, disposal station, rental boats, dock. Swimming, fishing, boating, waterskiing, hiking and equestrian trails. Contact: (916) 988-0205.

Lake Oroville State Recreation Area, 7 miles east of Oroville on State 162 (Butte County); 212 campsites, 75 sites with hookups, disposal station, rental boats, marina, en route camping. Swimming, fishing, waterskiing, hiking trails, visitor center. Contact: (916) 538-2200.

Woodson Bridge State Recreation Area, 6 miles east of Corning on South Avenue (Tehama County); 46 campsites, disposal station. Swimming, fishing, hiking trails. Contact: (916) 839-2112.

LAKE TAHOE

D. L. Bliss State Park, 6 miles south of Meeks Bay on State 89 (El DoradoCounty); 167 campsites (summer), disposal station. Swimming, fishing, hiking trails. Contact: (916) 525-7277.

Donner Memorial State Park, 3 miles west of Truckee on Donner Pass Road (Nevada County); 154 campsites (summer). Swimming, fishing, hiking trails, museum. Contact: (916) 587-3841.

Emerald Bay State Park, 8 miles north of South Lake Tahoe (El Dorado County); 100 campsites (summer), dock. Swimming, fishing, boating. Contact: (916) 541-3030 (summer) or 525-7232 (park district headquarters).

Grover Hot Springs, 4 miles west of Markleeville off State 89 on County Road E1 (Alpine County); 76 sites (May–October), hot spring pool. Swimming, fishing, hiking trails. Contact: (916) 694-2248.

Sugar Pine Point State Park, 1 mile south of Tahoma on State 89 (El Dorado County); 175 campsites, disposal station, dock. Swimming, fishing, hiking and ski trails, museum. Contact: (916) 525-7982.

Tahoe State Recreation Area, ½ mile northeast of Tahoe City on State 28 (Placer County); 39 sites (summer), dock. Swimming, fishing, boating. Contact: (916) 583-3074 (summer) or 525-7232 (park district headquarters).

NORTH COAST

Fort Ross State Historic Park, 11 miles north of Jenner on State 1 (Sonoma County); 25 campsites (April–November). Reconstructed Russian trading post and fort. Fishing, museum, visitor center. Contact: (707) 847-3286.

MacKerricher State Park, 3 miles north of Fort Bragg on State 1 (Mendocino County); 143 campsites, disposal station.

Fishing, hiking and equestrian trails. Contact: (707) 937-5804.

Manchester State Beach, 7 miles north of Point Arena off State 1 (Mendocino County); 45 campsites, disposal station. Fishing. Contact: (707) 937-5804.

Patrick's Point State Park, 5 miles north of Trinidad off U.S. 101 (Humboldt County); 123 campsites. Fishing, hiking trails, museum. Contact: (707) 677-3570.

Russian Gulch State Park, 2 miles northeast of Mendocino off State 1 (Mendocino County); 30 campsites. Fishing, hiking trails. Contact: (707) 937-5804.

Salt Point State Park, 20 miles north of Jenner on State 1 (Sonoma County); 130 campsites, disposal station. Fishing, riding. Contact: (707) 847-3221.

Sonoma Coast State Beach, north of Bodega Bay on State 1 (Sonoma County); 128 campsites, disposal station. Primitive 11-site environmental camp (April–November only). Fishing, hiking and equestrian trails. Contact: (707) 875-3483.

Van Damme State Park, at Little River on State 1 (Mendocino County); 72 campsites, disposal station, en route camping. Fishing, hiking. Contact: (707) 937-5804.

Westport–Union Landing State Beach, 16 miles north of Fort Bragg on State 1 (Mendocino County); 130 campsites, en route camping. Fishing. Contact: (707) 937-5804.

REDWOOD COUNTRY

Grizzly Creek Redwoods State Park, 18 miles east of U.S. 101 on State 36 (Humboldt County); 30 campsites. Swimming, fishing, nature trails, visitor center. Contact: (707) 777-3683.

Humboldt Redwoods State Park, 45 miles south of Eureka off U.S. 101 near Weott (Humboldt County); 214 campsites, disposal stations, en route camping. Swimming, fishing, hiking and equestrian trails, visitor center. Contact: (707) 946-2311.

Richardson Grove State Park, 8 miles south of Garberville on U.S. 101 (Humboldt County); 169 campsites, disposal station. Swimming, fishing, hiking trails. Contact: (707) 247-3318.

Standish-Hickey State Recreation Area, 1 mile north of Leggett on U.S. 101 (Men-

docino County); 162 campsites. Swimming, fishing. Contact: (707) 925-6482.

SHASTA-CASCADE

Castle Crags State Park, 6 miles south of Dunsmuir off Interstate 5 (Shasta County); 64 campsites, en route camping. Fishing, hiking. Contact: (916) 235-2684.

McArthur–Burney Falls Memorial State Park, 11 miles northeast of Burney on State 89 (Shasta County); 128 campsites, disposal station, en route camping. Swimming, fishing, boating, waterskiing, hiking trails. Contact: (916) 335-2777.

Golf Courses

If you take your golf game on the road, you'll find an ever-increasing choice of courses to play in Northern California. Because of their popularity, you need to reserve tee times well in advance. Our sample of public, resort, and semiprivate courses allowing public play gives some idea of what's available. For a complete roundup, contact local visitor bureaus. Yardage listed is from the regular tees.

BAY AREA

Half Moon Bay Golf Links, 2000 Fairway Dr., Half Moon Bay; (415) 726-4438. Very scenic Palmer/Duane public course; 18 holes, par 72; 6,447 yards; rating 71.0, slope 130.

Pebble Beach golfers

Harding Park Golf Course, Harding Rd. and Skyline Blvd., San Francisco; (415) 664-4690. Municipal course with narrow, tree-lined fairways; 27 holes, par 72; 6,586 yards; rating 71.3, slope 119.

Lincoln Park Golf Course, 34th and Clement Sts., San Francisco; (415) 221-9911. Scenic, hilly public course; 18 holes, par 68; 5,149 yards; rating 64.5, slope 106.

Pasatiempo Golf Course, 18 Clubhouse Rd., Santa Cruz; (408) 459-9155. Semiprivate Alister MacKenzie course overlooking Monterey Bay; 18 holes, par 71; 6,154 yards; rating 71.4, slope 134.

Tilden Park Golf Course, Grizzly Peak Blvd. and Shasta Rd., Berkeley; (415) 848-7373. Hilly public course with lots of trees; 18 holes, par 70; 5,823 yards; rating 67.8, slope 114.

MONTEREY PENINSULA

Del Monte Golf Course, 1300 Sylvan Rd., Monterey; (408) 373-2436. The Monterey Peninsula's oldest public course; 18 holes, par 72; 6,007 yards; rating 69.5, slope 119.

Laguna Seca Golf Club, 10520 York Rd., Monterey; (408) 373-3701. Robert Trent Jones public course with many bunkers and two lakes; 18 holes, par 71; 5,711 yards; rating 68.5, slope 119.

The Links at Spanish Bay, 2700 17-Mile Dr., Pebble Beach; (408) 624-6611, ext. 66. Authentic Scottish links public course bordering Pacific Ocean; 18 holes, par 72; 6,078 yards; rating 72.1, slope 133.

Pacific Grove Municipal Golf Links, 77 Asilomar Blvd., Pacific Grove; (408) 648-3177. Scenic coastal public course; 18 holes, par 70; 5,553 yards; rating 66.3, slope 114.

Pebble Beach Golf Links, 17-Mile Dr., Pebble Beach; (408) 624-3811, ext. 228. Popular resort course famed for magnificent ocean views; 18 holes, par 72; 6,357 yards; rating 72.7, slope 139.

Poppy Hills Golf Course, 3200 Lopez Rd., Pebble Beach; (408) 625-2035. Robert Trent Jones, Jr. public course with tree-lined fairways and rolling greens; 18 holes, par 72; 6,288 yards; rating 71.7, slope 134.

Rancho Cañada Golf Course, 1 mile east of State 1, Carmel Valley Rd., Carmel; (408) 624-0111. Public course set against Santa Lucia Mountains. *East:* 18 holes, par 71; 5,822 yards; rating 67.3, slope 111. *West:* 18 holes, par 72; 6,071 yards; rating 69.6, slope 120.

Spyglass Hill Golf Course, Stevenson Dr. and Spyglass Hill Rd., Pebble Beach; (408) 625-8563. Outstanding, challenging Robert Trent Jones resort course; 18 holes, par 72; 6,277 yards; rating 73.1, slope 135.

SIERRA

Edgewood Tahoe Golf Course, Loop Pkwy. at Stateline, NV; (702) 588-3566. Scenic resort course on south shore of Lake Tahoe; 18 holes, par 72; 6,960 yards; rating 72.8, slope 133.

Graeagle Meadows Golf Course, State 89, Graeagle; (916) 836-2323. Public course in towering pines of Plumas National Forest; 18 holes, par 72; 6,655 yards; rating 70.7, slope 118.

Incline Village Championship Course, 955 Fairway Blvd., Incline Village, NV; (702) 832-1144. Resort course on Nevada side of Lake Tahoe; 18 holes, par 72; 6,446 yards; rating 70.5, slope 124.

La Contenta Lakes Golf & Country Club, 1653 State 26, Valley Springs; (209) 772-1081. Gold-country public course nestled in foothills; 18 holes, par 72; 6,409 yards; rating 71.3, slope 127.

Lake Tahoe Golf Course, State 50 West, South Lake Tahoe; (916) 577-0788. Public course with mountain and lake views; 18 holes, par 71; 6,169 yards; rating 67.9, slope 110.

Northstar-at-Tahoe Golf Course, Basque Dr., off State 267, Truckee; (916) 587-0290. Robert Muir Graves resort course; 18 holes, par 72; 6,294 yards; rating 69.3, slope 130.

Tahoe Donner Golf Course, Northwoods Blvd., Truckee; (916) 587-9440. Resort course, tight fairways lined with huge pines; 18 holes, par 72; 6,595 yards; rating 71.5, slope 127.

Tahoe Paradise Golf Course, State 50, Tahoe Paradise; (916) 577-2121. Hilly public course with lots of trees; 18 holes, par 66; 4,070 yards; rating 60.0, slope 95.

WINE COUNTRY

Napa Municipal Golf Course, 2295 Streblow Dr., Napa; (707) 255-4333. Championship public course with lots of water; 18 holes, par 72; 6,506 yards; rating 70.7, slope 115.

Silverado Country Club & Resort, 1600 Atlas Peak Rd., Napa; (707) 257-0200. Challenging championship resort courses. *North:* 18 holes, par 72; 6,351 yards; rating 70.9, slope 126. *South:* 18 holes, par 72; 6,213 yards; rating 70.4, slope 123.

Sonoma Golf Club, 17700 Arnold Dr., Sonoma; (707) 996-0300. Top-rated public course; 18 holes, par 72; 6,583 yards; rating 72.3.

OTHER AREAS

Bodega Harbour Golf Links, 21301 Heron Dr., Bodega Bay; (707) 875-3538. Seaside resort course designed by Robert Trent Jones, Jr.; 18 holes, par 70; 5,630 yards; rating 69.2, slope 125.

Haggin Oaks Golf Course, 3645 Fulton Ave., Sacramento; (916) 481-4506. Municipal golf course close to downtown. *South:* 18 holes, par 72; 6,344 yards; rating 69.3, slope 110. *North:* 18 holes, par 72; 6,660 yards; rating 69.9, slope 112.

Lake Shastina Golf Resort, 5925 Country Club Dr., Weed; (916) 938-3201 or (800) 358-4653 in California. Partly open, partly wooded Robert Trent Jones, Jr. resort course; 27 holes, par 72; 6,594 yards; rating 70.9, slope 109.

Skiing

Many Northern California skiers head for Lake Tahoe, with its concentration of top resorts. Other ski areas are in the central Sierra, south of Lake Tahoe, and in the Shasta/Lassen area.

LAKE TAHOE AREA

Alpine Meadows, Alpine Meadows Road off State 89 between Truckee and Tahoe City; (916) 583-4232. Lifts: 1 quad, 2 triple, 8 double chairs; 2 pomas. Summit: 8,637 feet.

Boreal Ridge, Castle Peak exit off Interstate 80 at Soda Springs near Donner Summit; (916) 426-3666. Lifts: 1 quad, 1 triple, 8 double chairs. Summit: 7,800 feet.

Diamond Peak at Ski Incline, 2 miles off State 28 at Incline Village, NV; (702) 832-1177. Lifts: 1 quad, 6 double chairs. Summit: 8,540 feet. Cross-country: 35 km of groomed trails.

Donner Ski Ranch, on old U.S. 40, 3 miles east of Interstate 80 (Norden/Soda Springs exit); (916) 426-3635. Lifts: 1 triple, 3 double chairs. Summit: 7,835 feet.

Granlibakken, on Granlibakken Road off State 89, 1 mile south of Tahoe City; (916) 583-4242. Lifts: 1 poma, 1 rope tow. Summit: 6,500 feet.

Heavenly Valley, on Ski Run Boulevard off U.S. 50, South Lake Tahoe; (916) 541-1330. Lifts: 1 quad, 7 triple, 9 double chairs; 1 aerial tram, 6 surface. Summit: 10,100 feet.

Homewood, on State 89, 6 miles south of Tahoe City; (916) 525-7256. Lifts: 1 quad, 2 triple, 2 double chairs; 5 surface. Summit: 7,880 feet.

Mount Rose, 11 miles northeast of Incline Village, NV on State 431; (702) 849-0704. Lifts: 1 quad, 3 triple, 2 double chairs. Summit: 9,700 feet.

Northstar-at-Tahoe, on State 267 between Truckee and Kings Beach; (916) 562-1010. Lifts: 2 quad, 3 triple, 3 double chairs; 1 gondola, 2 surface. Summit: 8,600 feet. Cross-country: 40 km of groomed trails.

Soda Springs Ski Area, on old U.S. 40, 1 mile east of Interstate 80 (Norden/Soda Springs exit); (916) 426-3666. Lifts: 1 double, 2 triple chairs. Summit: 7,352 feet.

Squaw Valley U.S.A., on Squaw Valley Road off State 89, 5 miles north of Tahoe City; (916) 583-6985. Lifts: 3 quad, 7 triple, 16 double chairs; 1 aerial tram, 1 gondola, 4 surface. Summit: 9,050 feet.

Sugar Bowl Ski Resort, on old U.S. 40, 2 miles east of Interstate 80 (Norden/Soda Springs exit); (916) 426-3651. Lifts: 1 quad, 7 double chairs; 1 gondola. Summit: 8,383 feet.

Tahoe Donner, on Donner Pass Road ½ mile off Interstate 80 (Truckee–Donner Lake exit); (916) 587-9444. Lifts: 2 double chairs, 1 tow. Summit: 7,350 feet. Cross-country: 68 km of groomed trails.

CENTRAL SIERRA

Badger Pass, on Glacier Point Road in Yosemite National Park off State 41; (209) 372-1330. Lifts: 1 triple, 3 double chairs; 2 surface. Summit: 8,100 feet. Cross-country: 57 km of groomed trails.

Cottage Springs, on State 4, 27 miles east of Angels Camp; (209) 795-1209. Lifts: 1 double chair, 1 surface. Summit: 6,500 feet.

Dodge Ridge, off State 108, 32 miles east of Sonora; (209) 965-3474. Lifts: 2 triple, 5 double chairs; 4 surface. Summit: 8,200 feet.

Iron Mountain, 42 miles northeast of Jackson at State 88 and Mormon Emigrant Trail; (209) 258-4672. Lifts: 2 triple, 3 double chairs. Summit: 7,800 feet.

Kirkwood, on State 88 at Carson Pass, 35 miles south of South Lake Tahoe; (209) 258-6000. Lifts: 4 triple, 6 double chairs; 1 surface. Summit: 9,800 feet. Cross country: 80 km of groomed trails.

Mount Reba/Bear Valley, on State 4, 52 miles east of Angels Camp; (209) 753-2301. Lifts: 2 triple, 7 double chairs. Summit: 8,500 feet.

Sierra Ski Ranch, off U.S. 50, 12 miles west of South Lake Tahoe; (916) 659-7453. Lifts: 1 quad, 2 triple, 6 double chairs. Summit: 8,852 feet.

Sierra Summit, on State 168, 64 miles northeast of Fresno at Huntington Lake; (209) 893-3316. Lifts: 2 triple, 3 double chairs; 4 surface. Summit: 8,709 feet.

SHASTA/LASSEN

Lassen Park Ski Area, on State 89 in Lassen National Park, 49 miles east of Red Bluff; (916) 595-3376. Lifts: 1 triple chair, 2 surface. Summit: 7,200 feet.

Mount Shasta Ski Park, between Mt. Shasta City and McCloud off State 89 on Ski Park Hwy.; (916) 926-8610. Lifts: 2 triple chairs, 1 poma. Summit: 6,600 feet.

Plumas-Eureka Ski Bowl, 5 miles off State 70 at Johnsville; (916) 836-2317. Lifts: 3 pomas. Summit: 6,150 feet.

Boat Cruises

 Viewing Northern California's waterways from the deck of a boat is usually the best, and certainly the most scenic, way to get to know them. We've rounded up a sampling of what's available; for a complete list of area cruise operators, check with the visitor bureau for that region (addresses at the front of each chapter).

FERRIES

Bay Area. *Golden Gate Ferries,* Ferry Building at foot of Market Street, (415) 332-6600; runs between the city and Sausalito/Larkspur in Marin County. *Tiburon–Angel Island Ferry,* Tiburon, (415) 435-2131; shuttles to Angel Island State Park daily in summer, weekends and holidays the rest of the year.

Sacramento River. *Princeton Ferry,* State 45, Princeton; river's last-operating car ferry, free 2-minute trip.

SIGHTSEEING CRUISES

Bay Area. *Blue & Gold Fleet,* Pier 39, (415) 781-7877; 1¼-hour bay cruises beginning at 10 A.M., 3-hour dinner-dance cruise departing at 8 P.M. weekends. *Hornblower Dining Yachts,* Pier 33, (415) 394-8900; lunch and dinner cruises aboard a re-created 1900s motor yacht. *Red & White Fleet,* Pier 41, (415) 546-BOAT; 45-minute narrated bay cruises departing daily from 10:45 A.M. from Piers 41 and 43½, round-trip ride to Marine World/Africa USA in Vallejo, Alcatraz, and Angel Island State Park. *Questuary,* foot of Broadway, Oakland, (415) 452-2214; 1-hour cruises of the Oakland-Alameda Estuary Wednesday through Sunday.

The Delta. *Delta Riverboat Cruises,* Sacramento, (916) 372-3690; 1- and 2-day cruises between Sacramento and San Francisco. *Matthew McKinley,* (916) 441-6481, and *River City Queen,* (916) 448-7447; paddle-wheeler cruises on Sacramento River, Old Sacramento Waterfront. *Island Queen,* Stockton, (209) 941-4835; paddle-wheeler cruises on the San Joaquin River.

Humboldt Bay. *M.V. Madaket,* foot of C Street, Eureka, (707) 445-1910; 75-minute narrated cruises daily at 5 P.M. May through September.

Lake Tahoe. *M.S. Dixie,* Zephyr Cove, (702) 588-3508, Emerald Bay cruises daily spring to autumn, south shore cruises Tuesday through Saturday afternoon in summer. *North Tahoe Cruises,* Round House Mall and Marina, Tahoe City, (916) 583-0141; 2-hour historical trips on northwest shore daily late spring to autumn.

Tahoe Queen, foot of Ski Run Boulevard, South Lake Tahoe, (916) 541-3364; Emerald Bay sightseeing and dinner cruises year-round, winter ski shuttle to north shore.

Monterey Bay. *Spellbinder Sailing Tours,* Fisherman's Wharf, Monterey, (408) 655-2281, harbor cruises aboard a 50-foot wooden yacht.

Napa River. *Napa Riverboat Co.,* Napa Valley Marina, 1200 Milton Road 8 miles southwest of Napa, (707) 226-2628; 3-hour cruises on Napa River.

Whale Watching

 After feeding all summer in the Bering Sea and Arctic Ocean, California gray whales head south each winter to birthing and breeding grounds 4,000 miles away in Baja California. This migration (mostly during December and January) brings the large mammals so near the shore that they can be seen from land at several points.

Males and noncalving females begin trickling north again in March. Cows with calves appear beyond the surf line from April into May.

One of the best places from which to watch the parade is at Point Reyes National Seashore (see page 69). Arrive early on weekends; you might wait up to 2 hours for a shuttle from the visitor center to the lighthouse. Call (415) 669-1534 for information.

Other good sites (from north to south) include these coastal headlands: Redwood National Park's Crescent Beach, at the end of Endert's Beach Road 4 miles south of Crescent City; Mendocino Headlands (whale festival in March); Salt Point State Park, 20 miles north of Jenner; Bodega Head, at the end of Bay Flat Road, 4 miles west of Bodega Bay; and busy Point Lobos State Reserve, south of Carmel on State 1.

Several companies offer whale-watching excursions by boat. Contact the following operators directly for schedules and prices.

Bay Area. *Blue & Gold Fleet,* P.O. Box Z-2, Pier 39, San Francisco, CA 94133, (415)

781-7890; *Dolphin Charters,* 1007 Leneve Pl., El Cerrito, CA 94530, (415) 527-9622; *Oceanic Society Expeditions,* Fort Mason Center, Building E, San Francisco, CA 94123, (415) 474-3385; *Whale Center,* 3929 E. Piedmont Ave., Oakland, CA 94611, (415) 654-6621.

Monterey Bay. *Monterey Sport Fishing,* 96 Fisherman's Wharf #1, Monterey, CA 93940, (408) 372-2203; *Princess Monterey Cruises,* 90 Old Fisherman's Wharf #1, Monterey, CA 93940, (408) 372-2628; *Randy's Whale Watching Trips,* 66 Fisherman's Wharf, Monterey, CA 93940, (408) 372-7440; *Shearwater Journeys,* P.O. Box 1445, Soquel, CA 95073, (408) 688-1990; *Tom's Fisherman's Supply,* 2210 E. Cliff Dr., Santa Cruz, CA 95062, (408) 476-2648; *Wharf Charters,* P.O. Box 396, Capitola, CA 95010, (408) 462-3553.

North Coast. *King Salmon Charters,* 1110 King Salmon Ave., Eureka, CA 95501, (707) 442-3474; *New Sea Angler & Jaws,* P.O. Box 1148, Bodega Bay, CA 94923, (707) 875-3495; *Pacific Adventures,* P.O. Box 268, Cotati, CA 94928, (707) 795-8492; *Lady Irma II Cruises,* Noyo Harbor, P.O. Box 103, Fort Bragg, CA 95437, (707) 964-3854.

River Runs

 Take a raft full of people, mix together with a wild and scenic river, and you've got the adventure known as white-water rafting. Commercial outfitters design trips to combine thrilling plunges down untamed rapids with relaxing floats on tranquil pools.

Trips can last from a few hours to a few days. Longer excursions include camping and planned activities such as hiking and gold panning. Plan on spending $50 to $120 (includes lunch) for a one-day excursion, depending on location.

Outfitters operate on these major Northern California rivers: Klamath (near the Oregon border), upper Sacramento (north of Redding), Trinity (northwest of Redding), Salmon (west of Yreka), Middle Fork of the Eel (northern coast), East Carson (south of Lake Tahoe), American (east of Sacramento), Stanislaus (east of Modesto), Merced (east of Merced), and Tuolumne (southeast of Modesto).

For a free directory of river-rafting companies operating in Northern California, call (800) 552-3625. The list, published by the California Western River Guides Association, briefly describes trips.

The California Office of Tourism (address on page 4) can also furnish a list of operators.

Spelunking

 Strictly speaking, spelunking is exploring caves left in their natural state, wiggling along on hands and knees through narrow passages and tight spaces. But most of the caverns open to the public in Northern California can be visited on a walk-through basis, via guided tours. Others, such as Lava Beds National Monument (see page 93) and Pinnacles National Monument (see page 57) can be explored on your own.

California Caverns at Cave City, P. O. Box 78, Vallecito, CA 95251; (209) 736-2708. John Muir wrote eloquently about his visit to the West's first commercially developed cave; other early tourists carved their names in its walls. A 1½-hour guided tour ($5.50 adults, $2.75 children 6 to 10) leaves every hour daily from 10 A.M. to 5 P.M. in summer, 10 A.M. to 4 P.M. in autumn; true spelunking is offered by reservation. From State 49 in San Andreas, take Mōuntain Ranch Road east about 8 miles to the turnoff.

Lake Shasta Caverns, P.O. Box 801, O'Brien, CA 96070; (916) 238-2341. Visits here have a novel flair. First a catamaran ferries you across an arm of Lake Shasta; then a bus drives you up to the cave, 800 feet above the lake. Dazzling formations include rocky draperies as grand as those in any opera house. Daily tours ($12 adults, $6 children 4 to 12) are offered hourly from 9 A.M. to 4 P.M. April to October and 10 A.M., noon, and 2 P.M. November through March. Total tour takes 2 hours. From Interstate 5, exit on Shasta Caverns Road, 15 miles north of Redding.

Mercer Caverns, P.O. Box 509, Murphys, CA 95222; (209) 728-2101. This earthquake-born, mostly vertical cave (visitors descend and then climb 440 stairs) is bounded on one side by a sheer rock wall. The 1-hour tour ($4.50 adults, $2.25 children 5 to 11) visits 10 "rooms"; it's offered 9 A.M. to 5 P.M. in summer, weekends the rest of the year. From Murphys, take Sheep Ranch Road north 1 mile.

Moaning Cavern, P.O. Box 78, Vallecito, CA 95251; (209) 736-2708. There are two ways to get the bottom of this cave: on a spiral staircase or by rappelling down (no experience needed) on secure ropes. Guided tours of the cavern ($5.50 adults, $5 seniors, $2.75 children 6 to 12) take place daily from 9 A.M. to 6 P.M. in summer, 10 A.M. to 5 P.M. in winter. The adventurous can continue deeper on a 3-hour spelunking expedition (reservations required). From Vallecito on State 4 take Parrotts Ferry Road south 1½ miles to the turnoff.

Subway Cave, Lassen National Forest, 55 S. Sacramento St., Susanville, CA 96130; (916) 257-2151. On a self-guided ⅓-mile tour of this lava tube, interpretive plaques explain the sights in colorfully named chambers. Bring a flashlight. To reach the cavern (always open), take State 44 east from Redding to Old Station; the cave is just north of town on State 89.

Train Rides

If riding the rails is your passion, Northern California offers some nostalgic excursions and interesting museums. Several trains operate year-round; others are geared for summer vacationers. Reserve space on the Napa Valley train 6 to 8 weeks in advance; it's also wise to have reservations for the Skunk on summer weekends.

Blue Goose–Short Line Railroad, Yreka, CA 96097; (916) 842-4146. A 3-hour run from Yreka to the old railroad town of Montague offers views of the countryside around Mount Shasta. The line operates from Memorial Day to Labor Day. Diesel trains ($7 adults, $3.50 children) leave at 9:30 A.M. Wednesday through Friday; steam trains ($9 adults, $4.50 children) depart at 10 A.M. weekends.

Central Pacific Freight Depot, Front and K Sts., Old Sacramento, CA 95814; (916) 448-4466. On a visit to the renowned California State Railroad Museum (see page 113), you can enjoy steam train rides May through Labor Day weekends (no trains on July 4th weekend). Trains depart on the hour from 10 A.M. to 5 P.M. from a circa-1867 reconstructed station. Fares for the 45-minute, 7-mile run are $3 adults, $1 children 6 to 17. Tickets are good for a same-day museum visit.

Napa Valley Wine Train, 1275 McKinstry St., Napa, CA 94559; (707) 253-2111 or (800) 522-4142. The train's elegant decor and fine food and wine make it a favorite with tourists, though many residents resent its intrusion. The 36-mile, 3-hour tour (no stops) operates daily Tuesday through Sunday plus holiday Mondays. Excursion fare is $25 weekdays, $29 weekends. Add $22 for champagne brunch (weekends) or lunch, $45 for dinner.

Niles Canyon Railway, (415) 862-9063 (for recorded information). Diesel- and steam-powered engines pull open-air passenger cars through a deep, wooded gorge between the East Bay towns of Sunol and Fremont. The 45-minute round-trip excursions follow the route of the old Western Pacific *California Zephyr*. Volunteers offer rides from 10 A.M. to 4 P.M. on the first and third Sunday of the month. Donations help maintain the line. The Sunol train station is at the junction of Main Street and Kilkare Road.

Railtown 1897, P.O. Box 1250, Jamestown, CA 95327; (209) 984-3953. This state historic park can make a number of claims to American railroading fame: it boasts the oldest steam locomotive still riding the rails, uses the only standard-gauge steam roundhouse, and has been a filming site for more than 200 television shows and movies. In summer, guided roundhouse tours (including a film on the line's history) take place from 10 A.M. to 4:30 P.M. daily ($2 adults, $1.25 children). On summer weekends and holidays, 1-hour runs carry passengers over 8 miles of Sierra countryside. Fares are $7.95 adults, $3.95 children 3 to 12.

Roaring Camp & Big Trees Railroad, P.O. Box G-1, Felton, CA 95018; (408) 335-4400. You'll travel a sinuous, narrow-gauge track up a summit and through the redwoods of the Santa Cruz Mountains aboard this 1880 steam train. Narrated 75-minute trips take place daily. Hours vary depending on the season. Admission is $10.50 adults, $7.50 children 5 to 17. The simulated logging camp of Roaring Camp (Graham Hill and Mount Herman roads near State 17) offers weekend barbecues and picnic grounds.

Santa Cruz, Big Trees & Pacific Railway, P.O. Box G-1, Felton, CA 95018; (408) 335-4400. The Suntan Special, another excursion from Roaring Camp (see above), leaves the redwood-covered mountains for a several-hour stop at Santa Cruz's beach and boardwalk. Trains run week-

ends in spring and autumn and daily in summer, with an extra train on moonlit Saturday nights. Southbound trains depart at 10:30 A.M. and return at 4 P.M.; the northbound express leaves Santa Cruz at noon, returning at 6:30 P.M. Round-trip fares are $16 adults, $8.50 ages 5 to 17.

Skunk Train (California Western Railroad), P.O. Box 907, Fort Bragg, CA 95437; (707) 964-6371. This old logging train through the redwoods between Fort Bragg on the coast and Willits on U.S. 101 dates back to 1885. It's affectionately dubbed the Skunk because old-timers said you could smell the yellow, self-powered railcars before you could see them. The 80-mile, all-day round-trip ride includes a midpoint stop at Northspur (refreshments and souvenirs); half-day trips to Northspur from either Fort Bragg or Willits are also available. In summer a Super Skunk steam train puffs out from Fort Bragg every morning. Round-trip fares are $20 adults, $10 children 5 through 11; half-day fares are $16 adults, $8 children. Reservations are suggested for summer and holiday weekends. Call for schedules.

Western Railway Museum, 5848 State 12, Suisun City, CA 94585; (707) 374-2978. Located at Rio Vista in the Delta, the 25-acre museum and park complex (open weekends only) showcases a grand collection of vintage rolling stock. Your entrance fee ($4 adults, $2 ages 12 to 17 and seniors, $1 ages 3 to 11) includes unlimited rides on electric trolleys and, on some weekends, 12-mile round-trips behind a diesel engine. Grounds include an attractive picnic area and a large bookstore.

Yosemite Mountain–Sugar Pine Railroad, 56001 State 41, Fish Camp, CA 93623; (209) 683-7273. Near the southern entrance to Yosemite National Park, an old logger steam train and Jenny rail cars loop through the Sierra National Forest on 4-mile tours. The steam train operates daily from mid-June through August, weekends only in May, September, and October, departing at 11 A.M. and 12:30 P.M., with extra trains at 2 and 3:30 P.M. from June through August. Jenny rail cars operate daily from late March through October.

Steam train fares are $8.50 adults, $4 children 3 to 12. Jenny fares are $5.75 adults, $3 children 3 to 12. An evening ride (barbecue and entertainment) is held on Saturday nights June through September. A museum on the grounds is free.

Index

Super Skunk train excursion